SARTRE AS
BIOGRAPHER

SARTRE AS BIOGRAPHER

Douglas Collins

HARVARD UNIVERSITY PRESS
Cambridge, Massachusetts, and London, England
1980

Printed in the United States of America

Publication of this book has been aided by a grant from the Andrew W. Mellon Foundation.

Library of Congress Cataloging in Publication Data

Collins, Douglas, 1945–
    Sartre as biographer.

    Includes bibliographical references and index.
    1. Sartre, Jean Paul, 1905– —Criticism and
interpretation.   2. Biography (as a literary form)
3. Authors, French—Biography.   I. Title.
PQ2637.A82Z597   840'.9   79–25863
ISBN 0–674–78950–4

Acknowledgments

Among those to whom I should like to express thanks are, first, my mentor, Bonner Mitchell, of the University of Missouri. A more patient and attentive reader cannot be imagined. The results of his improving suggestions are found on every page. Special thanks are due to Joseph Bien, Michel Rybalka, and Benjamin Suhl, who read the manuscript as a whole and offered extended, energetic, and helpful reactions. An early version was also read by Richard Dixon, Adèle King, Paula Sommers, and Allen Thiher, who offered suggestions and encouragement. I have profited from brief but invaluable conversations with Jean Bruneau, Richard Zaner, and Alexander von Schoenborn. While attending the "Sartre aujourd'hui" conference at Cerisy in June 1979, I had the opportunity to benefit from discussion with other "Sartrophages," as Alain Robbe-Grillet termed us, including Anne Clancier, Alain Costes, Thomas Flynn, Manfred Frank, Traugott König (Sartre's heroic German translator), Josette Pacaly, Oreste Pucciani, Robert Stone, and Philip Wood. I owe particular thanks to Dr. Clancier and Mme. Pacaly for giving me confidence in my judgments.

Spurred by Dean Andrew Minor, the Graduate School of the University of Missouri provided funds for travel and clerical assistance. I owe a debt of gratitude to my typists, Corinne Davis and Tess Lambrecht, and to Jeaneice Brewer and Marilyn Voegele of the Ellis Library staff. My wife Marcia provided the necessary "valorization" that Sartre describes in his life of Flaubert.

I would like to thank Gallimard for permission to quote from Sartre's works, and to thank as well the publishers who hold English language rights: New Left Books for *The Critique of Dialectical Reason*, George Braziller for *Saint Genet*, New Directions for *Nausea* and *Baudelaire*, and the University of Chicago Press for *The Idiot*.

Contents

SARTRE AS
BIOGRAPHER

The utopia of knowledge . . . has
utopia as its content.

Theodor W. Adorno

I

Truth and Alterity

The immense appetite that we have for biographies is born of a profound passion for equality.

Baudelaire

Biography is a fallen genre. In eighteenth-century England the life study had a prestige that has not been duplicated in modern literature. The frontispiece of *The British Nepos,* a late-century work of collective biography, suggests the high status and mission that the genre was assigned. Torch in raised hand, the Genius of Biography guides two youths up a mountain at whose summit appears a pantheon decorated with busts of the great and virtuous. Not yet understood as a dispassionate quest for fact, biography was unashamedly didactic and normative. Its power to teach wisdom was generally accepted. Samuel Johnson argued that "no species of writing seems more worthy of cultivation than biography, since none can be more delightful, or more useful, none can more certainly enchain the heart by irresistible interest, or more widely diffuse instruction to every diversity of condition."[1] Novelists such as Defoe and Fielding exploited the prestige of moralizing biography to mask and justify their fictions. An equivalent status was not enjoyed by biography in France, although during the revolutionary period the classical biographers had considerable vogue. Napoleon was a careful reader of Plutarch, and the night before assassinating Marat, Charlotte Corday prepared herself by studying exemplary figures of Stoic morality in *The Lives of Famous Men.*

During the eighteenth century the Genius also strayed onto less ascendant paths to biographical truth. An undidactic, sensational strain appeared, the exclusively moral conception of the genre began to crumble, and the social threshold of describability was dramatically lowered. Whereas biography once had the almost exclusive function of portraying the great of church and state, of justifying their authority and commemorating achievements and lofty qualities, accounts were now written about subjects from all classes, including the lowest. The public eagerly read of the lives and sufferings of the eccentric, the humble, and the abused. Books appeared on the lives of dwarfs, contortionists, pirates, and cheats. At the end of the century this spectacle of unjustified renown moved one Vicesimus Knox to complain: "Biography is every day descending from its dignity. Instead of an instructive recital it is becoming an instrument to the mere gratification of an impertinent, not to say a malignant curiosity."[2]

The lost dignity of biography has never been fully recovered. An enormous number of biographies were written during the nineteenth century, and the genre had significant friends in Wilhelm Dilthey, Hippolyte Taine, Ernest Renan, Charles-Augustin Sainte-Beuve, and the Sartrian arch-fiend, Louis Napoleon, who produced a life of Caesar. The romantics preferred the unmediated exhibition of self, historians swayed by Hegel preferred to follow the traces of the Idea, and positivists doubted the possibility of a final psychological knowledge. For Victor Cousin, "The individual by himself is a miserable and petty fact . . . Humanity has not got the time and cannot bother to concern itself with individuals who are nothing but individuals."[3] François Guizot felt that "Man can barely know himself and he is never more than guessed about by others."[4] Mark Twain revived the objections of the positivists when he wrote that "Biographies are but the clothes and buttons of the man—the biography of the man himself cannot be written."[5] In *Bouvard and Pécuchet,* Gustave Flaubert mocked biography as a vain, impossible thing. The two clowns of knowledge undertake a life of the hopelessly banal Duke of Angoulême, but their project aborts when they are faced with contradictory evidence on the decisive phrenological question of whether the Duke's hair was curly or straight.

In the twentieth century, biography has often fared worse. The dignity, propriety, possibility, and ethics of biography have been repeatedly questioned, and enemies operating from within the genre have abused it by employing harshly reductive systems of knowledge that undermine the reality of the individual whom they pretend to set in relief. Freud felt that most biographers were guilty of nostalgic quests to revive infantile conceptions of their fathers. For structuralist critics, biography perpetuates the illusion that the intentional "I" can be the source of meaning. According to Claude Lévi-Strauss, the goal of the human sciences is to dissolve man. Michel Foucault has questioned the legitimacy of a science of the individual, not because it is unfeasible, but rather because the very category of the individual and the attendant desire to rivet his particular essence serve the control needs of the state and modern economic production. Since the seventeenth century Western man has lived in a golden age of confession. He has found himself surrounded by an ever growing crowd of priests, physicians, psychiatrists, and other experts whose task is to serve the requirements of a control-obsessed disciplinary society by interpreting and judging the secrets they elicit. Because of the totalizing character of the modern biographer's ambitions, and the fact that his task is often to drum intimate revelations from the dead, he is the most impertinent practitioner of a malicious epistemology. Perhaps E. M. Cioran suspected that the genre was a tool of domination when he wrote, "It is incredible that the thought of having a biographer has not caused anyone to renounce the idea of having a life."[6]

The best of this century's novelists have had little love for biography. Marcel Proust resented the prying eye of Sainte-Beuve who sought to reduce art to the status of biographical document. "Psychoplagiarism" was Vladimir Nabokov's rude term for the genre; "biografiend" was James Joyce's epithet for the practitioner.[7] By unveiling the "biographical fallacy," the New Critics formalized the animosity of the aesthetes. Thomas Mann discovered in Hermann Hesse's *The Glass Bead Game* "the parody of biography and the grave scholarly attitude," which may also be sensed in his own *Doctor Faustus*.[8] D. H. Lawrence argued that all attempts to nail someone down in literature must be unsuccessful, for either the author nails his subject dead, or the subject walks off with the nail.[9] The biographer's position is impossible. He has a choice between mutilating a person by reducing him to his objectivity, or having his own methods mocked by an elusive subject who is refractory to all attempts at isolation. Most recently Bernard Malamud invented an anti-Plutarch who writes the lives of others because he cannot handle his own. Throughout *Dubin's Lives* the existence of the biographer is shamingly vicarious, for it is lived through and for the life of another. The biographer is a relative man, displaced and decentered, in that the thoughts and words of his subject crowd out his own, and his own truth becomes confused with his chase after the essence of the other. "Anyone turning biographer," concludes Dubin, "has committed himself to lies, to concealment, to hypocrisy, to flattery, and even to hiding his own lack of understanding: for biographical truth is not to be had, and even if it were it couldn't be useful."[10]

For Sartre, on the contrary, biography is possible, and the successful biographer is a hero, however ineffectual, who demonstrates the possibility of human life. The work that faithfully discloses its subject to be what Sartre calls "the singular universal"—a being who is both totalizer and totalized, at once the subject and the object of history—is the ideal that Sartre himself has pursued with vigor, for he feels that the demonstration of its possibility makes an important social point. Those who deny the validity or necessity of biography play into the hands of those who find it expedient to insult human possibilities. Sartre would agree with Twain that a person cannot be the object of conceptual knowledge, but this inability by no means precludes a person from being comprehensible. If this were not so, Sartre explains, solipsism and domination would be the world's lot. The lazy or methodologically ill-equipped biographer, on the one hand, bears false and demoralizing witness that contributes to the mystification of social relations, arming the master and pacifying the slave. For the philosophically lucid biographer, on the other hand, ethics and epistemology are one, because "A liberation that proposes to be total must start from a total knowledge of man by himself."[11] If altruism depends upon the possibility of a full recognition of the reality of the other person, then establishing the feasibility of a faithful life study becomes the most critical of philosophical tasks. If biography can never take the form of altruistic knowledge, then existence can never assume a human face. Truth in its original sense, Sartre remarks, is the liquidation of alterity. If biographical truth is possible, then so is a world in which man is not a wolf for man.

"What can one know about a man today?" asks Sartre at the start of *L'Idiot de la famille* (1971, 1972), his three-volume life of Flaubert.[12] The question echoes insistently through his own life and works. On the first page of the *Critique of Dialectical Reason* (1960) he queries, "Do we have today the means to compose a structural and historical anthropology?"[13] "What do I know about him?" puzzles the biographer protagonist of *Nausea* (1938) over the elusive Adémar de Rollebon.[14] Merleau-Ponty reports that one day in front of a crowded Gare de Luxembourg, Sartre said to him, "I can't help myself, these people interest me."[15] Simone de Beauvoir recalls that from the earliest years of their acquaintance Sartre was an obsessive people-watcher. Sartre and his friends could pass hours analyzing a single gesture or vocal inflection. The goal he sought was a global and concrete understanding of the individual, "because the individual alone exists."[16] The biographies of Charles Baudelaire, Jean Genet, and Flaubert represent an increasingly systematic effort by Sartre to arrive at that complete knowledge of particular men which de Beauvoir describes as one of his earliest ambitions.

This comprehensive understanding of the individual cannot be distinguished from biography. Even before his extended brush with Marxism, Sartre felt that knowledge of the past is essential to comprehension, not because it plays a determining role but because one can make a new decision only on the basis of one's past. A person is free to reject the past, but an option to do one thing or another can only be understood with reference to what has gone before. The early Sartre would have agreed with Henri Bergson that "The profound states of our soul, those which translate themselves through our free acts, express and summarize the entirety of our past history."[17]

The publication of L'Idiot forced recognition of the crucial place of biography in Sartre's writings. Since the war he has devoted far more pages to biography than to anything else. Most commentators have considered that this genre is for him a secondary one, in which he merely applies and dilutes the conceptual tools that he has elaborated elsewhere. But he himself clearly considers the biographies to be more than relative or parenthetical creations. They reconfirm a conclusion to be drawn from his multifarious activities in literature, journalism, polemics, and political activism; namely, that his primary interest is applied philosophy. For Sartre, the test of a system of ideas lies in its ability to perform in the real world, and this ability is best revealed in its capacity to reconstruct the life of an historical individual. A philosophical system is thus subordinate in interest to the biography it generates, because in the biography that system's success or failure is ultimately evaluated. Rather than being the bastardization of philosophy, biography is its legitimation.

In the Search for a Method (1960) Sartre, for example, makes clear that his main reason for judging orthodox Marxism negatively is its inability to produce satisfactory biography, that is, biography which does not lapse into abstraction and which fully recognizes the historical individual as a free and unique subject, not just the object of history that he also necessarily is. The inability of a banalized Marxism to produce anything but a bankrupt form of biography is not just regrettable as a failure within a secondary and innocuous literary genre. Its abstract errors also reflect an insensitivity that has pernicious consequences for the daily lives of millions who live under Marxist regimes where callous philosophy has personal horror as its routine result. Sartre has explained that he wrote the Critique of

Dialectical Reason in order to be able to write the more intimate, altruistic philosophy of *L'Idiot,* the proof lying in the frequent mentions of Flaubert in the *Critique.*[18] Even if biography were for Sartre, as it is not, strictly the application of a philosophy that has been more abstractly developed elsewhere, it would still not be mere application, mere watered-down philosophy, but the all-important moment of the concrete and systematic revelation of the contempt or respect these ideas hold for the lives of real men. Works of technical philosophy form a necessary plinth which is nevertheless subordinate in interest to the human likenesses that rise above.

Sartre's three lives reveal that for him, of all forms of literary criticism, biography is the most serious. As he remarks about *Madame Bovary,* "If we do not regress continually . . . in the process of reading, to the author's desires and ends, back to the total enterprise of Flaubert, we would quite simply make a fetish of the book . . . just like a piece of merchandise, considering it as a thing and not as the reality of a man objectified by his work."[19] Criticism at its best, for Sartre, involves what Nietzsche termed "the backward inference from the work to the maker, from the deed to the doer, from the ideal to those who need it, from every way of thinking and valuing to the commanding need behind it."[20] Biography also permits Sartre to ask a more important question than the one posed in the other pieces of literary criticism. The one asked in the biographies is, "What can we know about a man today?" In the other essays the principal question is, "Does this work appeal to human freedom?" Both questions refer to quite different ethical concepts and paradigms of dealienated human relations.

To consider the lives simply under the rubric of literary criticism, however, would belittle their ambitions and would fall directly into the trap of intellectual detail function, against which Sartre complains so bitterly. Although literary criticism may be found in these pages, it is always in the service of something larger: discovery of the laws of a new moral science. Sartre consciously caused *L'Idiot* to appear in a Gallimard philosophy series. The biographies of Genet and Flaubert each contain passages of extraliterary significance which complete, clarify, and correct the works of technical philosophy. All three lives, particularly the Flaubert, treat such an astonishing variety of crisscrossing themes that their assignment to the genre of literary criticism constitutes a serious vitiation of their broadest aims. In these audacious books, psychology, economics, social and cultural history, political philosophy, aesthetics, and ontology are fused by an overriding concern with the problem of the creation of an ethical anthropology.

Together, Sartre's biographies form a twentieth-century Laocoön group. Two small figures, Baudelaire and Genet, together with a much larger one, Flaubert, struggle with and are compositionally united by a single formidable serpent, whose multiple and anarthrous attitudes bind them, rendering defensive strategies all but impossible. Alienation is Sartre's name for this ubiquitous monster. Although today the word has been coopted to label the most prosaic complaints, for Sartre alienation forms the crux of his thought. Because of it, the biographies flow into one another and interact with the philosophical works providing their conceptual support. Sartre's career has been a long search for the tools to understand men from the point of view of their freedom. But since men are often disposed to hold their freedom in horror, or to steal the freedom of others, he has been obliged to approach the issue principally from the negative, to study how men have refused freedom, how it has been refused them, and how they have either acquiesced in or rebelled against this theft of their substance. Approaching the biographies from the point of view of Sartre's various concepts of alienation leads to an understanding of them that is not abusively reductive, which rather simplifies their contents while retaining all their intended levels of meaning. To read these books without continuous reference to the idea of alienation is to ignore their fiercely political impetus.

Sartre did not always consider biography a meaningful task. In *Nausea,* his first novel, it is portrayed as a decadent, gratuitous, and bedeviled genre, whose goals are ultimately impossible. The failed pursuit of biography is chosen as a metaphor for the inevitability of solipsism and the illusionary character of any notion of a coherent, aesthetically shaped life. "Is there a Truth of man?" Sartre asks in the *Critique.*[21] In *Nausea* the answer seems to be no.

The protagonist of the novel, Antoine Roquentin, is a feckless biografiend, disenchanted by his clerkly efforts to improve the real by imposing on it an arbitrary order. For the past three years Roquentin has been in Bouville, engaged in the futile and faintly comical project of a life of Adémar de Rollebon, a dimly recalled eighteenth-century figure of court intrigue. A footnote about Rollebon which Roquentin had read ten years before had seduced him and become the genesis of the project. At first Rollebon lived vividly in Roquentin's imagination, and he took enormous pleasure in making sense of the devices of the Marquis: "How I loved M. de Rollebon that year! I remember one evening—a Tuesday evening: I had worked the whole day at the Mazarine; I had just discovered, on the basis of his correspondence from 1789–90, the magnificent manner in which he tricked Nerciat. It was night, I went down the Avenue du Maine and, at the corner of the Rue de la Gaîté, I bought some chestnuts. How happy I was! I laughed to myself as I thought of the expression Nerciat must have worn when he returned from Germany."[22] The understanding of the Marquis provides a privileged moment, for in comprehending the life of another, Roquentin has provisionally redeemed his own life from ambiguity and flux. Biographical tidiness offers a temporary antidote to his nausea: the sense of a lack of necessity in the world, the feeling that everything could be other than it is, that anything can happen.

But just as Roquentin thinks he has nailed the Marquis dead, Rollebon walks off with the nail. After finishing a chapter on the Marquis' equivocal dealings in Russia, Roquentin becomes troubled by an inability to attribute motivations to his ambiguous behavior. Rollebon's role in the assassination of Paul I, his spy mission to the East, and his betrayal of Alexander for the profit of Napoleon do not fall patly into any perceivable pattern: "What is missing in all these reports is stability and consistency. It is true that they don't contradict, but neither do they agree; they don't seem to concern the same person." Conventional psychological categories are of little aid in Roquentin's efforts to circumscribe the behavior of the mercurial Marquis: "I don't think that the profession of historian disposes one to psychological analysis. In our game we deal only with coherent emotions that we label with generic names such as Ambition, or Self-Interest." This mechanical division of the psyche into a mosaic of fixed instincts has to result in a failed representation. In the past, according to Roquentin, Rollebon "needed me to exist and I needed him in order not to feel my existence . . . He had delivered me from myself."[23] The two had worked out a cozy symbiotic relationship, each providing the other with sense and shape. For Roquentin, however, biography loses its charmed, accident-proof status when the subject proves refractory to all attempts to impose cohesion. The collapse of the biographical project functions as a negative epiphany. The disjointed Marquis can now function only as a correlative of the biographer's own elusive and incoherent existence—and as the final proof that language and psychological categories are traducers of the reality of life.

Faith in representations of the individual is undermined on other occasions in the novel. Sartre introduces the fiction of an insipid scholarly editor who has prepared the journals of Roquentin for publication. His desiccated introduction and footnotes contrast starkly with the rich and intense firsthand experience they are intended to frame. In the municipal museum of Bouville Roquentin also finds himself surrounded by mendacious images. In a gallery given over to commissioned portraits of past dignitaries, Roquentin comes upon a painting of Olivier-Martial Blévigne, a five-foot, squeaky-voiced reactionary whom the powers of art have transformed into a superb and threatening figure.

Roquentin is initially disturbed by the fact that the only way of making sense of the shards of Rollebon's life is through constructing hypotheses that derive from the imagination rather than from facts. His realization that the characters in a novel seem more true than the real but problematical Marquis leads Roquentin to relinquish the attempt to find consistency. He recognizes that an aesthetically patterned life is not possible in the world of existence. Instead, he entertains the idea of basing a work of fiction on the life of Rollebon, resorting frankly to the imagination as the only, if illusory, means to retrieve the life of the Marquis and his own in the bargain.

The failure of Roquentin as biographer can be attributed in part to an inadequate method and a failure of will after discovering the proper tool within his grasp. His epistemological nihilism is premature. If he had been a careful reader of Bergson, as Sartre was, his life of Rollebon might have been less painful. Although it is a tradition to begin an account of the formative influences on Sartre with the impact of Edmund Husserl, a study of Sartre as biographer must take into account the influence of Bergson which predates that of Husserl. Roquentin's insight that generic psychological labels are inadequate for dealing with human psychology has a Bergsonian feel. Sartre's protagonist expresses unhappiness over being a prisoner of what Bergson calls analytic or associationist thought, a methodology that inappropriately relies on atemporal, spatial models when confronting dynamic psychological realities. This method considers mental states in isolation, as detached fragments, and finds nothing in psychology but a welter of atomized drives. Any attempt to reconstitute the personality by juxtaposing these separated elements misses the essential unity of the subject. Analytic thought seeks to reconstruct other minds from the outside, having recourse only to inflexible, readymade categories.

Bergson believed that personality has a unity which must be grasped through intuition or "sympathy," if one is to arrive at a lived and indivisible apprehension rather than at an enumeration of qualities. Intuition places itself, through an effort of the imagination, within the dynamic subject. Only with this method is it pos sible to discover what is essential and unique about another person. Roquentin thus should not have been frightened of the uses of the imagination in his search for consistency.

That the influence of Bergson's methodology continues to be evident in the biographical method of the late Sartre is clear from his remark in the Genet biography, entitled *Saint Genet* (1952), "Let's try to understand, that is to say, to sympathize."[24] It is evident as well when Sartre explains that he does not consider *L'Idiot* to be a "scientific" work because:

> The term scientific would imply a rigor of *concepts*. As a philosopher I try to be rigorous through *notions,* and the distinction I make between concept and notion is the following: a concept is a definition in exteriority which is likewise atemporal; a notion . . . is a definition from the inside, which includes in itself not only the time supposed by the object whose notion it is, but also its own time as [an act of] knowledge. In other words, [a notion] is a thought which incorporates time. Thus, when you study a man and his history, you can proceed only by notions.[25]

Both Bergson's rejection of a form of knowledge that is external and atemporal and his suggestion of a superior knowledge that is a knowing from within are evident here. Another feature of Bergson's method that Sartre continues in his biographies is the idea that the goal of knowledge—an indivisible, lived grasp of the unique—can be achieved only by stepping outside of the traditional language and forms of philosophy and relying on genres and language usually associated with the artist.

Bergson's influence is as noticeable in the thematic content of the biographies as in their methodology. Sartre has remarked that his views on human consciousness had their original inspiration in Bergson's *Essai sur les données immédiates de la conscience*. Sartre's ideas on this subject seem to have derived, at least in part, from Bergson's distinction between spatial and temporal experience. The unconditionally free self of the early Sartre appears to be modeled on the free self of Bergson who experiences human reality as something that cannot be defined, as pure movement into the future.

According to Bergson, we determine ourselves; we are the result of our own choices. We are free "when our acts emanate from our entire personality, when they express it."[26] We are free when we experience ourselves as a flight into the future, but become unfree when we impose upon the experience of "duration" the vocabulary and experience of spatial categories, when we experience consciousness as a thing. We are unfree when we fix the activity of the self, when it is experienced as static, when our spontaneity is interfered with by the imposition of inappropriate perspectives which distort our experience of ourselves as always in the process of creation and hence refractory to measures and labels.

As Bergson remarks: "Most of the time we live externally to ourselves, only perceiving a colorless shadow of ourselves, a shadow that pure duration projects onto homogeneous space. Our existence thus transpires in space rather than in time: we live for the external world rather than for ourselves; we 'are acted upon *(sommes agis)*' rather than ourselves acting. To act freely is to retake possession of oneself, to replace oneself in pure duration."[27]

Recalling these words, Sartre says in *L'Idiot* of the young Flaubert, "he never had the impression of being an agent, but constantly that of being acted *(agi).*"[28] The ideal of self-possession found in Bergson, and the negative idea of not being in control of one's destiny, of experiencing oneself from the outside rather from within, appear on practically every page of Sartre's biographies. Because Baudelaire, Genet, and Flaubert experience themselves as labeled by themselves and by others, because they experience themselves from the outside and are hence narcissistic, they are unfree, beyond their own control.

In Bergson there is an implicit connection between ethical and epistemological ideals. People are not free unless a certain variety of knowledge is universalized. If men are objects to each other, then no man can ever be free. But if they have a form of knowledge based on a sympathetic reliving of the experience of the time world of the other, if spatial categories are eliminated from their view of their fellow men, then they can experience one another as free. This intimate connection between ethics and epistemology appears throughout Sartre's biographical enterprise, but particularly in *L'Idiot*.

A number of factors relating to Sartre's interest in biography—factors which help to explain both his fascination with the genre and the methods he employs—are rooted in his discovery of the phenomenology of Husserl, although on occasion Husserl offered less of a starting point than a confirmation of what Sartre had already learned from Bergson. In his first philosophical writings Sartre is preoccupied with the thought of the German teacher. He wrote articles on the idea of intentionality in Husserl, on Husserl's concept of the ego, and on emotions and the imagination from the phenomenological point of view, and he gave *Being and Nothingness* the subtitle *An Essay on Phenomenological Ontology*.

One of the most important features of Husserl's thought for Sartre is the theory of intentionality. For Husserl, consciousness is intentional, meaning that it is a consciousness of something, subject or object. Philosophy, by consecrating itself to describing the world through intuition, can achieve a naive point of view uncontaminated by a priori concepts. The phenomenological method begins with an accurate description of the objects of the real world as they appear to consciousness. From this point there must be no movement into metaphysics, for the goal is to preserve the immediacy and uniqueness of the thing as it appears to consciousness, to focus exclusively on the idiosyncratic individual phenomenon rather than on the class.

Phenomenology resembles literature in its ambition to individuate and to confront the concrete, and it respects literature as a means of revealing the nature of human consciousness. Sartre was early aware of these implications in his acquaintance with phenomenology: "Husserl reinstituted the horror and the charm of things. He has restored to us the world of artists and prophets."[29]

The phenomenologist's assertion that it is not possible to speak of consciousness outside of its real context is in part responsible for the idiographic character of Sartre's thought, its focus on the individual, the particular, the unrepeatable. Sartre's need to anchor his thought in real experience and the individual phenomenon brings his philosophical work close to literature. This concrete imagination is most strikingly displayed in the anecdotes used to illustrate technical philosophical points in *Being and Nothingness,* such as the histrionic waiter swallowed up in his own legend or the embarrassed voyeur. An approach to the abstract through the concrete is one of the most characteristic features of Sartre's manner of philosophising. All of his activities in the literary genres, journalism, and biography reveal this tendency of his thought to move from the conceptual to the concrete, felt experience which he has previously articulated in a more abstract form.

For phenomenological analysis, confrontation with the object, is finally subordinate in Husserl's thinking to making sense of other selves.[30] Knowledge of the experience of another is not, as Descartes thought, comparable to knowledge of an object, for the other is an object who is also a subject. Knowledge of the other originates in the solipsistic stage of inquiry but must also go beyond it. The other must be accounted for as another subject, or as another self-constituting stream of experience with the same world. The subjectivity of the alter ego must be correlated with the activity of the subject to whom it is given. By analogy with one's own experience, one grasps the experience of the other. One understands the other as an analogue of oneself. But as the other is more than this, because his experience is not identical with one's own, a further step is required. A person must imagine what he would feel from the other's point of view. Through this imaginative projection one's image of the other acquires a vivacity that it would not otherwise have, and at the same time it secures an independence with regard to its own perspective.

This experience is necessarily a fiction, for one is not the other, but it represents an advance, for it constitutes a liberation from a personal point of view and a true movement into the point of view of another. The result is, as Ricoeur remarks, "A transfer into another life in imagination and sympathy."[31]

Sartre could have found in this theory of Husserl additional justification for adopting the method of Bergson. Throughout Sartre's remarks on the tools required by the biographer are references to the ideas of sympathy and of imaginative projection into the experiences of the other. The necessary roles of imagination and sympathy in biography were not, however, the discovery of German phenomenology. In 1750 Samuel Johnson observed, "All joy or sorrow for the happiness or calamities of others is produced by an act of the imagination, that realizes the event however fictitious, or approximates it however remote, by placing us, for a time, in the condition of him whose fortune we contemplate; so that we feel, while the deception lasts, whatever emotions would be excited by the same good or evil happening to ourselves."[32] Iris Murdoch has argued that "The novelist proper is, in his way, a sort of phenomenologist . . . [more] a describer than an explainer."[33] If the biographer attempts to seize the world as it appears to the subject and to apprehend that person in his pristine reality without recourse to preconceived notions, the biographer may also be said to be a phenomenologist. Sartre's methods, however, do not always permit this label.

Another feature of Husserl's thought that perhaps influenced Sartre's biographical practice is the emphasis on phenomenology as an eidetic rather than a factual science. The phenomenologist strips off the layers of accidental attributes and reduces facts to those that reveal essence. The method does not involve accumulating a vast catalogue of facts regarding an individual but rather focuses on a few features or incidents that disclose the individual's essence. Similarly biography for Sartre is not the accumulation of a constellation of details of an individual's life but the discovery of his essence by focusing on a few moments of truth.

Together with Bergson's concept of consciousness, Husserl's idea of intentionality seems to have had a critical role in the genesis of the single most prominent concern of Sartre's writings: his concept of freedom. Sartre's obsession with this theme in turn has implications for his use of biography, both in providing an important justification for it, almost seeming to make cultivation of the genre an imperative task for the philosopher, and in requiring the development of biographical methods that preserve respect for the free subject. From Bergson, as well as from Husserl's idea that consciousness is consciousness of something, Sartre has drawn the conclusion that transcendance is the constitutive structure of consciousness. Consciousness is born oriented toward a being which is not itself. It is purified of thing-hood or determinism of any kind. He rejects Husserl's contention that the ego is the origin of intentionality, maintaining instead that the ego is itself an object of consciousness. The for-itself is prepersonal and prereflexive; it is an emptiness, a self-transcending, spontaneous activity. From this notion Sartre deduces the total freedom of the self.

The early Sartre believed that a person is free to choose himself, regardless of the circumstances in which he finds himself. Later Sartre modified this concept of freedom to take into account the dimension of history. Today he rejects the concept of freedom which holds that a person is free to make of himself what he will no matter what his situation. In Sartre's present view of freedom, circumstances play an overpowering if not wholly determining role. It is "the small movement that makes of a totally conditioned social being a person who does not simply reflect back the totality of what he has received from his conditioning."[34] The change is significant. Man is still a free subject, but circumstances impose conditions. Freedom is ontologically given but historically taken away. To account for a person, one must not study him exclusively as an object, as Sartre claims anthropologists are prone to do; one must rather recreate him as a free subject. Sartre believes, however, that one must add to that understanding of man as a free, transhistorical subject a view of him as an object of history. Man must be studied as object-subject, consideration being given to both the transhistoricity of the historical man and the historicity of the transhistorical man. Man is irreducible to history but is nonetheless rigorously conditioned by it.

Phenomenology has considerable implications for psychoanalysis. Angelo Hesnard, with whose works Sartre is acquainted, examined these implications in *Apport de la phénoménologie à la psychiatrie contemporaine*. This work explains how Sartre's methods follow from a phenomenological attitude and incidentally suggest the possible influence of Hesnard on Sartre. The rejection of an unconscious identified with an instinctual drive seems to follow as naturally from Husserl's ideas as from those of Bergson. For the phenomenologically oriented psychologist, according to Hesnard, consciousness has as its essential characteristic the fact that it is not hidden from itself. Instead of the conscious and unconscious, Hesnard speaks of the "lived that is present (vécu actuel)" and the "lived that is not present (vécu inactuel)," by which he means an awareness that can be conceptualized and verbalized and one that is latent and unformulated. Psychoanalysis "is but a search for the meanings of structures that are *lived (vécues)* before being thought. An 'unconscious' thought would be a thought that does not think itself—which would be contradictory."[35] Sartre too, instead of accepting the usual idea of the unconscious, believed in what he called the "lived," which is clearly modeled on Hesnard's concept. In adopting this term, Sartre notes that he "wanted to give the idea of an ensemble, the surface of which is completely conscious and of which the rest is opaque to this consciousness and, without being unconscious, is hidden from you."[36]

If there is no determining unconscious, Hesnard argues, then human psychology is founded upon the subject's relations with others. Psychoanalysis is the study of intersubjective links; it is a study of man's being in the world, his communication with others and his experience of his objective context. Sartre becomes fully aware of this only in *Saint Genet* and *L'Idiot*. A major cause of neurosis, according to Hesnard, is the radical devaluation that a child may experience in early youth. One of the consequences of this traumatic devaluation is a defective relationship with words. The distressed individual creates, as a defensive strategy, "a language without dialectic," which is "more speaking than spoken."[37] Communication with others dissolves into a meaningless discourse. Sartre makes use of these ideas in *L'Idiot,* where Flaubert is described as having been persuaded by his parents that he was without intrinsic value, for which he compensated by constructing an imaginary world that included a language based on a refusal to communicate.

Sartre believes that the task of philosophy is to show man as an actor. The philosophy that does so he calls "dramatic philosophy." Kierkegaard was a founding father of this kind of philosophy because he introduced into it "biography as buffoonery, or as drama."[38] But philosophy, strictly speaking, does not concern itself with the specific individual. Kierkegaard, whose point of departure is autobiographical, is thus labeled an "antiphilosopher" by Sartre. In order to come to terms with Sartre's conclusions concerning man as irreducible subject, the philosopher must become an antiphilosopher, that is, a biographer.

Together with pure literature, biography has been Sartre's means of approaching the ideal of making philosophy coincide with experience. Explaining his interest in biography, Sartre has observed, "To understand Adam is to become Adam."[39] If man is a free subject and one seeks to understand him as such, there can be no dissociation between knowing and feeling, between comprehension and a concrete re-experiencing of all the dimensions of his life. Empathy becomes a condition of understanding: "To understand a man empathy is the necessary attitude."[40]

Perfect empathy that does not exclude a retention of individuality is one of the most frequently expressed ideals of the later Sartre. Hell is no longer other men but is rather the impossibility of empathy. *"You are not me,"* Goetz cries in *The Devil and the Good Lord*, "it's unbearable. I don't understand why we are two and I would like to become you while remaining myself."[41] This kind of empathy which does not preclude a freedom-saving distance is the central feature of Sartre's biographical method, although it manifests itself fully only in the last two biographies.

Kierkegaard is joined in his role as founding father of dramatic philosophy by Hegel, the philosopher who studied man in action as the object of history. According to Sartre, Hegel's descendant Marx, together with Kierkegaard, propose the essential question of philosophy. The task of philosophy suggested by these two men is to discover the singularity of the universal and the universalization of the singular. This practical task can be nothing other than the study of the life of an individual man. It is mainly the Kierkegaardian approach to understanding men as transhistorical subjects that dominates *Baudelaire,* but in *Saint Genet* and *L'Idiot* the question jointly suggested by Marx and Kierkegaard is answered in progressively more systematic fashion.

The wish for empathy expressed by Goetz in Sartre's play is closely related to another wish expressed by the same character later on: "Give me the eyes of the lynx of Boeotia so that I penetrate under this skin."[42] The ideal of transparency expressed directly here, as well as implicitly throughout the biographies, is one that Sartre has often voiced: "A man must exist entirely for his neighbor, who in turn ought to exist entirely for him."[43] This ideal has been pursued in Sartre's private life as well as in his writings. De Beauvoir reports of her early years with Sartre that they had a horror of private thoughts, "these gardens where refined souls cultivate delicate secrets . . . where all the devices of bad faith are at play." To dissipate these shadows, the two friends made a pact to expose fully to one another their thoughts and feelings. "Sartre was as transparent to me as I was to myself: what tranquility."[44] In *The Age of Reason* (1945) Mathieu and Marcelle make a similar agreement. Sartre has largely renounced any private inner life. Commenting on the possibility of the publication of his letters and other personal documents, he has stated, "So much the better if that permits me to be as transparent to the eyes of posterity—if it is interested in me—as Flaubert is to mine."[45] Sartre maintains that the primary responsibility for spoiling the relations between people belongs to the fact that "each conserves in his relations with the other something hidden, and secret." The remedy lies in the Edenic condition of universal mutual transparency: "I think that transparency must always take the place of the secretive, and I can well imagine the day when two men will no longer keep secrets from one another, because they will keep none from anyone, because subjective life, as well as objective life, will be totally offered, given."[46]

Sartre's acceptance of the idea of intentionality and his rejection of the existence of a preconstituted ego brought him to the concept of consciousness (the for-itself) as a void, a pure, transparent, nonsubstantial, prepersonal nothingness. The for-itself may experience the in-itself (unconscious matter) as either a threat or a temptation. During a hallucinatory experience with the chestnut tree, Roquentin is terrified of the danger that it holds for the integrity for the for-itself. Consciousness may experience its own indeterminancy as anxiety and may envy the ontological status of a thing, seeking to escape its unease through a coincidence with the massive and non-transparent object. This urge, which Sartre calls bad faith, is a threat to transparency and hence to the freedom of consciousness.

Sartre's equation of positive culture with the search for transparency is freighted with political implications. His hostility to a culture of opacity, the expression of the ideal of the impenetrable man, is related to his antipathy to all forms of authority and inequality. A person who is transparent cannot hold power over another. This thought appears in the words of the Archbishop in *The Devil and the Good Lord:* "If the end of this day brings me news of my defeat, my usury will be so great that they will see through my person: and what, Lord, will you do with a transparent minister?"[47] Transparency makes power impossible, for to be transparent means to be experienced as a subject, and as Sartre explains in *Saint Genet*, a leader cannot be a subject to his subordinates, unless he is willing to relinquish his authority.[48] When biography is driven by the ideal of transparency, it forms a protest against the idea of one man having power over another. The leveling, subversive function of biography for Sartre is clear at the end of his autobiography, where he reports that his goal in that work has been to display himself as "Wholly a man, composed of all men, the equal of all, and no better than any."[49] For the late Sartre, successful biography is an anarchistic act.

If consciousness has unobstructed access to itself, as Sartre maintains, then two things obtain: there can be no determining unconscious in the Freudian sense, and the reality of one consciousness may be thoroughly revealed to another, on the condition that a means of expression is found. For the late Sartre, all is communicable. To Pierre Verstraeten he said, "I think that there is nothing that cannot be said."[50] He regards incommunicability as one of the major pernicious myths of bourgeois literature of the nineteenth and early twentieth centuries. To debunk it, Sartre wrote L'Idiot, which for him demonstrates "that ultimately all is communicable and that one can achieve, without being God, being a man like any other, if one has the needed elements, a perfect understanding of a man."[51] To accept the concept that a biological unconscious determines behavior, or to insist that no psychological reality can be communicated, is to permit the consciousness to disallow the unconditional freedom of the for-itself and to appropriate it to the mute and opaque world of things.

This obsession with transparency is also evident in Sartre's language ideal. He has remarked that poets use words as if they were nontransparent things. The attention of the reader is focused on the sensuous surface of the word and hence does not pierce easily beyond that surface to the thing it designates. In prose the reader does not dwell on the word as an object but moves directly to what is signified, or as George Orwell described it, "Good prose is like a window pane."[52] Because such language is a faithful image of the free for-itself, the reader experiences it as an appeal to his own freedom. Sartre has pointed out a regressive use of words which he terms "creation-appropriation." In this case language does not have communication as its end but aims rather at the magical creation and possession of the object that is evoked. For Sartre, Flaubert typifies this attitude. Such an infantile use of language must be held in check for the sake of improving communication. It is understandable that Sartre, with his ideal of psychological gymnosophism, would refuse other men their secrets and, with his faith in the complete expressibility of another life, should turn to the genre most obviously suited to giving flesh to these convictions.

Because modern poets, according to Sartre, make a choice in favor of opacity, they are saying that communication and hence human life is impossible, that solipsism and power are inevitable. If poetry bears witness to the defeat of man, it is the task of biography to prove this witness false. If successful biography must be antiphilosophy, it must also be antipoetry.

Foucault has noted that the eighteenth century discovered two related but ultimately opposed concepts of transparency.[53] In his invention of the panopticon, Jeremy Bentham provided an architectural solution for the needs of institutions, such as hospitals and prisons, that required surveillance of the many by the few. The panopticon involves two complementary structures. A building in the shape of a ring is divided into cells for the inmates. Each cell has two windows, one facing outward, the other facing toward the center of the ring. Light is allowed to pass through the cells, permitting a warden in an observation tower at the center of the ring an unobstructed vision of the activities of the residents. This variety of transparency was developed to serve the needs of a centralized, unshared disciplinary power. Rousseau envisioned a transparent society of a very different kind: a world of total visibility that would not serve but would rather put an end to privileged power. Men would have unrestricted access to one another; they would communicate freely, without mediation. There would be no more obscurity behind which unjust authority can hide. It has been charged that Sartre's imperialistic biographical methods result in his creation of "a panopticon in which the analyst plays a godlike game in his totalizing 'look' at the other."[54] However, Sartre's biographical enterprise as a whole shows rather that the model suggested by Rousseau is more relevant.

At the heart of each of Sartre's major philosophical statements lies a biographical method. The tenets of Sartre's Bergsonian system of existential psychoanalysis are elaborated in *Being and Nothingness* (1943), and the progressive-regressive method is explained in the *Search for a Method*. Although he has come to realize that existential psychoanalysis can provide only part of the truth about a man, he uses this tool throughout the three biographical essays.

In describing existential psychoanalysis, Sartre cites a passage on Flaubert from Bourget: "In his early youth he seems to have experienced as his normal state a perpetual exaltation, composed of a simultaneous feeling of grandiose ambition and invincible strength . . . The effervescence of his young blood took the form of a literary passion, as happens in about the eighteenth year to those precocious souls who find in the energy of style or the intensity of fiction something to stave off the need to act or feel too intensely that torments them."[55] Sartre uses this comment to launch an attack on conventional empirical psychological analysis. Bourget has reduced the personality of the adolescent Flaubert to a few basic, universalized drives. Overweening ambition, a desire for violent action, and intense feeling all join together to produce a permanent state of exaltation. For Bourget, this psychological pointillism provides a satisfactory explanation of Flaubert's urge to write. For Sartre, it is unacceptable.

Flaubert's literary temperament cannot be explained simply by a particular confluence of universal desires. They fail to account for his specific calling. Flaubert the individual has disappeared behind the play of abstract forces and drives. Bourget cannot tell why Flaubert turned to literature rather than to the other arts. Sartre is disturbed by the fact that this sort of psychology dominates biography: "Open a biography at random, and this is the sort of description you will find there, more or less interspersed with narrations of external events and allusions to the great speculative idols of our time, heredity, education, milieu, constitution, and physiology."[56] Roquentin was just such a biographer; he tried to glue Rollebon together with universal concepts, but the Marquis fell to pieces. The connection between the forces of ambition and self-interest and his acts was too loose and too abstract. One cannot portray character by successive strokes, reconstructing a person by adding together his inclinations and then stopping.

As Sartre perhaps learned from Bergson, each man is a totality founded upon a radical decision that he has made about himself. This is the psychic irreducible from which all else follows. And since the essence of man is this freely decided original "project," each of his inclinations expresses this choice in its entirety. The search for this "project" or choice is the task of existential psychoanalysis: "The irreducible unification that we must find, which *is* Flaubert and which we ask biographers to reveal to us, is thus the unification of an original project."[57]

In all men this original project derives from the character of the for-itself. It is defined ontologically as a lack of being, which is synonymous with freedom. The for-itself chooses a project in order to cease experiencing itself as a void. That being which the for-itself lacks is the in-itself with which it desires to coincide in order to form the impossible object, the for-itself in-itself. Sartre equates this unrealizable fusion, this consciousness that is no longer a nothingness but a thing, with God, and man becomes defined as the desire to be God. Men seek this end in their particular empirical situations. The infinite catalogue of the original projects of men derives from, and is reducible to, this original project of human reality. The varieties of first choices are the different ways of concretely symbolizing this fundamental desire. In Sartre's early thought he defines the for-itself in-itself ahistorically as the end of all human striving, but he later calls it "this spiritual nothingness." In *L'Idiot* it will appear as the ideal of a society in which the commodity is the universal structuring principle.

Sartre's focus on the decisive and ubiquitous choice imbues his portraits with a rigidity and austerity that has analogues in the medieval saint's life, or in the tradition of the Theophrastan character sketch as represented by such authors as Jean de La Bruyère, Thomas Overbury, and John Earle. By briefly describing a series of characteristic traits, each of these authors demonstrates how his subject represents an ethical type. Like Sartre at times, the Theophrastan is a deductive portraitist. Because of a desire to achieve coherence and to make the subject truer than reality, the author omits or adjusts details to fit the simple, imposed frame. In the nineteenth century Taine maintained that in every man one could discover the "master faculty" that motivated his every action. This same idea, perhaps owing to the influence of classical literary theory, was much in evidence in eighteenth-century English biography. In his life of Horace Walpole, William Coxe explained that the task of the biographer was to seek out "one grand principle of action."[58] More immediately relevant is the psychoanalytic case study that seeks to understand a single forcefully present impulse by discovering its origins in the impressions of earliest childhood. Like Freud in his imaginative reconstruction of the youth of Leonardo, Sartre dispenses with most of the undramatic, atmospheric background material that has been associated with biography since Boswell. There are no words wasted on undecisive events, no anecodotes told for their own sake, no attempt to reproduce the formless flux of life, no effort to recreate the sensual world of the subject, no painterly touches—in short, no untendentious curiosity.

The search for the single organizing truth is responsible for the fact that Sartre's biographies upset some of the expectations that have been generated by more conventional examples of the genre. Sartre does not always seek to reproduce the original temporal order as lived. He may spend pages throwing a dramatic, Caravaggesque light on an obscure or even imagined childhood event, but discard great clumps of years because they disclose no subsequent conversion to a new self-image. In *L'Idiot* Sartre lurches wildly from one decade to another in order to discover secret passages within the life of the novelist. We are told that Flaubert died on September 4, 1870, long before the biological fact.

What counts are the moments of conversion or false conversion. Everyday events are nothing more than reflections of the ubiquitous choice. Between these traumatic moments, Sartre's subjects lead lives that have a comic quality, because they are only capable of living in repetition, continuously engaged in self-caricature. By being faithless to the calendar time of his subjects, Sartre is able to recreate the more essential internal experience of time that is founded in their relationship with the original choice.

The focus on the epochal choice brings these books into closer relation with works of art than with biography with scientific pretensions. Sartre's subjects have a frozen, flattened-out, overmanaged quality that causes them to ressemble characters in a *roman à thèse*. In his works of fiction proper, Sartre carefully avoids this impression, but in the biographies he seems to provoke it consciously. For him the interpretive understanding of a historical individual does not pretend to be a thorough copy but is instead a structural representation or summational fiction. Rather than grasping every experiential detail, Sartre seeks to establish an ideal order that is intentionally false to the ambiguity of actual experience. The reasons are given by Dilthey when describing his own concept of how the individual ought to be represented: "Artistic creation produces types which raise and intensify the manifold of experiences to an image and thus represent it. Thus, the opaque and mixed experiences of life are made comprehensible in their meaning through the powerful and clear structure of the typical. That which is elevated and connected in the type, what is seen to be necessary to the coherence of life from the vantage point of the life of the creator—that we can call the essential."[59] The biographer must make use of bold, unambiguous contours if the reader is to grasp the essence of his subject. He must be false to his subject, to a limited, selective extent, if he hopes to be true. Sartre's concept of the single choice leads him to violate most of his suggestions for the novelist, such as the use of a decentered point of view, rejection of the godlike narrator who sees into the minds of his creations, and presentation of characters who surprise because of their ambiguities. His biographical practice leads to the creation of works that bear a greater resemblance to the conventional novel than to the new model he suggests.

Sartre's totalizing method had an exponent in Roland Barthes, who in his biography of Michelet repeated Sartre's hunt for an individual's single truth. Barthes later concluded, however, that one cannot hope to isolate a final, ultimate truth about an individual.

In Derida's *Glas,* without mentioning Sartre by name, the author condemns a certain "ontophenomenologist of liberation" for his sadistic efforts to fix the meaning of Genet's life.[60] The mood of others has also turned decisively against this kind of knowledge of the subject. For Foucault, all attempts to isolate the particularity of an individual are the tools of power. André Glucksmann has condemned Wagnerian, totalizing interpretations that pretend to account for everything, holding them accountable for the political horrors of our time.

In accordance with this current reluctance to fix meaning, Barthes has suggested that the "biografiend" be suppressed in favor of the assembler of "biographemes," random scraps of biographical debris: bits of knowledge, images, and innocuous observations that are more likely to have aesthetic than tendentious value. Here, for example, are extracts from his brief, experimental life of Fourier: "Fourier hated old cities: Rouen . . . Inter-Text: Claude de Saint-Martin, Senacour, Restif de la Bretonne, Diderot, Rousseau, Kepler, Newton . . . His knowledge: mathematical and experimental science, music, geography, astronomy . . . His old age: he surrounded himself with cats and flowers."[61]

The neologism *biographeme* is unnecessary, for there existed in eighteenth-century England and France the biographical subgenre called the *-ana,* a largely uncontrolled cumulation of anecdotes from the life of an individual. Purged of the "one grand principle," deconstructed biography is innocent of power, taking pleasure in its unwisdom and its refusal to conclude or in any other way to radiate an assurance of mastery. For Sartre, the question of the biographical will to power is far from being a red herring. Biography has been known to take the form of the time-lapse mug shot. But the radical innocence achieved by the biographeme may also cause it to fall into the hands of power, for it is a form of knowing that is too diffuse to permit real empathy or to illuminate the causes of alienation.

The influence of Dilthey's romantic hermeneutics on Sartre's biographical method is perhaps even more substantial than the influence of Marx. It may also extend to the title of the *Critique,* for Dilthey wrote a work entitled *Critique of Historical Reason.* Although today Dilthey is little read in France, a Frenchman who knows his work well is Raymond Aron, at one time a good friend of Sartre.[62]

Dilthey's most signal achievement was the development of a systematic, multidimensional methodology for the human sciences. He believed that the basic unit of historical reality is not a collective mind, or will, but rather the individual human being. Biography and autobiography are the genres that form the trunk from which all other human studies branch. As a consequence of these views, he became a biographer, writing an unfinished life of Friedrich Schleiermacher and biographical sketches of Hegel, Frederick II, Schiller, Goethe, Bruno, and Dickens.

Dilthey recommended a biographical method that would bring to bear the disciplines of economics, history, sociology, psychology, and literary criticism. This synthetic approach to knowledge was called anthropology by Dilthey, as by Sartre. Influenced by Schleiermacher's concept of the dialectical relation between the universal type and the individual instance, Dilthey used a shuttlecock movement between the part and the whole, between the general historical background which conditions a person and that person as individual. This background Dilthey termed, after Hegel, "the objective spirit."

> I understand by it the manifold forms in which the common background subsisting among various individuals has objectified itself in the sensible world. In this objective mind the past is for us a permanent enduring present. Its realm extends from the style of life and the forms of economic intercourse to the whole system of ends which society has formed for itself, to morality, law, the State, religion, art, science and philosophy. For the work of genius too represents a common stock of ideas, mental life, and ideals at a particular time and in a particular environment. From the earliest childhood our self receives its nourishment from the world of objective mind. It is also the medium in which the understanding of other persons and their expressions takes place. For everything in which the mind has objectified itself contains in itself a factor common to the I and the Thou."[63]

It is necessary to focus on the objective spirit in order to discover in what way a person is unique. That Sartre was influenced by this concept is clear in the third volume of *L'Idiot,* which is largely devoted to a study of "the objective spirit" of Flaubert's day.

But this to-and-fro procedure is not sufficient to arrive at a complete understanding of a man. Like Bergson, Dilthey objected to the influence of the natural sciences in psychology, for he felt that the models they provide are inadequate for explaining man from the point of view of his changeability and freedom. Dilthey's system contained a romantic protest against the view that a person can be explained in the same way that material phenomena can be explained by the natural sciences. To avoid treating a person as an object, one must know that the "basis of human studies is not conceptualization but total awareness of a mental state and its reconstruction based on empathy."[64] A person cannot be understood exclusively from the outside but must also be explained from within. Dilthey's term for this empathy-based knowledge is *das Verstehen,* "comprehension." "Interpretation," he wrote, "rests on comprehension, which rests on a projection of the self into the other, and this is not an intellectual but an imaginative act."[65]

The details of the mental life of another can be interpreted only in terms of one's experience of the whole. Thus Dilthey rejected the mosaic theory and believed, like Husserl after him, that one cannot know another simply by accumulating a quantity of empirically verifiable data. Rather, one comes to understand another by examining the typical and crucial episodes of that person's experience. One must seek to grasp much in little, for the goal is to see the other as an integral whole. To follow the conventional procedure of the modern biographer, by recounting long trains of events covering months and years, is to work against this end. By rendering a portrait too diffuse, excessive, or unfocused, documentation can be a block to understanding.

Because Marxism furnishes the only valid interpretation of history, according to Sartre, it cannot be dispensed with. Marxism is the philosophy of our time, and we cannot go beyond it until we have surpassed the historical situation it accurately describes. Any so-called surpassing of Marxism today can only be the resuscitation of a pre-Marxist idea. For Sartre the only advance possible for the present would consist either in the rediscovery of a thought submerged, but already contained, in Marxism, or in new concrete applications of Marxist philosophy. One who sets out to make such a worthy contribution is not a philosopher but a "relative man," and what he creates is not a philosophy but an ideology, a parasitical system of ideas. Existentialism is just such an ideology, and its historical role is to return Marxism to its best and original instincts.

Marxism has ceased to evolve. It has expelled the free, evolving individual and become an antisubjectivist terrorism. For years, Sartre maintains, Marxist intellectuals believed that they were serving the party by violating experience, grossly simplifying data, and conceptualizing events or individuals before confronting them in their multidimensionality. Marxists have done violence to reality and their own cause by dispensing with detail. These superficial thinkers are guilty not only of consigning people to the tyranny of large social categories but also of explaining individuals and events in terms of raw economic factors, or economism. In short, man has become a thing. A focus on the typical in Marxist thought results in the suppression of the unique.

To understand Paul Valéry, for example, Sartre advises that it is

better not to consult the orthodox Marxist, for his inquiry is far
from comprehensive. He readily mentions the situation of Valéry's
social caste, the petite bourgeoisie, at the end of the last century and
how it was threatened on two fronts, by the demands of the working
class on the one hand and by the accumulation of capital on the
other. He speaks of a kind of idealism prevalent in Valéry's day,
at once analytic and tinged with pessimism, which was a defensive
reply to materialist rationalism. In this analysis the subject has been
properly situated, but he is merely situated. But much of Valéry
escapes this analysis, for he is far more than simply an ideological
reflex of class interest and has an element of autonomy that must
be accounted for. The integral man with his peculiar genius is thus
reduced to the role of a personage in a shadow play. Valéry was
indeed a *petit bourgeois* intellectual, but not every *petit bourgeois*
intellectual is Valéry. The specific man whom the Marxist claims to
consider has vanished from sight, for the individual personality does
not directly derive from the general fate of his class. A multitude of
mediating factors cannot be ignored.

It matters little that this aberrant thinking leads in literature to
This abstract approach is by no means endemic to Marxism.
Both Marx and Engels had denounced the reduction of the individual to *homo economicus*. Sartre does not question the basic Marxist
tenet that the material life of a given historical moment governs the
development of social, political, and intellectual life. He does, however, as did Marx and Engels, realize that each man lives these determinisms in a particular fashion and thus is not crudely reducible
to them. In its refusal to differentiate and its insistence on providing
only a dishonest caricature of the philosophy it pretends to apply,
contemporary Marxism is engaging in the terrorist practice of
liquidating the particular.

It matters little that this aberrant thinking leads in literature to
portraits more abstract than the reading public may find desirable,
but bleak consequences follow for millions of people who live in
political systems where individuals are both figuratively and literally
dissolved for the same reasons that they are in orthodox Marxist
biography. Sartre recalls a poster which appeared on the walls of
Warsaw in 1949: "Tuberculosis slows down production." This is
evidence of a fundamental misappropriation of the individual. For
Sartre, a certain variety of knowledge is the inevitable concomitant
of a world of reification. Freedom is inseparable from a respectful
knowledge of other men. A terrible epistemological shortcoming is
fatally involved in the workings of the society capable of inventing
the demoralizing form of encouragement that Sartre found in Warsaw. In the correction of the epistemic inadequacies of these super-

ficial Marxists, more is at stake than the theory of a secondary literary genre.

The progressive-regressive method is Sartre's antidote for the abstractions of an inhuman Marxist anthropology. This method demonstrates that men are free as well as determined, that they make their own history, though within an environment which conditions them. The seeds of such a method have always been contained within Marxism, and it is the historical task of existentialism, with its emphasis on the concrete man as the center of knowledge, to recall Marxism to its original interest in the specific human existence.

The new method is capable of revealing the dialectical movement of the "project," now defined by Sartre as the subjective surpassing of material pressures toward a self-objectification, and the poles of objectivity bordering this moment. The first of these poles is the determining set of economic circumstances, which are internalized and then externalized through the project by which a man creates the second pole: the production of himself in the world as a certain objective totality. The regressive moment of analysis discovers the historical particularity of the subject, his original circumstances, the society of the moment, and the political system and ideology in which the subject began to take form. With this first step in the regressive phase the slothful Marxist ends his task. He ignores the uniqueness that must be revealed at this stage, a uniqueness to be found in what Sartre calls, borrowing a term from Merleau-Ponty, the "differential." Sartre defines this as the disparity between the commonly held beliefs of a period and the particular attitudes of the individual.

The progressive phase of the investigation involves the study of the project. Only psychoanalysis can allow one to eliminate chance as an explanation while still passing from general and abstract determinisms to elucidation of the particular traits of an individual. It allows one to discover how a person lives his relationship to his class. During the progressive phase one must examine both a person's attitude toward the economically conditioned options open to him and his urge to objectify himself in a certain way. One must study a person's production and be attentive to its relationship to the original project, its adherence or deviation from the individual's choice of himself. Sartre reveals a further refinement of thinking regarding the dynamics of the project: "a life develops in spirals; it always passes again by the same points but at different levels of integration and complexity."[66] In *Being and Nothingness* the mechanics of psychological development are ignored. Like the dialectic of Hegel and Marx, the project manifests itself in a spiral pattern, appearing each time at a new level of integration. Sartre's use of the dialectic in this context is possibly evidence of the further influence of Hesnard, who recommended that the Hegelian dialectic be used to describe individual psychology.[67]

In the *Critique* Sartre illustrates his method with a condensed analysis of the life of Flaubert. It is reported in literary manuals, notes Sartre, that Flaubert is called the father of realism, yet during a trip to the Orient he conceived of writing a tale about a mystic virgin of the Netherlands who would be the symbol of his cult of pure art. Sartre asks how Flaubert could have held within himself these antithetical tendencies. How could he have been responsible for such apparently disparate works as *The Temptation of Saint Anthony,* which deals in a confusing fashion with great metaphysical themes of the day, and *Madame Bovary,* which seems dry, banal, and objective? Sartre first turns to the verifiable data of Flaubert's life. The literary work can be useful for clarifying the biography, though the work never reveals biographical secrets and can only serve to give the study some direction. The works reveal narcissism, idealism, solitude, dependence, and femininity, traits that suggest the presence of particular social factors and a unique childhood drama.

Sartre then turns to a study of the early childhood of Flaubert and his family relations. The family is for Sartre a mediation of crucial importance, being the particular context in which the individual experiences adherence to his social caste.[68] Sartre considers more generally young Flaubert's whole context, what determined the lives of families like his, such as the intellectual *petite bourgeoisie* which was created during the Empire, the halt in the advance of family capitalism, the conditions of the working class, and the return of landed proprietors. To discover the differential, Sartre compares Flaubert's family with other families of the period of a somewhat higher caste, such as that of Baudelaire, or that of the Goncourts, *petits bourgeois* who had been ennobled at the end of the previous century. In studying these families, their social characteristics and their ideological and professional loyalties, Sartre casts light on the complex situation of the Flauberts and the dominating contradiction in the life of Gustave, namely the conflict between the bourgeois spirit of analysis and religious emotion. At this point, when Sartre has revealed much of his subject, Flaubert nevertheless remains an abstraction.

Sartre next demonstrates the second progressive phase of the investigation, explaining how Flaubert's project appears and reappears throughout his life in a spiral pattern. As a child, Flaubert felt that he was deprived of the affection of his father, who lavished attention on the gifted elder brother, Achille. The very young Gustave proudly refused to resort to the obvious ruse of imitating the favored traits of his brother and settled on a pattern of distinguishing himself negatively. Entering school, he again found himself confronted with Achille, who nine years earlier had won all the awards and greatly pleased the father. The younger brother, choosing to be different from the prize-bedecked ghost, decided to be an average student and hence to disgrace the family. The honors awarded to other students were experienced by Gustave as a humiliation, because they once again reminded him of his inferiority to Achille.

The project is once again in evidence when Flaubert reluctantly agrees to study law. To prove himself different by demonstrating inferiority, he chooses to hate the profession, turns against his class, and resorts to fits of hysteria, idealism, and mysticism. *The Temptation of Saint Anthony* expresses this original project in all its purity. Flaubert's friends Louis Bouilhet and Maxime du Camp condemn the work's formlessness and excess, urging Flaubert to draw his inspiration instead from a contemporary incident. They press him, that is, to return to an accepted literary vehicle of the day, the realistic novel. Flaubert the metaphysician and mystic bends his will to their advice and deviates from his personal project. He objectifies himself as the author of *Madame Bovary,* the *petit bourgeois* whom he was reluctant to admit that he was. Because the original project is no longer discernible in his self-expression, *Madame Bovary* is an alienated objectification, a work that has escaped its author.

Returning to the regressive phase of the study, Sartre finds that contemporary with the publication of *Madame Bovary* there was a hopelessly banal school of realism whose adherents included Gustave Courbet and Louis Duranty. Although Flaubert professed contempt for this movement and reserved his devotion for a cult of pure art, the public read *Madame Bovary* as a representative piece of this kind of realism and refused to see within it the idealism, art, misanthropy, and spite for the bourgeoisie that Flaubert had expressed and which Baudelaire alone at the time understood. Flaubert's project had already been distorted on one level, and this incompletely faithful self-objectification was now compromised on a new level. Another moment of alienation was apparent. Flaubert no longer recognized himself in his novel as the public had chosen to understand the work. He had lost control of his objective existence.

Valéry observes that the biographer has two alternatives: he "can try to *live* his character, or instead to *construct* it."[69] Although for Valéry these options are mutually exclusive, for Sartre they clearly are not. Knowledge of man the object, which Sartre calls "intellection," must be complemented by comprehension of man the agent. Comprehension, as defined in *Search for a Method,* is the act by which one provisionally becomes the other, by which we exist his project. In this nonconceptual form of knowledge, being and knowing are fused. As Sartre phrased it, "To comprehend Adam is to become Adam. Our comprehension of the Other is never simply contemplative: it is but a moment of our praxis, a way of living, in struggle or in connivance, the concrete and human relation that unites us to him." In perfect knowing the knowledge of man the subject and man the object are joined: "This perpetual dissolution of intellection in comprehension and, inversely, the reverse movement that introduces comprehension into intellection as the dimension of rational nonknowledge at the heart of knowledge, is the very ambiguity of a discipline in which the questioner, the question, and the questioned are one." Comprehension establishes that man is not necessarily an object for man, that one can respect the freedom of the other by becoming that freedom without ceasing to be oneself. If this form of knowledge is not possible, then neither is human life, for "human existence and the comprehension of the human are not separable."[70]

Not only did Sartre's discovery of man the free subject require an excursion into biography, but his discovery of man the subject-object of history required a certain kind of biography. It might seem that the tools outlined in *Search for a Method* could only result in an archaeology of alienation, for today, Sartre remarks, and throughout all of past history, only the alienated man exists. But the method accomplishes more than showing how man exists his fate and struggles against it; it also affords an indirect view of an unrealized world of spontaneous empathy, one in which man is not merely an object for man. Through the method one experiences the fact that the present or past state of affairs it describes can be negated, for it portrays a world of alienation that is at once conserved and surpassed. What was, or is, and what ought to be are experienced in the same moment. As Dilthey noted: "A historical consciousness which is no longer abstract or conceptual and, therefore, does not dissolve into unlimited ideality, forms a basis for the unity of mankind."[71] Because of its focus on the blighted existence of the embattled individual, biography is the genre that most pointedly calls into question the condition of man in a world of scarcity and exploitation. But if biography is the site of the most telling demonstration of the irrationality of the whole, it can also reveal a glimpse of a utopian world in which the whole has become rational.

II

Proteus and the Rat Trap

This Proteus, endlessly defeated, but endlessly restored to
life behind a different mask: alienation.
This rat trap: the imaginary.

Sartre

Time and again Sartre has been referred to as the philosopher of
freedom. After a certain point in his development, however,
this label loses exactness. In the course of an interview about *L'Idiot*,
Sartre mentioned that Flaubert appeared to have been destined to
passivity by his status as the youngest in the family. "Destined?"
queried his interlocutors in apparent astonishment. "You risk surprising those who see in you the philosopher of freedom." Sartre
replied, "I feel that we are not free—at least provisionally—because
we are alienated."[1]

Sartre is today, and has been for some time, the philosopher of
alienation. During the war and the years that followed, when he discovered the existence of decisive social forces, the absoluteness of
freedom in his thinking underwent an erosion. He came to realize
that humans are not, as he had once confidently thought, unconditionally free, and that circumstances sometimes rob them of their
transcendence. During this period he reached a conclusion that has
dominated his writings and activities up to the present: "The freedom that I was implied that of all. And all were not free."[2]

In the *Critique* Sartre argues that the philosophy of freedom is
quite impossible today and can only be imagined as a thing of the
future. He does not mean that freedom does not exist. As he commented in 1975, "Everything that I have tried to write or do in my
life was meant to stress the importance of freedom."[3] That which
does not exist is the world of freedom that the philosophy of freedom
would be called upon to describe. Although the substance of con-

sciousness, considered abstractly, is indeed freedom, the antagonistic world of today is one of alienation, a vampire world in which
freedom is sensed indirectly and obscurely because it can be felt only
as an absence or, at best, as a perilously fragile thing. "When I say
'free,' I hope I am understood," Sartre observes. "There is spontaneity, but it is founded on a prefabricated essence."[4]

But if alienation exists, it is only because freedom exists. Alienation is a negative category, but at the same time it is positive, for
one cannot alienate an unfree man. To say that Sartre is a philosopher
of alienation is not at all to deny that he is a philosopher of freedom,
but rather affirms that he is a philosopher of a particular kind of
freedom which is hardly in evidence, but which would truly exist
except for a world of scarcity and exploitation. For Sartre, to speak
of freedom is necessarily to speak of its opposite: "freedom preexists
in the individual, in the sense that it appears in him from the very
beginning as exploited, and alienated. But everyone, in his very
alienation . . . grasps his freedom as the deviated affirmation of his
sovereignty."[5] It follows that human freedom can be seen only in
the biographies of alienated men.

Concrete description of the avatars of alienation becomes the
necessary complement to an abstract theory of freedom: "I think
that a theory of freedom that does not explain at the same time what
are alienations, to what an extent freedom can be manipulated, deviated, turned against itself, such a theory can cruelly deceive someone who assumes that freedom is everywhere."[6] Sartre defines the
sort of person who can facilitate Marxist revolution as one "who is
totally conscious of his alienation and, in the face of it, sees in the
future the possible existence of a society in which men would no
longer be alienated."[7] The principal task unifying Sartre's three-part
martyrology is to demonstrate the meaning of alienation and hence
indirectly to show the extent to which freedom might exist if historical conditions were otherwise.

Neither of Sartre's two major theories of alienation is totally original. The concept as it appears in *Being and Nothingness* is heavily
influenced by Hegel and perhaps also by Husserl, while the idea in
the *Critique* is almost completely Marxist. Sartre has an important
place in the history of ideas, not because he developed a distinctive
definition but rather because he broadened and applied the earlier
ideas in new and unexpected ways. Only by reading Sartre in the
context of his predecessors can one discover where the originality lies.

The concept of alienation as formulated by Sartre had its origins
in Hegel, who applied the term in several situations.[8] For Hegel,
human nature has its essence in "universality"; its significance there-

fore depends on its making itself comfortable with the universal. Since one of the manifestations of universality is social existence, man's unity with his society is desirable. Acute consciousness of oneself as existing individually, in disunity with society, is called alienation, which, as a falling away from universality, constitutes a separation from one's human essence and thus from harmony with oneself. Any turning away from the social world, such as solipsistic self-cultivation, falls into the category of alienation. Hegel also uses the term to designate the opposite phenomenon—the overcoming of alienation in the sense of separation. Man returns to universality and his human nature through alienation of his self-alienation, through surrender of his separateness and fusion with the social fabric. Another form of estrangement from man's essence occurs, according to Hegel, when he loses independence in the sense of being forced to rely on others for the vehicles through which to manifest his own individuality. Both Marx and Sartre were influenced by these ideas.

Another feature of Hegel's thought, the idea of objectification, had a great impact on subsequent thought about alienation. Although there is disagreement over Hegel's use of the term, both Marx and Sartre thought that Hegel equated it with alienation and criticized him for doing so.[9] Objectification became the point of departure for Marx's theory, and it was also the starting point for the *Critique*.

For Hegel, the *Geist* is all of reality. This Idea, or Spirit, is constantly engaged in a progressive motion: "The Spirit is essentially the result of its own activity: its activity is transcending of immediacy, negating it, and returning to itself."[10] The movement of the Spirit is a process of self-alienation and subsequent dealienation. The first variety of movement characteristic of the Spirit is self-externalization, or objectification. The Spirit externalizes itself, makes itself manifest in time and space, through displaying itself in an external, objective entity that is outside, hence alien, and seemingly hostile. The Spirit was formerly all of a piece, pure undifferentiated self-awareness, but at the stage of objectification it becomes conscious of being split off from itself in the foreign entity that it has generated. But the otherness of this alien and hostile self-projection is illusory because it is nothing other than the Spirit itself. It is a delusion of the *Geist*. The Spirit views this separation negatively because of its urge to be infinite, absolute knowledge of Spirit knowing itself as Spirit. Confronting its spatial and temporal projection, the Spirit experiences the "sorrow of finitude."[11] To experience itself as an objective and external phenomenon is to fall into localization and contingency. In the final phase of its history the Spirit overcomes the phase of self-estrangement by discovering that it has been self-deceived and that the objectification is nothing but an insubstantial reflection of itself. The alien projection is extinguished as a separate and hostile object, and the estrangement concludes with the Spirit, through knowledge, becoming reunited with itself.

The idea of objectification also has a more concrete application for Hegel. An essential human feature is the action which the human spirit takes to objectify itself in the world in a deed or the creation of an object. For Hegel this process results in alienation only when the individual ceases to identify with his objectification of himself as it appears in the world. Sartre, in *Being and Nothingness,* concludes that any self-expression results in alienation, not because of the relation between the for-itself and the matter upon which it inscribes itself but because of the presence of the hostile Other who steals this objectification.

The dominant influence on Sartre's early theory of alienation was Hegel's description of the relations between master and slave, his mythical account of the primitive sources of human history.[12] According to Hegel, the condition of self-consciousness is the presence of another self. The initial reaction of a consciousness when faced with another is to assert its own existence as a self against the other. The master seeks to assert himself by destroying the self of the slave. He founds his subjectivity upon the ruins of the subjectivity of the slave, existing as a subject to the extent that the slave exists as an object. The slave is reduced to the level of a thing, a mere instrument of the pleasure of the master. In Hegel's system the slave may definitively escape his relative status by a series of cognitive acts. It is not necessary to change the world to become free. The impact of this Hegelian model is found in most of Sartre's works, particularly *Saint Genet.*

The role of the idea of alienation in Marx's thought is harder to evaluate. Only in his early writings does the term figure centrally; later it appears sporadically and, on occasion, as a subject for ridicule. Sartre, among others, nevertheless insists that alienation is the major theme uniting all of Marx's writings.[13] The work with which Sartre is most clearly acquainted, and in which the term figures most prominently, is the *Economic and Philosophical Manuscripts* of 1844.

The point of departure of Marx's concept is Hegel's idea of objectification, which he adapted for his own very different purposes. Whereas Hegel had seen man as being a disembodied mind, Marx found man to be a natural being, corporeal and sensuous. He assumed the task of giving concreteness to his predecessor's abstractions about history and alienation, both of which he explained in terms of the play of economic forces. The phenomenon of alienation, according to Marx, represents the terrible effects of the capitalist economy on human beings, on their mental, physical, and social lives. It is a disease of the total social body and requires a total cure.

Marx discusses several types of alienation; religious, political, and most important, economic, which is the generator of all other forms. Common to all of these varieties is the sense of having lost to someone or something the essential feature of one's human nature: the control of one's own existence. Under capitalism, Marx claims, all of life is under the sway of inhuman power. In the case of religious alienation, man forfeits his nature to a god. His essence is transferred away from him and placed in an imaginary location. Religion is the imaginary realization of the human essence. De-alienation would entail its abolition and the rescue of the ideal freedom, which is the human essence, from its estranged position in a mythical being and its restoration to its proper location in real people. Speculative philosophy becomes a similar species of alienation when, as in Hegel's *The Phenomenology of Spirit,* it reduces man to an abstract mental process, estranging him from his concrete nature. As for political structures, they are nothing but formalized expressions of the alienated relations between men in a capitalist society.

In the *Manuscripts,* Marx catalogues four major ways in which the worker is alienated and reduced to a pathetic remnant of himself. He is estranged from his work, from the product of that work, from his fellow man, and from his human nature. Man is generically a worker: it is his nature to desire to express himself freely in his work. But in his labors in a capitalist society, the worker feels estranged from his work and hence from his essence as a human being. Under capitalism, labor is a sacrifice of life, for it belongs to someone other than oneself. The overlord capitalist decides on the kind of work, the character of the product, the conditions of work, and even whether the laborer can work at all, hence eat and live. In such a system a man does not feel his work to be a free extension of himself but rather a self-denial. A natural man works to satisfy freely and directly a personal need, while in a capitalist economy man works to satisfy a need which is not his own, and he is permitted to satisfy his physical requirements only indirectly through the earning of a wage. In a capitalist system labor is divided; an individual performs a single, limited, and repetitive task. He is thus estranged from the exercise of the full array of his abilities.

Alienation appears as well in the relationship with the product of labor, the object into which the worker pours his life. The self-objectification is alien in that it is not a self-expression: a person is unable to recognize himself in the result of his labor. He cannot use the object to stay alive or for purposes of self-development; once it leaves his hands, he has no control over what becomes of it. The worker's life is no longer his own but belongs to the object he has been forced to waste his life in producing. Having sucked the life out of the worker, the object takes on a malevolent and independent life of its own. It becomes a power which confronts him, a parasitic force which drains his vital substance and capriciously changes in value in the course of its movements on the market place. Sartre uses this model to explain both Flaubert's relationship to *Madame Bovary* and the relationship of the bourgeois to the world he has created.

The third major form of alienation is found in a man's relations with his fellow men. The worker is seen by Marx to be estranged from both the capitalist overlord and his own colleagues. If a man's product confronts him as an alien power, it is because the product belongs to another, and if a man's product is independent and hostile, the master of this product is viewed similarly. The capitalist does not retain his imperium over the worker by divine right or simply by wealth, but ironically by the repeated acts of the worker himself, who with each gesture ensures the dominion of the man who does not produce.

The fourth category is alienation from the "species," Marx's term for that assemblage of qualities which sets humans apart from other creatures. Whereas in a communistic society a man is free to develop these features fully, in a capitalist world the potential is necessarily stunted. Labor, for the worker, becomes strictly a means to the perpetuation of brute physical existence. The opportunity for free and spontaneous productive activity, which is the characteristic desire of the species, is taken from him since the capitalist dictates both the nature and the product of the worker's activity. A man's work becomes merely the crude means to perpetuate an existence empty of truly human features.

Alienation for Marx, however, is not located simply in the relations of the worker to his activity, product, fellow man, and species. It permeates the whole of the capitalistic society, dominating all of its members, institutions, and intellectual and spiritual expressions. The capitalist may well have a greater relative freedom than the worker, but he is nonetheless alienated. In producing alienated material objects, the worker spreads alienation through all the classes that have relations with the products. The products are carriers of the infec-

tion. Because everyone lives in the realm of alienation, universal
human emancipation will result from the freeing of the worker. The
nonworking capitalist is dominated by social handicaps that follow
in the wake of alienated labor: an inability to relate to his workers
or peers, a deforming desire to accumulate wealth, and an economic
uncertainty generated by the market fluctuations of his wares. He is
passively controlled by the product he offers for sale. Necessary to
man, for Marx, is a direct, personal, and active relationship with
production. Thus the parasite deprives himself of this requirement
for human fulfillment and, just like the worker, is in no position to
develop the full range of his potential. Since the means of production
determine consciousness—a claim Sartre embraces enthusiastically
—none of the occasions of human expression—religion, politics, law,
art, literature, family life, morality, or science—can be free of alienation if their context is a realm of alienation.

To the Hegelian and the Marxist theories of alienation, which have
had a clear influence on Sartre, must be added Husserl's concept,
traces of which appear in *Being and Nothingness* and perhaps as well
in Sartre's ideal of comprehension. According to Husserl, a person
perceives others in two ways, the first of which is through empathy.[14]
In this case the other is revealed as another subject, another "I."
Others are also revealed through sensuous perception, and in this
manner they are experienced as objects as well as subjects. When
a person comes to understand that he exists as an object for others,
he feels himself alien, estranged from his subjective aspect in the
others' experience. At every moment there is "the possibility of
becoming the object of the experience of the other."[15]

Alienation in *Being and Nothingness* appears in two basic forms,
both characterized by a distorted relationship between the for-itself
and the in-itself. In one case, consciousness, intentionally or not, reduces another to the status of an inanimate thing among things. In
the other case, a man experiencing anguish before the perpetual
flight of consciousness seeks artificially to mask this experience by
falsely constituting himself, to himself and others, as an in-itself.
The first variety of alienation involves an external modification of
the for-itself, the second variety involves an internal modification. In
both, a person is separated from what he is by nature. The first kind
of alienation, reminiscent of Hegel's master and slave, is a necessary
feature of the perpetual struggle between liberties that characterizes
the interpersonal relations of men.

According to Sartre, true community is categorically impossible.
The very fact that a man lives in a world of other men, that he is one
transcendence surrounded by others, results in a conflict of freedoms,

each struggling, both intentionally and unintentionally, against the Caesarism of the Other, in whose freedom his own discovers its limits. In the present world, at any moment the Other can rise up and alienate a man's for-itself from its free nature and confer upon it the status of a thing. A person seizes the characterizing event of the glance of the Other as a solidification of his own possibilities. While his freedom has for the moment been destroyed by the look of the Other, the Other's freedom, affirmed in his glance, remains inviolate. In the Other, a man's transcending powers are transcended. To be alienated in such a manner means to exist for the Other. One becomes an in-itself for the Other, but only for the Other. One continues to be all of the possibilities for oneself, a free for-itself but at the same time, the look of the Other relieves one of these possibilities. One becomes his means, his tool, and one's world is swallowed up and negated by his. One is the slave of the Other, in that the Other may think anything of one he cares to, imposing freely his own values without intervention. Every man is, like Gogol's gnome King Viy, the possessor of a glance that kills.

Precisely homologous is the problem of language, for to speak is to act under the glance of the Other. Every word, gesture, and expression establishes the Other's alienating powers. When a person speaks or writes, he has the agonizing certainty that the words are escaping him to take on unpredictable meanings determined by the Other. Verbal expression quickly ends in the theft of thought, because thought has need of the cooperation of the alienating Other in order to be constituted as an object. Language thus inevitably betrays one. To use it in the presence of the Other is to exist for him. To live in the world of other men is to live in perpetual danger of being named and shaped. Biography is thus, for the early Sartre, the melancholy genre, the genre of the fallen, centered self, the self that has been contracted into an adjectival existence.

To describe concretely the procedure of alienation, Sartre describes a man in a corridor, anxiously peering through a keyhole and straining to listen to what is occurring on the other side of the door. Caught up in what he is experiencing, the man is a pure prereflexive consciousness of things, a transparent for-itself freely flowing into the future, with no fixed, external identity. Unconscious of himself, totally absorbed, he loses himself in what is going on in the room. He is nothing but that which he is experiencing. Suddenly he finds himself the victim of an ontological ambush. He hears footsteps in the hall and realizes that someone is looking at him. At this point drastic changes occur in his structure. Reflexive consciousness is born of the encounter. He now sees himself because someone sees him, and he becomes an object for the Other. The specular captive is conscious of losing his autonomy to become what the Other chooses him to be, the Other being free to make of the compromising posture what he will. Sartre also speaks of a community alienation, which occurs when a group experiences itself collectively as a "we-object," a frozen aggregate of dead possibilities. Writing of himself, Roland Barthes speaks for Sartre's man: "He tolerates unwillingly any *image* of himself, and suffers when named."[16]

In this moment of objectification the victim experiences shame, which Sartre describes as a feeling of fallenness, a recognition that one's self is held up before the Other, a recognition that one's liberty escapes to become a given object. Shame, for Sartre, does not have its usual sense of an awareness that one has done wrong, that one is reprehensible to society because of breaking a code. Shame is "the sensation of having my being *outside* of myself, engaged in another being and thus without any defence, lit up by an absolute light that emanates from a pure object."[17] In pride and fear a person is especially conscious that he has become an object for another. Both Genet and Flaubert, like Sartre's man in the corridor, are "caught in the act." For both, the experience of shame, the subjective reaction to alienation, is the dominant experience of everyday life. Baudelaire also experiences the look, but in his case it is self-generated. Willingly or not, each of Sartre's subjects is ravaged by a foreign gaze.

To know another is also to subject him to an ontological humiliation. Knowledge of other persons involves a relation of superiority, one in which there is a victor and a victim. In the altruistic epistemology developed in the *Critique,* this alterity disappears, for although the biographee does not cease to be the object of the biographer, he is simultaneously recognized as a subject as well, an impossibility for the early Sartre. In *Being and Nothingness* biography can only confirm the fact that man is the enemy of man.

These imperial designs of the Other cause drastic alterations in the victim's structure, but the duration of these modifications is fully within the control of the objectified subject. He has a defense: he can reciprocate by making a retaliatory raid on the Other, putting an end to his prerogatives by an identical process of petrification. Liberation requires essentially no more than a simple cognitive act. A man can reclaim his world in an instant, but can lose it just as easily in the next. Sartre describes the Other, experienced as an object, as an explosive device which must be handled with care, for at any moment it might detonate and blow the world away. Life is a constant series of volatile confrontations. At every moment a man is either author or victim of a glance. No demilitarized zone, no green patch, separates Sartre's warriors, for "Always, wherever I am, someone is looking at me."[18]

For Sartre, dealienation would require one of three things, all of which are impossible. The first is the elimination of the subject-object relation. The second is realization of the Kantian ethic, grasping the freedom of the Other as an unconditioned end, which is quite out of the question: "respect for the freedom of the other is an impossibility: even if we were able to entertain the idea of respecting this freedom, every attitude that we would take toward the other would be a violation of this freedom that we were pretending to respect."[19] The third impossible escape from the instability of the subject-object relation is the ideal of the simultaneous grasping of the freedom and objectivity of the Other. In *Saint Genet* these strategies emerge once again, but all three are no longer considered impossible.

Although a permanent sanctuary from alienation is not possible in *Being and Nothingness,* a definitive objectification is the ultimate fate of all. Death is a terminal alienation for it hands us over to the uncontestable grasp of the Other. The for-itself is changed eternally into an in-itself because, having lost its future dimension, it disappears into the past. Life is transformed into destiny. This is the case of the characters in *No Exit:* because the recourse of a display of self-transcendence is no longer available, they exist in a state of permanent alienation.

For the person who seeks solace in unfreedom and relishes the experience of the fixed image of himself held by the Other, a number of devices are available to encourage the development of alienating relations. One of the most common is a belief in a God, for "God is the concept of the Other pushed to the limit." Such a being is a transcendental subject which in no way can become an object to another. If I believe in God, "I posit my being-an-object-for God as more real than my for-itself. I exist alienated and I cause myself to learn what I must be from outside my being."[20] All three subjects know the temptation.

The project of loving is a more complicated phenomenon, based as it is upon a contradiction. To love is to desire to be loved, to be appropriated. Within the amorous dyad, each one seeks to appear as a precious object to be possessed. This involves alienation. Each demands that he be an object, but he in turn requires that the Other be a free subject in order to perform the desired process of alienation. When a person demands that the Other love him, he asks him to relinquish the role of object which is his project as the beloved. He insists that the Other have a totally free will, being free to choose to love him and to choose the opposite at the same time. Each is alienated to the exact extent to which he demands the alienation of the Other. The masochist differs in that his project consists in an attempt not to fascinate the Other by means of his objectivity but rather to cause himself to be fascinated by his objectivity for Others. He strips himself of his subjectivity by losing it in that of another. He experiences a pleasurable vertigo before the abyss of the subjectivity of the Other. All of these insensate projects are doomed because they seek to alter the inalterable character of the human condition.

As for the opposite, men in quest of the illusion of an entirely recuperated freedom can resort to a variety of means to suppress the alienating glance and bring shame, fear, and slavery to the Other. One solution is solipsism, to eliminate from a person's thinking the possibility that the Other is a glance who can fix his possibilities. For this, indifferent Others are consciousless forms who pass in the street. Sartre finds this strategy in Flaubert's fiction. To evade the Medusan eye of God and to confer the status of object on the absolute subject, the believer may resort to black masses, profanations, or diabolical associations. Such an effort is doomed to failure because of the contradiction involved. Generosity appears as another project within this category of futility because, as Sartre explains, to give is to enslave. In hatred, willing the death of an enemy and through his death that of all men, a person seeks another magical solution to the threat of the loss of his nonsubstantial freedom as a for-itself. By seeking the death of a specific individual, he seeks the symbolic destruction of the general idea of the Other. The sadist is another radical in search of an impossible, unconditional freedom. In mortifying the flesh of the Other, the sadist seeks to snuff out the Other's liberty, which if freely displayed would have a corrosive impact on his own.

Each of Sartre's varieties of bad faith entails a denial of one of the two essential but irreconcilable ontological features of man, a facticity and a transcendence; or to employ one of Sartre's gnomic paradoxes, man is "a being who is what he is not and who is not what he is." One species of bad faith seeks to deny the physical body; the other, offering the apparently greater temptation, seeks, without the aid of an external agent, to immobilize a person's own free for-itself. "Thus we feel anxiety in trying to seize ourselves *from the outside* as another or as *a thing*." This form of bad faith, this desire to become something which haunts every human choice, must thus be termed an autoalienation, clearly following in the pattern of the alienation of one consciousness by another.

At one point Sartre seems to rule out the possibility of such an equation: "I cannot be an object for myself, for there is no way I can alienate myself."[21] Self-alienation is therefore clearly impossible. But the logical impossibility of a phenomenon in no way precludes the possibility that men might find it highly desirable. Indeed, according to Sartre, that ideal to which all men aspire, with no chance of success, is the utopian fusion of the for-itself and the in-itself, an impossibility which Sartre equates with God and beauty, both equally nonexistent in the real world. The very impossibility of self-alienation is itself an additional justification for equating it with bad faith, for bad faith is also declared to be impossible. It is a lie that one tells oneself, something which might well be attempted but is necessarily unrealizable because the liar and the lied to are one and the same person. A person cannot lie to himself for the same reason that he cannot become a pure object to himself. He may however try his best to do so. Each man is a single consciousness, but he can falsely establish himself as a double being, one being imposing alienation on the other, in order to mask the experience of freedom.

In the case of both forms of alienation in *Being and Nothingness*—the form that is self-imposed and the form that the self submits to from outside—it is up to the victim to save himself, to recuperate his liberty either by petrifying the Other in turn or by recognizing the impossibility of the falsehood he has offered himself as the truth. The temporary escape—for a momentary dealienation is all that is possible—is a relatively simple and localized operation. In *Being and Nothingness*, alienation and dealienation occur almost entirely without reference to historical conditions. With his conversion to Marxism, Sartre discovered the world of history which destines men to alienation, and he saw that the isolated individual's struggle against his object state counts for little. Dealienation, to whatever degree it is possible, can come about only through the collective struggle of desperate men.

Although, as Richard Schacht insists, the ideas on alienation in *Being and Nothingness* mostly do not show Marx's influence, there is one reference to an alienation that is not ontologically necessary: "Work, when it is not strictly meant to serve the personal ends of the worker, is a form of alienation."[22] These words suggest, according to Fredric Jameson, that Marxism played a role in the development of Sartre's first philosophy.[23] An historically conditioned alienation does make a very brief appearance in *Being and Nothingness*, but for Sartre it seems to be worthy of only the most perfunctory interest.

The category of bad faith subsumes another species of self-alienation that Sartre discusses in *L'Imaginaire* (1940). Although it has long been apparent that Sartre equated a certain use of the imagination with bad faith, the only explicit statement appears in the third volume of *L'Idiot:* "The essence of the image is bad faith, a lie, the insoluble problem falsely resolved."[24] Sartre considers his autobiography *The Words* and his two most recent biographies as further studies of the imaginary and of men who have chosen it as a way of life: "If I wrote *The Words,* it was to reply to the same question that was posed in my studies of Genet and Flaubert: How does a man become a writer, someone who wants to speak of the imaginary?"[25]

According to Sartre, an image is not a sensation or perception recalled and altered by the intellect. To create an image is to form an analogon of the real outside the margins of the real; it is to hold the real at a distance and to negate it. This denial of the world, which is the imagination, is not a distinct faculty of the mind but is co-extensive with free consciousness as it realizes its liberty. The imagination is human freedom itself in its negativity and unfettered spontaneity. But as in the case of bad faith, freedom can be used against itself. In the *Critique* Sartre calls this *"the moment of the trap."*[26] Imaginary objects offer the opportunity to escape the constraints of the world: "They seem to present themselves as a negation of the condition of *being in the world,* as an antiworld."[27] In this alternative domain there are no possibilities, because the options among which human freedoms navigate suppose the existence of a real world and an historical present which the imagination has obliterated. "The imaginary world offers itself as a world without freedom: neither is it determined. It is the opposite of freedom; it is fatal."[28]

Men can be divided into two categories, depending on whether they prefer to live a real or an imaginary life. The subjects of the three biographies chose the later strategy. Genet and Flaubert did so because they found themselves in impossible situations. Because they were completely powerless the only ruse available to them was their power to negate imaginatively their crushing reality, transforming it into a controllable analogon of itself. This is the one exit available when all is lost, a substitute gratification of the most desperate variety. But this use of the imagination is a rat trap, for by leaving the real, the victim relinquishes any hope of reversing his situation, thus ensuring the uncontested dominion of the Other. This is bad faith, for freedom is used against itself. But the late Sartre sympathetically realizes that bad faith is sometimes the only means a person has to assert himself, the falsely saving mask for a total impotence that cannot be remedied. Sometimes, as Theodore W. Adorno writes, "Only estrangement is the antidote to alienation."[29] Although the image is always the negation of the real, the imagination is not always in bad faith. It is if the real were negated for the purpose of negating the real. In *What Is Literature?* (1947) Sartre describes an imagination that is in good faith, one that negates the real in order to intensify the experience of the actual, one that lies in order to tell the truth.

A hostility to this negative variety of imagination has a Marxist pedigree. It is man's end, Marx claims, to become fully human. This he cannot do if he feels that he can realize himself only through religious fantasies. Such imaginary achievement is ineffectual, for it plays directly into the hands of unjust authority. For Marx, the criticism of religion is the beginning of all criticism. Similarly for Sartre, the criticism of the imagination in bad faith is the starting point for much of his criticism of the world of the bourgeois. For him, as for Marx, "the demand to renounce illusion . . . is a demand to renounce a situation that required illusions."[30] The study of alienation is necessarily tied to a study of both correct and self-destructive uses of the imagination.

There is an emphasis on the literary and cultural aspects of alienation not only in the biographies but also in *What Is Literature?* The subject of the essay is the alienation of literature and the alienation of men and how the two relate. Sartre employs the term in a clearly Marxist sense for the first time, but also in a different and distinct sense, and he succeeds in interweaving the two concepts by demonstrating that the elimination of one can contribute to the demise of the other.

The use of the term *alienation* that is original with Sartre occurs in an explanation of how literature becomes alienated from its nature. The essence of a work of prose lies in its being an act of freedom revealing itself as such and thereby appealing to the liberty of the reader. "The essence of the literary work is freedom unveiling and willing itself as an appeal to the freedom of other men."[31] It is thus an act of generosity.[32] At the heart of the aesthetic experience of the ideal work of prose is hidden the moral imperative to treat each person as an absolute end. For a moment the experience of reading magically brings into being what Kant termed the kingdom of ends, that utopian realm in which no one is a means or object for another. In order for this "concert of good wills" to come into existence, the author must demonstrate in his work that his creative process has been uncontaminated by the conditioning of an unfree passion or a freedom-denying individual, institution, or ideology. For the work to be an act of confidence in the freedom of the reader, it must be pure presentation, an absolute end, not a vehicle to manipulate the audience. As such, it reveals the world as though it had its source in human freedom.

If these conditions do not exist in the author-reader relationship, alienation is present. A negative, unfree relationship comes into being when the author seeks to overwhelm the reader by saturating his work with emotional coloring. The reader must not be able to divine the author's feelings. Literature is also alienated when other factors contaminate the author-reader relationship: "I say that the literature of a specific historical moment is alienated when it has not succeeded in achieving an explicit awareness of its autonomy, and when it submits itself to temporal powers or to an ideology, in a word, when it considers itself as a means and not as an unconditional end."[33] According to Sartre, such a period was the twelfth century, when literature, unworthy of the label, subordinated itself to the church and the political oligarchy. The literature of the classical moment in France addressed itself exclusively to an elite, to whom it held a flattering looking glass. Literature was then reduced to innocent psychologizing and became an instrument for ridiculing those who deviated from social conventions. Nineteenth-century bourgeois literature, by developing a more utilitarian emphasis on psychology, submitted to the pressures of the ruling class, providing it with the techniques of seduction and domination that its instrumental rationality required.

Sartre makes use here of Marx's notion of the worker's alienation from the product of his work. In an alienated society the worker's product is stolen from him. The experience of literature, as it demonstrates the possibility of free production, suggests the idea that there is an alternative to alienated work. But the dealienating mission of literature is not completed by the simple expression of its autonomy, its free essence. Literature must also be concrete. The good will of the reader must be historicized: "It is our task to convert the city of ends into a concrete and open society."[34] The good will of the reader must be channeled into concrete projects. Otherwise the kingdom of ends will remain an abstraction and dissipate as the reader puts down the book. To obviate this outcome, Sartre recommends that each book propose a concrete freedom from a particular alienation. One cannot stop at the momentary and abstract reciprocal recognition of freedoms which occurs in the author-reader experience of autonomous literature: "We shall have done nothing unless we show him as well, within the plot of the work, that it is quite impossible to treat men as ends in contemporary society."[35]

After autonomous literature has been achieved, the greatest danger to literature is to subside into abstraction which fails to contest specific alienations. In order to accompany man in his efforts to transcend his current alienation toward a better world, literature must include some things in its subject matter and avoid others. Escapism must be eschewed. Authors must present themselves and their characters as situated in a particular historical context and having the limitations of all men. All-knowing narrators are unacceptable. The minds of men must be sympathetically presented as partially confused and partially lucid. To be avoided is what Sartre terms "the literature of consumption," which instead of presenting men as freely producing the world in order to encourage them to overcome an alienated relation with their product, shows them as passively consuming it. Falling into this literary category, according to Sartre, are Barrès' *Culte du moi,* Larbaud's *Journal de A. O. Barnabooth,* and Gide's *Nourritures terrestres.* In this negative literature, "to be is to appropriate," and the work "pretends to be pleasure or the promise of pleasure."[36] Reading in these circumstances ceases to be creation and unconditioned action.

In a society largely oriented toward the ideal of consumption, literature does not feel at home because it wishes to represent the free man of a society of production. Only in a utopian society— dealienated, socialist, and in a state of permanent revolution—can the practice of literature become fully congruent with its essence. Since literature is the appeal of one freedom to another, only in these circumstances is the reader free to take the requested action. Material freedom is thus a condition for the realization of this ideal harmony of author and reader. It does not suffice to accord to the author the freedom to say all; he must have the opportunity to address a public which has at its disposal the freedom to change all. The author's freedom may then fully reveal the liberty of his audience. "Thus in a classless society, without dictatorship, and without stability, literature would finally awake to a full consciousness of itself." When these conditions are met, the written word becomes "total literature."[37] Although Sartre has come to doubt literature's social efficacy, he still retains this ideal as a model of dealienated human relations. In 1974 he commented on the necessity "to struggle for a certain kind of freedom of thought and life that is implied by the very idea of writing."[38]

The *Critique* is the key to most of Sartre's later writings, literary and otherwise. The ideas of alienation in the *Critique* help in understanding *Saint Genet,* especially in discovering its failings, and are a prerequisite for the biography of Flaubert. According to Sartre, the major themes in *L'Idiot* correspond to "that part of the *Critique of Dialectical Reason* where I describe alienated freedom."[39] As Benjamin Suhl points out, when Sartre functions as literary critic, he is the philosopher as literary critic.[40] His literary works can therefore be wrenched out of their philosophical context only at the price of a total misunderstanding of their function in Sartre's *oeuvre* and their place in the history of ideas. The volumes on Flaubert, which are freighted with cross references to the *Critique,* were clearly not intended to stand alone.

In the *Critique* there are two basic varieties of alienation: one is historically contingent, the other is not. In *Being and Nothingness* Sartre maintains that alienation results from the ubiquitous glance of the Other. But in the *Critique* the only species of alienation that is not said to be eliminable results from the fact that man objectifies himself in the world in an act or physical product but subsequently discovers that this self-objectification returns to him as Other. Alienation is due to the fact that man becomes praxis. The fact that there are other men in the world has no bearing. Sartre criticizes Marxists for ignoring this particular reality, which underlies all of the historically removable, socially problematic, kinds of alienation: "History is more complex than a certain simplistic Marxism believes it to be. Not only does man have to struggle against Nature, against the social context that created him, and against other men, but also against his own action when it becomes Other. This primitive form of alienation expresses itself through other forms of alienation, but is independent of them, and serves as their foundation." As a courtesy to the readers of *Being and Nothingness* Sartre resorts to his earlier vocabulary: "It is the for-itself, as agent discovering itself as inert . . . in the milieu of the in-itself."[41]

Self-objectification is positively described by Sartre as a man's means of producing his life. It is his vehicle for transcending himself and disengaging from the status of the thing. At the same time, however, when a man plows a field or creates a tool, he reduces himself to the inorganic, to an object with an inert future which always returns to him as something alien. The act of objectification does not in itself constitute alienation but necessarily results in alienation. Sartre, assuming Hegel to have equated objectification with alienation, dismisses this idea and then proceeds to redefine objectification in such a way that it can once again be considered a form of alienation: "Hegel's error was to believe that within everyone there is something to objectify and that work reflects the individ-

uality of its author. In fact, the objectification as such is not the goal,
but the consequence that is later attached to the goal."[42]

   In *L'Idiot* Sartre seems to change his mind about the appropriate-
ness of the word in this case. He remarks that in the hypothetical
socialist society of abundance of the future a man can objectify himself in the world without having the experience of his product returning to him as Other. This is possible because this man incorporates into his object the awareness that he, the agent, is both a
transcendance and a facticity, and hence to an extent always has
imperfect control over what he creates as it assumes an inert future.
Because he realizes that what he does or creates "reflects him in
his facticity as well as in his liberty," his products cannot be said to
return to him as Other.[43]

   All other varieties of alienation in the *Critique* are historically
contingent because the factor that underlies them, material scarcity,
is eliminable. Sartre concludes that human history must be understood dialectically, that is, in the light of the antagonistic interaction between men and men, and men and their material environment.
Two facts make this observation possible. The first is the phenomenon of scarcity. Man is a creature of need and faces the threat
of extinction if his material requirements are not met. The earth,
however, is not characterized by an inexhaustible abundance of those
things that are necessary for the satisfaction of biologically given
needs. It is scarcity, or obstructed need, that sets the class struggle—
and history—in motion. Whereas the fact that the despotism of
physical requirements might be the root of alienation is merely
suggested by Marx in the *Critique of the Gotha Program,*
Sartre advances it to the foreground and implicitly criticizes Marx
for failing to ground alienation in something more fundamental
than exploitation. Without scarcity, history in the Marxist sense
would be inconceivable, and only societies based on stability and
repetition would be imaginable.

   Because of the monolithic fact that history is a struggle against
scarcity, the relations between men are mortally contentious, and
peaceful coexistence is impossible. Each man becomes a threat to
the Other, a menace of death, because he seeks to consume a life-
giving commodity of which the supply is limited. The Other in
this milieu becomes a man's demonic double. "For each, man exists
as *inhuman man,* or alternatively, as an alien species." In this world
the aim of each person is to suppress the freedom of the Other,
which is potentially fraught with mortal consequences to himself.
Sartre takes the utopian position that human relations can be based
on positive reciprocity only when "the Other than me *is also the*

same." But as soon as reciprocity is modified, as it always is, by scarcity, "the same appears to us as the antiman."[44] Hell is no longer other men but rather the fact that scarcity salts the earth of human relations.

This fact is central to the second major discovery of the dialectic: "man is mediated by things to the exact extent that things are mediated by man." In consequence, man is both free to act on nonhuman things and in danger of being alienated because of his necessary relations with this sphere. All forms of alienation must be understood through this quintessential discovery: "It is in the concrete and synthetic relation of the agent to the other mediated by the thing, and to the thing mediated by the other that we are able to discover the foundations of all possible forms of alienation."[45] If a man experiences alienation because the scarcity-contaminated object insinuates itself between himself and others, he also experiences alienation when his relations with the object he produces are interfered with by his demonic double.

The man in need is forced to attempt to overcome the brutish claims of biology by objectifying himself, by making tools and acting in the world. He must become praxis, purposeful activity in the world designed to overcome scarcity. In a domain of scarcity his relation with his product or action is always mediated by the Other. His product has a double character. As he creates it, it seems to have a positive meaning and to wear an innocent face, for it is designed to diminish scarcity, to increase the wealth of the whole community, and hence to reduce tension in the world. But its inertia permits it to absorb and return against each the efforts of others. His praxis is experienced by the Other as a threat; as it represents an attempt to perpetuate his existence, the Other understands it as a threat to his. Mediated by the Other's view of it, his object returns to him with an inhuman face. Because he understands it as a provocation, as a menace of death, it causes him to be vulnerable, it becomes a weapon that can be used against him. "In the most adequate and useful tool there is a hidden violence that is the opposite of its apparent docility. Its inertia always allows it to 'serve another purpose.' " Every product, to the extent that it is produced in a milieu of scarcity, designates the producer both to his fellows and to himself as Other: "It is the product that defines men as Others and constitutes them as another species, as antiman. It is in the product that each produces his own objectivity, that returns to him as an enemy, and constitutes him as Other than himself."[46]

In *Madame Bovary* Sartre finds an example of how the Other exploits a person's action for his own purposes and returns it in an unrecognizable form. Flaubert despised realism, but his public read his book as though it were representative of this school. Because of the willful misreading, Flaubert could not find himself in his objectification. In a context of scarcity every man is Other, and whenever he acts in this world, his action always returns redolent with this terrible and inescapable fact. In a socialist world of abundance, however, other men will not be hostile, and hence objective being will be homogeneous with the practice of objectification. His product will not return with an inhuman face.

For Sartre, alienation is not a necessary accompaniment of objectification.[47] The theft of praxis by the Other is clearly an historical rather than an ontological fact: "It is due to the development of exchange . . . that objective demand as a moment of a free *praxis* of the Other, constitutes the product as *Other*."[48] It is the obdurate, but nevertheless contingent, fact of scarcity that sets this process in motion. A multiplicity of men can share the same planet, and no theft of praxis will result, on the condition that each produces all that his needs require. But when scarcity results in an economy based on exchange, when men are forced to produce objects or actions that must meet the requirements of the Other, it may be said that a praxis, because of the mediation of the Other, has stolen the freedom of its producer.

A person's relation with his product also results in alienation when others convince him that his reality is exclusively located outside himself in this physical object. In the world of scarcity the Other seeks to define him by the inertia of his product. Because the aim of each is to suppress the threatening liberty of the Other, there is always the urge to reduce him to a thing, the thing that he produces that can be a means to his end. The Other seeks to mystify him, to convince him that he is nothing other than the thing he produces, rather than being the free movement that results in this object. A man is no longer his own product but instead the product of his product. His relation with it is mediated by the hostile Other who seeks his death.

Sartre holds capitalism responsible for the predominance of the negative community. Here men's relations are mediated by an object in an atmosphere of scarcity. The theme of the crowd, physically massed and unified superficially by a tacit agreement but spiritually isolated as individuals, is an old one in Marxist literature, going as far back as Engel's *The Condition of the Working Class in England*. To illustrate, Sartre cites an example from everyday experience. A group of individuals waits at a bus stop in front of the church in the Place St. Germain des Prés. Each comes from a different background and has a different destination; each seems to ignore the presence of the others. Sartre quotes Proust: "Each is very much alone."[49] These arbitrarily juxtaposed individuals hold only one thing in common: the collectivity in which they participate is united by the bus they await. The collective has no internal unity. What has brought them together is something outside themselves. Sartre calls such unifying forces the collective objects that are the physical signs of our alienation.

An additional, crucial fact about the bus is that it is an image of scarcity because its seating capacity is limited. Not all of those who are standing will be permitted to board. The separation of the hopeful future passengers automatically is transformed into a relation of cordial hatred, however diluted this antagonism may be by the relative banality and innocuousness of the circumstances. When men are united by matter in an atmosphere of scarcity, their cohesion can only be a mask for separation and hostility. Within this feckless aggregate each is radically Other, for the goals of each are mutually exclusive. The hostility of the Other, who seeks someone's place on the bus, enters that person's character. The scarcity-contaminated object causes him to be defined by his antagonism: "*identity* . . . becomes synthetic: each is identical to the Other inasmuch as he is formed by the others, Other acting upon the Others."[50] In the series a man is always the Other because he inevitably internalizes the threat he poses to his fellows.

For Sartre, alienation is the dominant fact of capitalist society, because such a society is serial in its organization. The capitalist world is formed of a large number of series arranged in a Chinese box pattern. Workers have their unity outside themselves in the factory in which they spend their days. The uncertain labor market is also an object which unifies the workers from without. It turns them against each other as they compete for the limited number of jobs and favors that the owner dangles before them to ensure that they remain separated and mutually hostile. The unselfconscious social class is a large series composed of smaller ones. Different companies, which produce the same product, are unified and separated by the competitive market for that product. Different industries struggle against each other for the same consumer dollar. Finally, each series has as its unifying collective object the capitalist system itself.

In this infernal system of mediations, the bourgeois is not exempt from the same fate that torments the worker. Ultimately the same collective object, the capitalist system, conditions his actions and pollutes his relations with others. The same means of production force both into a passive role. Flaubert provides a case in point. The novelist was a bachelor, an artist, seemingly in all respects socially passive. Despite his apparent withdrawal from the social maelstrom, he also experienced alienation in his role of landowner. His income and the value of his possessions fluctuated from day to day. Inevitably he interiorized this unsettlement. In *L'Idiot* Sartre shows how this experience had a crucial impact on the genesis of "The Legend of Saint Julian" and on the development of Flaubert's personality in his late years.

In the *Critique* Sartre describes how the bourgeois displays in all the aspects of his life his alienated relations with the worker. This analysis, in which Sartre's wit and skill as a psychologist reappear, constitutes one of his most original contributions to the history of the concept of alienation. Marx claimed that the bourgeois "does not do against himself what he does against the worker."[51] Sartre apparently disagrees. Using weapons both real and symbolic, the bourgeois seeks to guarantee the impotence of the proletariat. The most prominent of the symbolic weapons of the class war is the inherently comical idea of "distinction." This concept, which is a characteristic of bourgeois humanism, indicates how the dehumanization of the oppressed returns and becomes the alienation of the oppressor. Its end is to propagate the dogma that human characteristics are possessed by the bourgeois alone, and its corollary that the bourgeois has a right to oppress the worker. As such, distinction is an exercise of bourgeois liberty, which Sartre defines as the power of man over man.

The bourgeois displays distinction to the extent that he displays a victory over physical needs. Distinction is an antiphysis, a "secular puritanism."[52] In France, Sartre maintains, this strategy became especially noticeable after June 1848, when class hostility between the bourgeois and the worker became overt. The dictatorship of culture over nature was apparent in the bourgeois cults of sobriety, bloodless objectivity, and sexual frigidity, as well as in the constrictions of dress, such as corsets, stiff collars or shirt fronts, and top hats. The bourgeois dressed not to attract but to inform and, symbolically, to kill. Eliot's lines from "Gerontion" convey the situation: "Virtues/Are forced upon us by our impudent crimes." In *L'Idiot,* art for art's sake appears as one of the more devious avatars of distinction. In the social sphere the farce of distinction was re-enacted in the formalized ceremonies of high bourgeois bonhomie: salons, teas, soirees, and balls, which were ostentatiously nonproductive occasions of symbolic exclusion, mutual recognition, and self-congratulation. Through the public violence he visits on his own person, the bourgeois symbolically oppresses the worker. Through this revenge on the carnal, that disconcertingly universal human component, he squashes the working class, whose physical body is its sole source of sustenance. For the bourgeois, this machinery of denial is a sidewinding repression of the worker's revolt against hunger and fatigue. But by denying the humanity of his slaves, the master also abrogates his own. The oppression of the proletariat is internalized, putting limits on the freedom of the bourgeois. As Rousseau notes: "Whoever is a master cannot be free, for to reign is to obey."[53]

For Marx and Engels the proletariat is the sole catalyst of the new order. But Sartre's bourgeois is so unhappy, so grievously burdened by the costs of his symbolic satisfaction, that he acquires a revolutionary potential. This new, historically conditioned avatar of the first variety of bad faith seems to have a literary source. As Baudelaire describes the dandy, he is "above all enamored of *distinction.*"[54] Both Sartre and Baudelaire italicize the word. Baudelaire remarks that distinction consists in a haughty, cold, stoical, and highly disciplined air. The perfect dress of the dandy expresses a horror of the natural and is "a symbol of the aristocratic superiority of his spirit."[55] Sartre, both here and in *L'Idiot,* provides Baudelaire's concept with a materialist ground. Sartre's use of the expression "secular puritanism" leads to the suspicion that Max Weber's concept of the "worldly asceticism" of the capitalist may have contributed to the idea of distinction. Thorsten Veblen's ostentatious man of leisure may also have had a role in the development of the concept.

Presiding over a muddled universe is the demon force that Sartre calls the "practico-inert," a collective term for the objects around which the series are formed, for the totality of worked-on matter that makes its way into the social sphere and metastasizes as history progresses. As men objectify themselves in the world, they create a second nature, a system of reification that constrains their actions.[56] The field of the practico-inert surrounds and conditions, laying siege to the autonomous individual: "men are all slaves insofar as their life experience takes place in the field of the practico-inert, and to the exact extent that this field is originally conditioned by scarcity." Its influence results in the theft of man's free activity and the deindividualization and diffusion of power: "the field of the practico-inert negates each objectified praxis to the profit of passive activity as the common structure of collectivities and worked on matter." Sartre describes this sphere ominously, referring to it as "this inert and demonic negation" and "this place of violence, shadows, and sorcery."[57] Men cannot fashion tools to satisfy needs without introducing determinism into the world. Human objects of his own and other's making, through their inertness, weigh heavily on his destiny and deviate his free intentions. The milieu surrounds men with tools they have inherited and through which they must express themselves. Customs, objects, ethical systems, *idées reçues,* artistic traditions, means of production, and tastes implant necessity in the heart of free individual praxis. In *Madame Bovary* he finds an example of an objectification deviated by this force: Flaubert was pressured by his friends out of writing a work in a maverick form and persuaded to express himself through the realistic novel, the accepted literary vehicle of the day.

But one need not seek so far afield. The experience of the practico-inert insinuates itself into every moment of daily life. Simply by glancing out of a window, according to Sartre, one can experience its imperium: "I will see cars that are men, and drivers who are cars, a policeman who directs traffic at a corner, and, a bit beyond, a traffic light controls the same flow of cars with red and green lights. A hundred demands rise up from the ground toward me: pedestrian crossings, notices and prohibitions . . . all these appeals, all these demands do not yet concern me directly. Later I will go down into the street and I will become *their thing.*"[58]

Sartre here resorts to the grotesque, the violation of the human by the nonhuman, the eerie fusion of the animate and the inanimate, to describe a haunted realm in which men experience, through the objects of civilization, the oppressive and petrifying presence of other men, past and present.

The practico-inert also has the ability to rigidify a person within his social class. Within the concept Sartre includes what he calls the "class being," the consciousness of one's location in a class, the feeling of class as a fixed fact of nature, as a consequence of the purpose of the practico-inert, which is "the transformation of every free *praxis* into *exis.*"[59] This class being, through its practico-inert character, awaits one from the moment of birth. A neonate is a determined possibility, because the established system reproduces in his mind the ceremonies and objects that distinguish the class through which he enters the world. From the moment a person enters the realm of culture, it awaits him, ready to absorb him into its reign. The alienation-generating ability of this domain is fueled by the fact of scarcity and hence is historically contingent. Man will always live surrounded by a tangled forest of objects, values, and choices that are not of his own creation. But in a world of abundance this field will lose the authority it now has to dominate the free will and deviate its actions.

A more activist and directly intentioned form of manipulation is "extereo-conditioning," a phenomenon that Sartre claims to be dominant in capitalist societies. To explain, he describes an experience from his 1946 visit to the United States, during which he listened to a radio program whose purpose was to announce to its audience the ten best-selling records of the past week. This widely listened-to broadcast had the effect of increasing the sales of these records by between 30 and 50 percent. The message was that one should buy these records because others had done so in great numbers. Those who complied underwent the malefic fascination by the Other. A group, to further its own ends, to create a world in its own image, or to maximize profits, can resort to extereo-conditioning to create a passive unity among serialized men, a unity which is a travesty of the totality of men sharing a common, positive purpose of liberating themselves from a form of slavery. The man who purchases one of the records is a victim of the liberal notion of "taste." This accessory man feels that he is expressing himself freely with others through the act of his purchase, which is in effect imposed upon him from outside. This form of coercion "results in total alienation because the solitary ceremony consecrates him as Other even in his individual sensibility." By this act a man's will is plasticized by a collective which has as its goal the making of men into instruments through controlling their present and future choices: "each individual learns to be the expression of all the Others and, through them, to be the expression of his entire milieu."[60] None of this would be possible unless the serial man had been programmed from childhood to be conditioned in this fashion. Within this environment a true culture, one reflecting free human activity that is an end in itself, is impossible.

Closely related to the issue of thought control is the problem of imposed ethical values. Systems of ethics threaten the conception of praxis as uninhibited self-transcendance. Formalized value systems are a theft of free praxis, as they seek to impose a prefabricated future upon it. Value, if it inserts itself into free praxis, takes on an inert, passive, independent existence. It is the praxis of the Other that has been internalized. In this case the free praxis becomes a means to the realization of an abstract end. The for-itself is contaminated by the in-itself. Because value is the alienation of praxis, it must be eliminated. The only ethical relation between men consists in the respectful meetings of free praxis. "Every system of values, at the moment of its revolutionary efficacy, ceases to be a system and the values cease to be values."[61]

The alienation characterizing life in the series is overcome when this feckless aggregate reconstitutes itself as the unanimist utopia of the "group in fusion," Sartre's ideal of a volatile and ephemeral community of ends. The group gains a single-intentioned heart to replace the thing that had formerly been its organizing principle. This sort of group has a spontaneous and organic quality for which Sartre has great affection. In *The Words* he ardently describes the spontaneously formed groups of children in which he had participated, and in a 1974 interview he remarks: "I have always wanted to move from the series to the group. I always thought that it is better to think in groups than to think separately."[62]

The group in fusion, which is the sudden regeneration of freedom, comes into existence when a collectivity of men is moved by the sudden realization of a common praxis, when men recognize their collective alienation and join together freely and spontaneously to face an immediate material danger. In this anarchist idyll there is no question of self-subordination to the collectivity, no abandonment of freedom; rather, each is freely and spontaneously himself as the group acts. Within such a group there is no hierarchical organization, no division of tasks: "the leader is always me." Positive reciprocity, Sartre's ideal for human relations, is a concrete reality in the group, where there is "the comprehension of the Other as the same."[63] In this moment the epistemological ideal of *Search for a Method* is spontaneously realized. The Other ceases to be a limit to one's project because the goal of each is the goal of all. In *Being and Nothingness* freedom, to the extent that it is possible, was gained in a struggle against other men, through domination, or through an escape into solipsism. In the *Critique* it can be achieved only through the strictest solidarity with others.

As an example of the group in fusion, Sartre mentions the hungry and tired Parisians of the quartier St. Antoine who stormed the Bastille upon hearing that Louis XVI had had the city encircled by his army. The inert and passive object-man of the series had become a free subject acting in concert with other free subjects. For Sartre the fused group is the privileged moment of history. Here he joins the tradition of thinkers—such as Sorel in his myth of the general strike, Hegel in his view of the ancient Greek polis, and Nietzsche in his description of the old Dionysian rites—who sought to discover the conditions for a moment of perfect community that would replace a world of differences and boundaries.

In his first major philosophical work Sartre had criticized Hegel for excessive optimism in asserting that the multiplicity of consciousnesses is surpassable. Hegel had wrongly felt that "the plurality can and must be transcended toward totality." For Sartre this was an absurdity. The scandal of the plurality is permanent because of men's ontological separation. "The dispersion and the struggle of consciousnesses will never come to an end," he avowed.[64] But now, in describing the group in fusion, Sartre sounds somewhat more sanguine. Speaking of this paroxysmally formed collectivity, he writes: *"in praxis* there is no *Other, everyone is the same."*[65] The irreversible spell of solipsism that cursed the world of *Being and Nothingness* is broken. Alterity, formerly an ontological problem, has been transformed into an exclusively historical scandal.

For the early Sartre, alienation was a consequence of the subject/object relation and hence could only be overcome by overcoming this dualism. In the *Critique* the ineliminability of the subject/object relation is retained. According to Pietro Chiodi, if this duality is admitted, there are only two possibilities of eliminating alienation: "alienation is suppressed by suppressing the relation" or "the relation is preserved by preserving alienation."[66] What Chiodi terms the "ontological check" on the possibility of dealienation is overcome in Sartre's insistence that to itself the group in fusion is a single subject and a single object. It is a single will with a multiplicity of centers. Although the multiplicity of subjects can never be suppressed, in the group it is disqualified. In *Saint Genet* Sartre indicates that two men cannot be a single object, partaking in the same whole, except in the eyes of a single transcendental subject who plays the role of the objectifying third consciousness. But in the *Critique* he states that in the group in fusion each party plays this role. Thus at this moment all people are one meta-subject and one meta-object. Alienation is a consequence of the multiplicity of consciousnesses, of the fact that standing against a person is the Other; it is not an epiphenomenon of the subject/object dichotomy.

Such an assemblage of men is potentially subject to a cycle of degeneration that can close with a return to seriality. The first metamorphosis is into the "organized group" that is born when the material danger that threatens the fused group is no longer real but potential. The members take an oath to prevent their focused collectivity from lapsing into seriality. Sartre calls this new group "a freedom that swears an oath." As a free and mutual limitation of freedoms, the oath protects one's freedom. An intensification of the danger of dissolution leads to the group which he calls "the Terror." In this case conformity to the group purpose is enforced by the threat of death. The terror unites rather than separates the members. In the threat that betrayal will be punished by death is the fact that each has absolute power of life or death over each. In this new fraternity, individual freedom is alienated and transferred to the group, which remains free. Evident here is Sartre's ideal of translucidity: "It is *truly* the reciprocal translucidity of common individuals."[67]

When the group organizes itself and a division of tasks is required, subtle forms of alienation occur. No longer do all perform the common function in a common way, but instead the common goal is performed by many, each in a singular manner. Sartre takes his example from soccer. A team calls upon one man to be its goalie. For the general good he must now abandon all thought of eccentric displays of freedom. But within his formalized role he remains free to be the best goalie possible in order to further the common and freely chosen end of the whole group. But because tasks are parcelized and interdependent, individual projects can be deviated by others within the group. A player can make a perfect pass to a less expert teammate who proceeds to mishandle the ball. The result is the alienation of the praxis of the more practiced player; his design has been thwarted by another.

The organized group can degenerate into an institution, in a total return to seriality. Centralized, stable, and rigid authority appears. Whereas in the fused group authority has been thoroughly diffused, now it is sharply localized. Free choice resides alone with the sovereign, and others merely obey. Once again, as is characteristic of the series, unity lies outside the group. The institution plays the role of the collective object. Men are passive and separated, which makes authority possible. Obediently performing his functions, a person serves the freedom of the sovereign and becomes his instrument, a thing, and denies his own freedom. There is not longer a congruency of goals between the individual and the collectivity. Although there is a common objective, it is dictated by the sovereign rather than chosen freely by all. Even before birth the individual enters the grip of a broad range of institutions. Preceding generations corset the lives of their descendants through the institution, which will appear to them as their external and mechanical destiny. Two of the biographies reveal the shaping potential of this particular collectivity. Genet was saved because the institution he encountered was in effect an anti-institution. The contradictory pressures that the Flaubert family exerted on their second son resulted in a personal catastrophe that could be escaped only through the false solution of a self-destructive use of the imagination.

The description of the adventures of the fused group may be read as an alternative to Freud's myth of the society founding fraternal hoard. Although the two myths are structurally almost identical, the moving force in each case could not be more different. Each offers a necessary complement to the other. In *Totem and Taboo*, Freud imagines a primal hoard led by a powerful father, an unlimited despot, who refuses to share with his sons the women and goods over which he has total control. The brothers band together in a pure democracy to kill the tyrant. To avoid the otherwise inevitable wars of succession and the disintegration of the unanimous group in whose solidarity the brothers find their strength, they vow never to kill and never to approach the women whom their victory has won. The oaths are sealed in the key festival of totemic religion.

A totem animal, who stands for the father, is killed and mourned. The grief turns to rejoicing, and the animal is devoured. The meal, which is an expression of what Freud terms the inexorable law of ambivalence toward the father, simultaneously offers an opportunity to express remorse and to rejoice in the recollection of triumph. By devouring the animal the brothers also reaffirm their solidarity and ritually absorb and democratically share the envied power of the tyrant who is both loved and hated. In the course of time the bitterness toward the father lessens. As this happens, the original, unlimited democratic solidarity begins to decay. The once fatherless society slowly erodes into one with a patriarchal basis. In the group's effort to unburden itself definitively of guilt, the brothers reinstitute centralized authority as a love tribute to the murdered despot.

Both myths are unilaterally insufficient but gain strength when synthesized. Freud is insufficiently cognizant of the role of historical accident in social psychology. Sartre describes a hoard of eternally unrepentant sons. In his account, the wax and wane of physical threat is the motor of the history of groups. Purely psychological, historically invariable factors play no role. If the myth of the group in fusion is to aid in the understanding of change, the study of subjective factors, such as the father complex, must reinforce the description of strictly objective conditions.

"Will the disappearance of capitalist forms of alienation result in the end of *all* forms of alienation?" Sartre asks in the *Critique,* and he can offer only a partial answer.[68] A founding, socially unproblematic alienation is declared to have an ontological status. But Sartre does not risk an answer to the question of whether communism will bring to an end all of the historically variable forms of alterity, compulsion, and circularity. The *Critique* describes but does not predict. To speculate would be to reason on the basis of a future history that cannot be known. A reply will be possible only when readers cease to recognize themselves in the biographies of men whose lives were not their own.

III

Baudelaire and Bad Faith

If a man is a slave, his own will is responsible for his slavery.

Hegel

"I know the nineteenth century well," Sartre has remarked, having written more on the subject than all but a few of those who have devoted their lives to understanding the literature of the century.[1] The unmasking of the ideologies of the period, of a past that Sartre believes to live in the present, is a task from which he never strays for long. He is the century's self-appointed master ironist, designated to expose the cruel and farcical deceptions by which the bourgeois live and perpetuate their dominance.

Besides the biographies of Baudelaire and Flaubert, Sartre wrote essays on Jules Renard and Stéphane Mallarmé, the last a distillation of a longer study, the bulk of which has been lost. Arthur Rimbaud and Lautréamont are discussed in *Being and Nothingness*. Baudelaire is mentioned in *The Imaginary*. Many pages of *What Is Literature?* and of Sartre's introduction to the first number of *Les Temps Modernes* are devoted to the canonical postromantics. In "The Communists and Peace" and the *Critique*, Sartre discusses the violence of 1848 and 1871, when the secret structures of bourgeois society were revealed. In short, few of Sartre's writings or interviews lack any reference to the men or events of the nineteenth century. Sartre specifies that the drawing-room set for *No Exit* be furnished in the Second Empire style, because for him that century was a hell from which mankind has yet to escape. But the period simultaneously provided the tool that may enable men to bring history to a happy resolution: "Dialectical thought became conscious of itself, historically, at the beginning of the last century."[2] The set of *No*

Exit contains this possibility as well: the architecture of hell includes an open door.

The roots of Sartre's obsession with the nineteenth century are both prelogical and ideological. His first exposure to the myths and authors of the period is one of the themes of *The Words*. Young Sartre lived in what the practitioners of speculative fiction describe as a time warp, having spent his youth in a century that had ended five years before his birth. His grandfather Charles Schweitzer, with whom he lived, had pretty much ceased to read new literature since the death of Victor Hugo, and the only contemporary authors for whom he had any affection were Georges Courteline and Anatole France. These tastes dictated the range of Sartre's reading. Because of his early passion for the works of the literary figures of the century developed in his grandfather's library, Sartre claimed to have earned the right to treat them with the over-familiarity that has since irritated more passively reverent specialists: "On Baudelaire, and on Flaubert I speak without mincing my words. And when I am blamed for this I always want to reply: Don't butt into our affairs. They belonged to me, your geniuses, I held them in my hands, loved them passionately and in all irreverence. How can I be expected to treat them with kid gloves?"[3]

From Schweitzer and the authors represented on his shelves, Sartre learned the etiquette of the clerk that Julien Benda would later systematize. The clerk, product of a formalist illusion, has a special saving mission. This fraudulently disinterested intellectual occupies his spoiled leisure with meditations on the good and beautiful. Hovering above the unclean, ignorant fray, he redeems all of humanity in the eyes of history. Despite its silliness and barbarism, the human race can be confident of salvation as long as a single such mandarin remains alive to ply his abstract trade.

The ideologically related doctrine of art for art's sake was another major part of the intellectual baggage inflicted on the young Sartre: "The old scorn of Flaubert, the Goncourts, and Gautier poisoned me. Their abstract hatred of man, concealed behind the mask of love, infected me with new pretensions. I became a Cathar, confused literature with prayer, and made of it a human sacrifice."[4] The implicit misanthropy and sadism of art for art's sake is a major theme of *L'Idiot*. Although Sartre claims that by the time he was fifteen he had weaned himself from what he would later term "art-neurosis," Simone de Beauvoir reports that in their early years together Sartre had "an unconditional faith in Beauty that he did not distinguish from Art."[5] Faith in the redemptive powers of art seems to be operative still in *Nausea,* though undermined by self-irony and on the verge of turning into its opposite. Sartre has a habit of writing against himself, and the many pages he has devoted to postromantic literary devices and mythologies testify to this personal tradition. Through them he settles accounts with a former, captive avatar.

Sartre's reasons for exorcising the ghosts of the nineteenth century are not merely personal. For him, most of Western literary and political history is still traveling on a course that was fatally set in the nineteenth century. Modern man cannot hope to understand himself without coming to terms with the century that saw the triumph of the bourgeoisie, that social class for which Sartre has always had a special affection.

In "The Communists and Peace" Sartre analyzes the critical moments in the history of the last century and demonstrates their connection with the present time. The events of the years 1848 and 1871, are, for him, the two moments of truth in modern history. On these occasions the true nature of the class struggle was exposed and the bourgeoisie was forced to overt violence in order to protect its interests against the legitimate demands of the oppressed. Under the July Monarchy, Sartre maintains, "the French population was made up of animals and the bourgeois: the king was bourgeois, and the bourgeois was king, the bourgeois was man, and man was bourgeois. The animal was the animal; he was yoked to the machines."[6] But in June of 1848 the occult founding contradictions emerged, and the structures of society broke apart. The proletariat emerged as a class and tested its strength. Ever since, the bourgeois has pursued with resourcefulness the goal of preventing the worker from realizing that he is a person and a member of a historically contingent class. The social order requires that the beast be held in check, that he perceive himself as beast and not as man, and that he be discouraged from joining in common cause with his oppressed brothers.

Because the bourgeois normally prefers not to show his hand, his tastes run to covert devices of domination. He avails himself of two powerful symbolic weapons: the concept of "distinction" and analytic thought. This methodology, by which the bourgeois defines himself intellectually, is as much in evidence today as it was in the last century. Within its world view totalities appear to be nothing more than chance-determined aggregates of disassociated particularities. In *Being and Nothingness* Bourget's use of the method was seen. In the analytic view of society, "the individual, a solid particle . . . resides like a pea in a can of peas: he is round, closed in upon himself, not in communication with others."[7] The analytic society is a simple, serieslike juxtaposition of persons, just as the individual, according to the analytic psychologist, is a mosaiclike organization of universalized drives. In the analytic society genuinely associative life and collective action are beyond conceptual reach. This static world view is highly agreeable to those in authority.

Two corollaries of this principle are the idea of social irresponsibility and the related idea of incommunicability. The nineteenth-century bourgeois is enabled by his official intellectual methodology to disregard the notion of class and thus to avoid collective responsibility for the fate of others. He sees men only in psychological terms. A worker is simply another atom, whose condition is in no way tied to his own. For the bourgeois, human mutuality is an impossibility because social relations and language are founded on the notion of incommunicability. Time and again Sartre finds these features of analytic thought in the writings of the postromantic period.

In *What Is Literature?* Sartre spends more time on the nineteenth century than on any other because of its special relation with modern times. People today are still on the path set by the French Revolution. During the eighteenth century a unique harmony had existed between literature seen as an appeal to freedom and the requirements of the politically oppressed bourgeoisie. But with the political triumph of the middle classes, this harmony disappeared. The writer lost his privileged position. During the struggles of the eighteenth century he had played with profit the role of the double agent: while in the pay of the nobility, he had advanced the cause of his class of origin, which was seeking to seize the dominant role in society. Following its triumph, the bourgeoisie no longer required the services of the writer to advance its cause against the nobility. But the writer had contributed to his own destruction, for the nobles of good will were no longer in a position to provide his support. An escape from his native but detested class was no longer feasible. After its victory, the bourgeois audience demanded a new kind of literature that would praise bourgeois values and institutions and would reduce itself, as in the seventeenth century, to psychology. The instrumental spirit of this class required a psychological literature that would legitimize the domination and seduction of others. A conflict therefore developed between the character of literature as an appeal to freedom and the ideology of the bourgeoisie. The world of ends was asked to become the world of means.

Of most interest to Sartre are those writers who refused to cooperate. These he divides into two groups, according to their relation with the reading public of their day. Because of educational reforms, a new audience developed between 1830 and 1848 that was both

oppressed and literate. A few authors—principally Sand, Hugo, and
Michelet—discovered this potential audience, but because they had
not arisen from this class, they neither understood nor spoke its
language. The historical role of the proletariat escaped their grasp.
Their appeal to this audience was moreover premature, for the oppressed did not yet understand their need for the voice which these
authors sought ineptly to provide.

Another group of authors made a double refusal, declining to
comply with the requirements of their native caste but also refusing
to truck with the new audience of the exploited masses. They criticized the bourgeois world, but from the perspective of an already
surpassed social class, the nobility. Georg Lukács maintains
that "the culture of capitalism, to the extent that it truly existed,
could consist in nothing but the ruthless critique of the capitalist
epoch."[8] But as Sartre shows, because the criticism of capitalist
society found in the art for art's sake movement was leveled from the
perspective of an already devolved caste, it was entirely without
menace and ultimately irrelevant. Although the authors broke with
the bourgeoisie, their schism was purely symbolic and thus ineffectual. They were obtuse to the moral imperative implicit in the
acts of reading and writing. In their hands literature was pure
negativity; it became its own subject and indulged in abstract
gamesmanship. These authors wanted their works to be considered
anything but acts of communication. The rule of the bourgeois was
not contested because ultimately they perceived the bourgeoisie not
as a social class but as an immutable fact of nature whose reality was
psychological rather than historical and contingent. Writers with-
drew from commerce with their own context and lived in communication with the atemporal clerks. The audience was ahistorical.
Stendhal's audience was Balzac; Poe's was Baudelaire. Through
this "communion of the saints" authors sought posthumous glory,
which Sartre sees as a symbolic social ascent into a mythical realm
created in the image of the old aristocracy.

By becoming the martyr of pure consumption, an author, according to Sartre, adopts the ideology of the class he hopes symbolically to enter. In this role he produces literary objects that are
useless and conspicuously wasteful. Outside the realm of the arts
the postromantic author approves of only three things: love, travel,
and war, all equally useless, nonproductive, parasitic, and wasteful.
He develops a taste for the destructive and scorns banal but productive work. He destroys his own life by abusing alcohol or drugs,
but finds in his own work the most satisfying if meaningless of all
phenomena, for beauty is the most perfectly useless of categories.

It teaches nothing, reflects no immediately recognizable ideology, and considers all forms of communication to be impure. Art is the highest form of gratuitous consumption.

As Lukács notes, anything that culture produces can possess real cultural value only when it is valuable for itself, and cultural expressions reach their highest level only when the economic plays no perceptible role, when the artist makes clear that, in the words of Gautier, a novel is not a pair of boots.[9] Sartre shows, however, that willful obliviousness to utilitarian values does not necessarily constitute criticism of a world of exploitation but can rather pay esoteric homage to the aristocratic ideal of pure consumption. He describes such literature as a total negation of the temporal. Its project is to negate the world or to consume it. For Sartre, these motives are displayed in the most apparently dissimilar literary schools. Flaubert wrote in order to rid himself of men and things. Zola's naturalism crushes life, the typical subject of his determinist sagas being the slow degeneration of a man, a family, or an enterprise. Symbolism discovered the close relationship between beauty and death. This equivalence is in fact the central feature of all avant-garde literature of the last half of the century. It was entirely appropriate for Mallarmé to send congratulations to Zola on the occasion of the publication of *L'Assommoir,* for the message in the writings of both is identical, and that message is, according to Sartre, "life is an absolute shipwreck."[10]

Whereas *What Is Literature?* demonstrates the relation between ontological and historical freedoms, the life study published in the same year generally fails to connect the two points of individual and collective salvation. *Baudelaire* is a severe book, in which Sartre strictly applies the tools and the ethics of individual authenticity expounded in *Being and Nothingness. Baudelaire* is the only one of the three biographies in which Sartre unequivocally holds that a person is utterly responsible for what he is. It is also a relatively uncomplicated book, in that it expresses the doctrine that an original choice is manifest in all moments of a person's life. Baudelaire lived as the survivor of an epochal moment of choice: "Each event reflects back the undecomposable totality that he was from the first day to the last."[11] This totalitarian approach to the life of the poet leads Sartre both to startling insights and to embarrassing gaffs.

One work that had considerable influence on the first biography is *L'Individu et le sexe: Psychologie du narcissisme* by Angelo Hesnard.[12] Although Sartre makes no mention of this book in *Baudelaire,* a footnote in *Saint Genet* indicates his acquaintance with Hesnard's theory of narcissism, amplifying the concept discovered by Freud.[13] For Hesnard, narcissism is the basic human instinct. In its purest state, which Freud terms "primary narcissism," it appears in the primal incestuous relationship between mother and infant.[14] During this phase the child experiences his mother as an extension of himself and his happiness is unmitigated. In Sartre's parlance, the negations of consciousness are not yet operative. A critical moment occurs when the child is forcibly separated from the mother and learns, typically through the intervention of the father, that he and his mother do not constitute a seamless, self-contained, universally inclusive whole. Before Jacques Lacan and Melanie Klein, Hesnard showed that the father, as the third party in the oedipal situation, is not only the hated and feared rival but also the agent whose presence brings to a close the unlimited relationship between mother and child. If the separation of the child from the mother is particularly traumatic, the child becomes narcissistic. In despair and rage such children turn in upon themselves and *"seek within themselves* a compensation for the loss of the mother."[15] Out of spite the child decides to be completely self-sufficient, a world unto himself.

Henceforth the individual is rendered incapable of loving anything or anyone other than himself or of tolerating any reality other than his internal world. The world is conceived of as nothing more than a self-image. Finding the natural world repulsive, the narcissist seeks to redeem it by a blurring of the external world of objects and the internal world of dreams. The traumatized child finds only himself in his experiences of things and people. Since he takes pleasure in finding himself in the eyes of others, he has a passion to show himself, to cause himself to be seen. Because of his desperate desire to isolate and capture his own image, he is incapable of spontaneous behavior. The obsession with his lost childhood is never overcome; his whole life is a flight toward childhood, and because of his unrelieved focus on the past, "The future is nothing but a word."[16] The life of the little Narcissus is complicated by a troublesome ambivalence. Simultaneously he hates those who have put an end to the paradise of maternal incest and assimilates them and their values into his consciousness. His personality is divided into two ferociously opposed components, each perpetually contesting the other. Because of this self-hatred, the narcissistic individual is often suicidal.

Hesnard traces the appearance of the narcissistic instinct in literature, philosophy, and religion. The man of letters seeks to find himself in the events, objects, and characters he describes. The aesthetic experience is an "ecstatic state in which the subject and the object merge."[17] This definition, which is equivalent to Sartre's definition of beauty as the fusing of the for-itself and in-itself, raises the question whether the influence of Hesnard on Sartre predates the writing of the first biography. All the traits mentioned by Hesnard are found by Sartre in the life of Baudelaire. The correspondence between the two books is closer than that between *Baudelaire* and *Being and Nothingness,* which is more commonly noted. The Genet biography also exhibits many of the same characteristics. In Hesnard, Sartre has clearly discovered a system of psychoanalysis that he feels to be compatible and complementary to his own.

As in the *Critique,* Sartre in *Baudelaire* is most deeply concerned with the dissolution of the barriers separating individuals. He regards the six-year-old Baudelaire's state of mind after the death of his natural father as one of these privileged moments of fusion. The boy, who now had his mother to himself, "lived within the adoration of his mother; fascinated, surrounded by attentions, respect and care, he didn't yet understand that he existed as an individual, but he sensed himself united to the body and affections of his mother by a sort of primitive and mystic participation: he lost himself in the warmth of their reciprocal love" (p. 18). His existence is unconditionally justified: "precisely because he is entirely absorbed in another who seems to him to exist by necessity and by right, he is protected against all anxiety, and fused with the absolute" (p. 19). Like a fused group, the young Baudelaire was "completely penetrated by unanimous life." Sartre recalls Hesnard when he refers to the mother and son as the "incestuous couple" (p. 20).

For Hesnard as well as Freud, a fissure appears in this ecstatic union with the infant's first experience of rivalry. The child discovers that the father also has a claim on the mother. Angered by the loss of the paradise of union and omnipotence, the child wishes the death of the person responsible for his declension. Such is the case in Sartre's *Baudelaire.* In 1828 the little Narcissus receives his incurable wound when his mother marries General Aupick and the boy is later sent off to school. From this time dates the "wound." Baudelaire discovers the situation of everyman: solitude, individual existence, and freedom. The child's reaction is to make the original choice that will lurk behind all his subsequent thoughts and self-objectifications. Baudelaire feels that his only recourse is to make a virtue of his rejection and to establish himself as the source of his isolation. His aim will be to experience as completely and concretely as possible this self-imposed singularity.

Refusing to accept passively the domination of the Other and the threat to his omnipotence that it entails, the child chooses to portray himself as self-conceived and thereby to restore the integrity of the seamless world of the past. But the result of the strategy is a compromised narcissism because it absorbs the domination of the Other that the willing of separateness sought to annul. Into his self-conception Baudelaire has admitted the authority of the Other, who has decreed that he be forever separate. Baudelaire declares war on the force that has caused his fall from paradise, but nonetheless absorbs its will. Sartre uses this division, suggested by Hesnard, to explain the major paradoxes encountered in the life and writings of the poet.

Baudelaire is the story of a man who fell from one narcissism to another. The prehistoric paradise of maternal incest and archaic narcissism has been devastated, and reality revealed as repressive of the primitive edenic state. Wounded, Baudelaire reacts with a psychic reorganization. By resorting to a defensive retreat, he seeks to reestablish the narcissistic integrity on a new, more limited level: "He prefers himself to all, because he is abandoned by all" (p. 24). "He dreams of a sense of unity that can be grasped by sight, and by touch, and that fills you as a pure sound fills the ears" (p. 25). This experience must now be found within himself: "The original posture of Baudelaire is that of a man who is stooping down, leaning towards himself, like Narcissus" (p. 26). Singularity becomes his personal symbol of the coincidence of the for-itself and in-itself. Denied the illusion of the larger coincidence available in the original narcissism, Baudelaire retrenches to a secondary, restricted narcissism. Unable to coincide with something larger, he seeks to coincide with himself by making a fetish of his singularity, which was first imposed, then self-appointed. Like the café waiter, Baudelaire chooses self-alienation. Sartre's biography is a catalogue of the means by which Baudelaire sought to appropriate himself, to catch himself in the act, to be both the alienating glance and its captive. But as indicated in *Being and Nothingness,* such a project is foredoomed: "Baudelaire chose to see himself as if he were another; his life is but the story of this failure" (p. 32). The poet's ennui is nothing other than his deflated sense that this self-alienation is impossible, his awareness of an unavoidable freedom, of the necessary failure of his project of self-coincidence.

The speculative reconstruction of decisive moments of a subject's childhood has a long and problematical history in modern biography. In the eighteenth century Edward Harwood wrote a life of Christ in which he imagined childhood scenes that had no basis in scripture, and Parson Weems invented the incident of Washington and the cherry tree. More to the point are the speculative fictions of Freud, such as his attempt to patch together an early life of

Leonardo on the basis of the artist's dream of a vulture. In each of his biographies Sartre operates in a similar fashion. He works backward from what is known of the subject's later life and writings in order to arrive at a crucial scene that resulted in a decisive choice, which is used to begin the biography. Subsequent events are then shown to flow inevitably from the traumatic moment. This procedure gives his biographies a deductive tone.

Philip Thody maintains that [Sartre] "would have preferred Baudelaire to have been a third-rate early Socialist pamphleteer rather than a first-rate lyrical poet."[18] This is a serious misreading of the biography. To be sure Baudelaire is to be blamed, for at this point Sartre continues to believe that liberation from alienation requires no more than a unilateral cognitive act, something available to all. In *Being and Nothingness,* however, he remarks that because of man's penchant for self-deception the experience of anguish is "entirely exceptional."[19] Baudelaire's obsession with ennui earns from Sartre mixed praise. The poet's life and works have a substantial heuristic content because, like few others, he understood and expressed the human condition. He had an acute intuition of the free, anomic character of the for-itself. Sartre's scorn is thus energized by admiration. If Baudelaire deserves great blame, it is because he first proved worthy of so much esteem. Admiration, rather than scorn, is the gravitational center of *Baudelaire.* Homage is the heart of the affront.

According to Sartre, the quest for singularity does not lead Baudelaire to adopt an individual morality, as shown by the banal and compliant resolutions in the *Ecrits intimes* and by Baudelaire's refusal to defend *Les Fleurs du mal* against the charge of obscenity. The poet's taste in secondhand values stems from the original project of difference from which his fear of creative liberty derives. Although the child wants to feel and enjoy his singularity, the creative act does not permit such enjoyment, for he who creates, at least during the moment of creation, moves outside the realm of singularity into the world of pure freedom. He no longer is; he does. Baudelaire prefers to experience his singularity as a thing. He is a rebel rather than a revolutionary. Whereas the revolutionary seeks to change the world and invent a new moral order, the rebel takes care to leave intact the abuses against which he complains. He does not want to destroy or to go beyond the moral order, but simply to strike an opposing posture that is more theater than substance.

The same prostrate homage to traditional values is found in Baudelaire's use of the theme of evil. "Flowers of evil" are appealing, not in spite of the fact that they are forbidden, but precisely because they are prohibited. The deliberate creation of evil is acceptance and recognition of good. Good is assimilable for Baudelaire to the blaming look. The accusing, alienating glance of General Aupick, or of his mother is required for him to experience himself as the singular object he has chosen to be. The attraction to the figure of Satan evident in the poetry finds its source in the fact that the fallen angel is pierced through by the gaze of God, fixed into his devilish essence. To sin in public becomes an essential feature of the project for it evokes the petrifying glance of the Other, which provides the privileged state of damnation. For a moment the sinner grasps himself through the eye of another. Throughout Baudelaire's work is heard the stifled cry "I am Satan" (p. 124). For Baudelaire, the devil is the symbol of disobedient children who beg for a paternal glance that will fix them in their rebellious singularity.

Baudelaire's eagerness for the transfixing eye of the judge is also found in other themes of his life and poetry, such as his cult of the frigid woman, who is, explains Sartre, the sexual incarnation of the judge. The coldness of the unresponsive woman, her purity and freedom from original sin, were what qualified her for the role of the Medusa. Although the lists of addresses found among Baudelaire's personal papers suggest that he had a profound weakness for a very different sort of woman, his taste for impure revels is in point of fact only a relative taste which functions to exalt further the role of the woman-judge by providing this figure with occasions on which she can crush the poet with her reproving glance. Sexual debauchery calls down the transforming look of the immaculate judge.

Baudelaire's Old Testament-centered theology is of a piece with the original project. In *Being and Nothingness* Sartre remarked that belief in God is a form of autoalienation. Baudelaire's personal theology is constructed to set in relief this feature of religion. The exteriority of the divinity must be stressed. Intercessors must be eliminated, for the direct confrontation with the alienating look of the judge must not be vitiated. Because Baudelaire cares not to be saved but rather to be judged, he chooses the pitiless God of the Old Testament rather than that of the New. This terrible divinity Baudelaire does not at first distinguish from Aupick. After the death of the general, Baudelaire's mother assumes the necessary role.

Baudelaire never ceased to regret having been expelled from the secure and static world of his childhood, when he was nothing but an object of attention. He defined genius as the ability to rediscover childhood at will. What he misses from those years is the child's not having yet experienced the revelation of freedom, his ignorance of the fact that the world is his to make of it what he will. Baudelaire understands that the desperate role of the adult is to create his own truth rather than to be passively subject to the truth of another. Childhood is the paradise of the unrelieved alienating glance, the fixed essence imposed from outside. Baudelaire's parents remain for him hateful but necessary idols: hateful and to be punished because they provoked the collapse of the edenic ideal, but indispensable because as judges they function to institutionalize the project of singularity he has adopted in order to spite them. The truth is found in their eyes. Baudelaire's attitude toward his parents is ultimately masochistic, hence a species of self-alienation.

But the perfect solipsist, or narcissist, cannot remain content in his masochism. Baudelaire thus attempts to duplicate within himself the sadomasochistic couple. The sadist, as described in *Being and Nothingness,* alienates his partner. The poet becomes his own victim. Sartre explains the sadist's logic: "To cause to suffer is to possess" (p. 87). Baudelaire's "Heautontimoroumenos" fits neatly into Sartre's system. In the lines "I am the wound and the knife/The victim and the executioner," Sartre sees at its most unadorned the fundamental project of constituting a monstrous couple who will permit a final form of self-possession. But the effort will be in vain, for such self-alienation is an impossibility. Such a sadomasochistic "one-man band" is a kind of ontological onanism, which is less psychologically satisfying than provoking the sanction of the Other. It requires a suspension of reality that is difficult to sustain.

The narcissist is perpetually in pursuit of a mirror which, in the words of Valéry's Narcisse, is that "precious treasure that divides the world."[20] The resourceful Baudelaire uses the external world against itself. His centripetal urge goads him to transform perception of the natural world into a tool for self-recuperation. In his experience of perception, Baudelaire never forgets himself. Rather than simply contemplating a thing, he dwells upon his consciousness of it. Hence his relations with the objects of experience are without immediacy or spontaneity. "What matters the nature of reality that is outside of me, as long as it helps me to live, to sense that I am and what I am" (pp. 26–27). All surrounding objects are called upon to aid him in experiencing his singularity. Of a piece with this attitude is his definition of modern art in *L'Art philosophique* as "the creation of a suggestive magic that contains at once the object and the subject, the world external to the artist and the artist himself" (p. 27).

Baudelaire lived at a time when the future had been newly discovered. Marx, Flora Tristan, Jules Michelet, Proudhon, and Sand had all found the meaning of the present in the future. But this newly discovered temporal dimension is one of the avatars of freedom. Baudelaire felt more at ease with a present that derives its sense from the past. One of the ways he displayed his passion for the past was to establish to others and to himself that his nature had been long ago programmed for all time. Sartre gives Baudelaire the words, "I am my past" (p. 216). Another example of the poet's obsession with the past is found in his cult of the life and writings of Edgar Allan Poe. If Poe had not been dead, Sartre suggests, Baudelaire would not have been interested.

Baudelaire also flirted with the final form of self-alienation, which is suicide. To destroy oneself is to provoke artificially the final objectification. Self-destruction for Baudelaire has as its end a desire to return, not to nothingness, but rather to a definitive object state. But in order to take pleasure in this final self-recuperation, Baudelaire must be the survivor of his self-destruction. The logic of the situation requires a suicide that is purely symbolic. This he accomplishes by presenting himself as a pure essence of inactivity. An additional reason that Baudelaire's *felo de se* must remain partial and symbolic is that the goals of autoalienation and self-possession are of only limited compatibility. Eventually self-alienation can no longer serve Baudelaire's project. It is a tool that must be surpassed. At some point it becomes not merely useless but positively refractory, opposing the project of self-recuperation. If Baudelaire were to destroy himself totally, either physically or symbolically, he would permanently deliver himself over as an object for the other, thus contradicting the ends of self-possession and self-conception. Just prior to the achievement of complete self-alienation, Baudelaire must reverse his field if the integrity of the project is to be maintained.

To reclaim himself from the encroaching grasp of the Other, Baudelaire must make a sudden display of freedom. For, as Sartre says, "One possesses oneself on the condition that one creates himself" (p. 84). If one becomes a pure thing, one loses the freedom that is at the foundation of self-appropriation. Final possession of self cannot be achieved through definitive objectification. Complete self-recuperation is attained by becoming the impossible thing, the for-itself/in-itself, by flitting back and forth between free existence and the object state in the vain quest of its achievement. Baudelaire takes pleasure in experiencing himself as a thing in the eyes of the Other, but just at the point at which the Other is in a position to make a final claim and just as he is about to be completely absorbed into the reign of the Other, Baudelaire can and does step backward and assert his freedom. But from the display of freedom Baudelaire must shift quickly back to the object state. A permanent suspension within this paradox is the only means of retaining the project in its original purity.

As an example of this necessary display of travestied freedom, Sartre mentions the theme of antiphysis, one of the most familiar features of Baudelaire's writings. Sartre finds it in Baudelaire's fascination with city life, his pose of the dandy, and his taste for sterile landscapes and unresponsive lovers. His fear of abandonment to nature is evident in his lack of temerity in the face of the problems of inspiration and poetic practice. In *La Fanfarlo* Samuel Cramer, rather than having his mistress in the flesh, prefers to see her heavily made up and dressed in theatrical garb. Hostility to the natural reappears in Baudelaire's personal dress, which was restrictive and highly self-conscious. This was his way of saying no to his body and its functions. Here Sartre expresses an embryonic, unhistorical notion of "distinction," which perhaps justifies the suspicion that his familiarity with Baudelaire's work had a crucial role in the concept's genesis. Baudelaire is finally described as hating nature and seeking to destroy it because it has its source in God. Antiphysis is thus assimilated to sacrilege, understood in *Being and Nothingness* as the impossible attempt to subjugate the alienating glance.

Another area in which Baudelaire affirms his freedom is within his moral system. He chooses to accept a preconstituted conventional morality, but within this comfortably fixed world he opts to assert his freedom in a narrow and theatrical manner. When he resorts to the freedom of wrongdoing, it is only as a vehicle to experience himself ultimately as object: "Baudelaire submitted to the Good in order to transgress, and if he transgresses it is in order to intensify his experience of its authority over him, to be condemned in its name, and transformed into a guilty thing" (p. 122). This indirect compliance is Baudelaire's idea of living dangerously. He is a tightrope walker performing on a wire with a net two feet below. The freedom he dares to exert is mostly relative. With the experience of unconditional freedom he risks only slight contact. Baudelaire chooses freedom not as a means to achieve authenticity but as a temporary ruse to further his project of a secondary, limited narcissism.

His vacillation between the categories of freedom and thinghood is the key to that feature of his poetry which Baudelaire termed "the spiritual." For Sartre, this is the essential quality through which the poet hopes to appropriate the world. The "spiritual" is characterized by a hesitant participation in existence: remaining in suspense between being and nothingness, it is never there. Baudelaire demonstrated a consistent predilection for twilight, distant music, cloudy skies, and mute or indolent women—all of which seem to contain within themselves their own negation. Poems themselves are "embodied thoughts" (p. 223). Baudelaire imbues the in-itself with the for-itself, making of the object a physical analogue of an idea. Hence the attraction of Emmanuel Swedenborg's system of correspondences within which each of the objects of the natural world points beyond itself and constitutes an objectified transcendence. Baudelaire seeks to surround himself with a whole world which will be just such a freedom-object. In this world he will find his self-image: "Lightened, hollowed out, filled with symbols and signs, this world that surrounds him . . . is nothing other than himself; and it is himself that this Narcissus seeks to embrace and to contemplate" (pp. 227–228). The poet revels in this world because it represents the synthesis of the for-itself and in-itself, thoughts become things, that he has hopelessly sought to realize in his life and can achieve only in the domain of the imaginary.

Within the nearly unanimous chorus of negative response that met the appearance of *Baudelaire,* there were two major criticisms, one legitimate, the other not. The unjustified complaint was that Sartre displayed no understanding of poetry.[21] This criticism is beside the point because, as Michel Leiris notes, Sartre's intention was not to deal with the poetry as such but rather to "relive from the inside" (p. 9) the experience of Baudelaire. Sartre's book was in fact written to preface an edition of the *Ecrits intimes,* not *Les Fleurs du Mal.*

The legitimate reservation concerns the book's psychologism, its ignorance of the social determinants of mental life. Sartre does not reveal the sway of the universal, that is, of the society, within and over the individual. Georges Bataille remarks on Sartre's obliviousness to the fact that the experience of Baudelaire was historically conditioned.[22] Sartre's outlook is almost entirely monological. All is reduced to the subject. The world surrounding Baudelaire seems touched by history, while the poet himself is not. The fundamental question is not man's relation to others but his relation to himself. In the last analysis Baudelaire's neurosis is the result of a moral failure that is purely personal. He has freely chosen bad faith over authenticity. The psychological realm is seen as an autonomous, self-enclosed field of psychic forces. This refusal to consider the possible objective roots of Baudelaire's predicament follows directly from Sartre's early view of human freedom as unconditional. It does not allow him to understand the relationship between existence and actuality as described by Hegel: "Actuality is always the unity of universal and particular, the universal dismembered in the particulars which seem to be self-subsistent, although they really are upheld and contained only in the whole. A hand which is cut off still looks like a hand, and it exists, but without being actual."[23] Sartre's first biography is like the severed hand described by Hegel. It discloses a Baudelaire who exists, who is very real, but who is not actual. Sartre has yet to discover the world of mutual mediation, the world of the singular universal.

An awareness of the poet's historical context could have improved the book. Simone de Beauvoir explains that in *Baudelaire* "Sartre had yet to demonstrate a thorough understanding of dialectical thought and Marxist materialism."[24] In 1970 Sartre himself judged the study to be "very insufficient, extremely bad."[25] In the two biographies that followed it, Sartre provided his own auto-criticism of the failures of *Baudelaire*.

There are two levels at which criticism of the book is possible. One is the discovery in Baudelaire's life and works of things which do not fall easily into the predatory pattern of Sartre's argument. The extremeness of Sartre's claim renders him most vulnerable. He argues that "Every event reflects back to us the undecomposable whole that he was from the first day till the last" (p. 245). Everything must show Sartre to be in the right; a single fact that does not fit will undermine the absoluteness of the claim.

Baudelaire has those positive and negative features native to the art of caricature. The poet is relentlessly reduced to a portrait that at once enlightens because it exaggerates the importance of certain basic features and misrepresents for it is willfully ignorant of complexities that might stand in the way of the simplification. All aspects of Baudelaire's life are galvanized into conceptual identity. The choice of detail is flagrantly tendentious. Yet evidence that counters Sartre's argument is obvious. Sartre's assertion of Baudelaire's interest in Poe hangs on the fact that the American was already deceased, but at the time that Baudelaire conceived his passion for Poe's writings, the American was very much alive. The unexpected discovery in 1967 of a group of new letters from Baudelaire to Aupick, generally characterized by an affectionate tone, belies the intense hatred that Sartre claims the poet had for his stepfather. The man who felt comfortable only in the past made a point, in the *Salon of 1845* and elsewhere, of advising artists to seek inspiration in the anomic present. For Sartre, Baudelaire's espousal of the republican cause was the fancy of a moment, having more to do with family than with national politics, but both Ernest Prarond and Charles Toubin argue convincingly that Baudelaire was an active participant at the barricades and a sincere advocate of social reform.[26] It is true that Baudelaire expressed hostility to the republicans, especially in the *Salon of 1846,* but F. W. J. Hemmings shows that it was not the aspirations of the poor which Baudelaire opposed, but rather their dreamy and ineffectual theory-obsessed leaders.[27] Whereas Sartre's Baudelaire is profoundly ungenerous, the real poet's sincere efforts on behalf of the mad and indigent Meryon, and his aid to the needy Daumier are indisputable facts.

Baudelaire's texts that are most refractory to Sartre's thesis are the two articles on the poetry of Pierre Dupont. Baudelaire praises the poems of *Chants et chansons* for their direct, natural tone and populist spirit. Sartre portrayed the poet as a compliant, apolitical figure, indifferent to the plight of the masses, but the historical poet praises Dupont's poetry as a call to direct political action: "Was the song one of those volatile atoms that float in the air and form agglomerations that become a storm, a tempest, or an event?" Further along: "this resounding hymn adapted itself admirably to a general revolution in politics and in the applications of politics. It became, almost immediately, the rallying cry of the disinherited classes." The man whom Sartre says preferred the company of the defunct here says "I prefer the poet who is in permanent communication with the men of his time." The poet whom Sartre reported to have felt uncomfortable in an atmosphere of radical reform remarks approvingly that Dupont "arrived with flaming language to proclaim the sanctity of the insurrection of 1830." The poet who excised the future from his consciousness writes: "Go into the future singing, providential poet. Your songs are the luminous traces of hopes and convictions of the people."[28] It is impossible for Sartre's regulative image to absorb the Baudelaire of these pages. Although the essays on Dupont are far from typical, they reveal a Baudelaire unaccounted for in the biography. Sartre's work, though unquestionably presenting a generally faithful view of the poet, is certainly not the complete and final portrait that it purports to be.

It might be objected that the phenomenologically oriented psychologist rejects the accidental event of personal character in order to arrive at an understanding of the essence of the man. Certainly Baudelaire's remarks in the Dupont essays and his activities at the barricades in 1848 are far from characteristic. But the fact remains that Sartre's psychology here is oppressively static. He had not yet discovered the model of the biographical spirals that he would unveil in the *Search for a Method.* In *Baudelaire* Henry James's admonition to the biographer is not heeded: "To live over people's lives is nothing unless we live over their perceptions, live over the growth, the change, the varying intensity of the same—since it was *by* these things they themselves lived."[29]

Although it would be inappropriate to criticize *Baudelaire* from the point of view of Sartre's future-discoveries, the work may be criticized from the perspective of its own premises and of those in another of Sartre's works published in the same year.[30] *What Is Literature?* raises certain problems. In that essay two ethics are in evidence, each involving the overcoming of a species of alienation. The first is the ethics of individual authenticity, which an author demonstrates if he recognizes the free character of literature, and man, and displays this freedom in his work. There is also an ethics of collective salvation. People live in historical circumstances inimical to autonomy and must be saved through the experience of ontological freedom communicated by literature and gained ultimately through collective struggle.

In *What Is Literature?* these two ethics of individual and collective authenticity are neatly synchronized. Individual authenticity is said to contribute to collective, historical liberation. These same two value systems are again evident in *Baudelaire*. The poet is for Sartre an inauthentic, self-alienated man. Sartre also assumes an ethics of collective salvation when he speaks harshly of Baudelaire's indifference to the need for qualitative social change and his cowardly assimilation of bourgeois values. Sartre criticizes the poet for a lack of interest in the working man. The bourgeoisie is excoriated for crushing the legitimate aspirations of the proletariat. What *Baudelaire* misses is the symbiotic rapport between these two value systems that makes *What Is Literature?* a more complete and satisfying book. Whereas *What Is Literature?* has a stereoscopic approach, *Baudelaire* suffers from double vision. In the biography the two moral systems exist, for the most part, in splendid isolation, each seemingly irrelevant to the realization of the other. Individual morality is divorced from public ethics, and the primal bourgeois distinction between private and public is retained. In allowing this disjunction, Sartre is guilty of a form of analytic thought that he condemned the year before in the first issue of *Les Temps modernes*. Ultimately *Baudelaire* has conservative political implications.

Today *Baudelaire* has lost much of its sting. Two readers of the biography have remarked that it is in the perspective of *Being and Nothingness* that the book loses its harshness.[31] The denigration of the poet is not as relentless as it seems, they hold, since according to the early philosophy of Sartre all men are failures. But for Sartre the failure of Baudelaire and the endemic failure of the for-itself to achieve a utopian fusion with the in-itself are by no means equivalent.

The poet is a moral failure because he refused to recognize that he could be other than a lack of being, because he could not bring himself to act on the knowledge that consciousness can never achieve its desire, and he wasted his life in passionate pursuit of the impossible snarklike ideal that is the eternal hope of the for-itself. Baudelaire is to be condemned, not because all men are failures, but because he thought he could be a success.

It is from the direction of the later philosophy of Sartre, however, that Baudelaire's exculpation arrives. In view of Sartre's discovery that a person's responsibility for himself is far from thoroughgoing, the first biography assumes an entirely different look. Whereas earlier Sartre had hypostatized the for-itself/in-itself as the irreducible ideal behind all human questing, in *L'Idiot* he historicizes the goal, declaring it to be the socially conditioned ideal of an ethics of alienation. Within this perspective Baudelaire's hope to coincide with himself becomes understood somewhat less as a self-alienation than as an alienation from outside, something more undergone than self-imposed. According to the later Sartre, Baudelaire is largely a martyr of the nineteenth-century bourgeois world view rather than a victim of himself. To a not inconsiderable extent the poet is off the hook. The early Sartre assumes a concept of normality but will come to realize that any such formulation in a false society is invalid. The locus of responsibility, sharply focused in the early Sartre, has now become diffuse. The discovery of sociohistorical determinism and the companionate realization that exopathic alienation precedes and provokes bad faith leads the later Sartre to abstain from passing judgment on Flaubert. Instead he attempts to "relive *sympathetically* the neurosis of Gustave."[32] The inauthentic strategies that once moved Sartre to righteous, unmitigated wrath are seen as the understandable response of a desperate man who found himself in a untenable position, tethered to an oppressive family and a dysfunctional society that had drastically narrowed his range of available choices. This same indulgence now flows backward to Baudelaire.

In the complaint of Goetz, "*You are not me,* it's unbearable," is heard the primal Sartrean cry of pain.[33] Valéry asserts that "all blame is tantamount to saying: *I am not you.* That is why an element of cruelty enters into it—that is to say an insensitivity, an essential dissimilarity—as between a rock that falls and the animal it crushes." Blame can only perpetuate Sartre's central dilemma of solipsism which is the consequence of a flawed epistemology that has the darkest political implications. The cruelty of which Valéry spoke is present in *Baudelaire;* the unfortunate animal meets with a rock: the harsh ethics of *Being and Nothingness*. During the course of his arrogant sprint past Baudelaire, Sartre appears as the advocate of what Nietzsche called "cruel virtue," a virtue that is meant to shame both reader and subject. Throughout the first biography are the pride-filled tones of a man who has had a victory over another. Sartre will discover that, again to use the words of Valéry, "it is impossible to comprehend and to punish at the same time."[34] The understanding of another person is inseparable from the understanding and even the provisional adoption of his values. The aspiration to reprove must be superseded by an immanent critique, an empathy that does not preclude distance. Accompanying intellectual possession must be a dispossession of self on the part of the knowing subject in favor of the object that is known. The questioner and the questioned must be one.

IV

Genet and the Just

From our birth [the Principle of Revolution] invited us
to a long and terrible duel where liberty and slavery
were at stake. If you are stronger, he told us, I will be your
slave. I will be a very useful servant for you; but I will
always be a restless servant, and as soon as there is some
slack in my yoke, I will defeat my master and conqueror.
And once I throw you down, I will insult you, dishonor
you, and trample you under.

Fichte, after Marmontel

As for Baudelaire, life for Genet begins in a state of ecstatic harmony and freedom from specific identity: "Scattered through
nature, he lives 'in sweet confusion with the world.' He caresses himself in the grass, in the water; he plays. Through his empty trans-
parancy passes the entire countryside. In short, he is innocent."[1] At
the age of seven the orphaned Genet is placed in the care of Morvan
peasants. Sartre imagines the decisive misfortune: one day, while
playing in the kitchen, Genet opens a drawer and reaches in. Someone catches sight of the incident and resoundingly declares the
child to be a thief. Like the man at the hotel door, like Baudelaire's
double, Genet is "caught in the act," the victim of an ontological
holocaust. In an instant he is individualized, his possibilities are
frozen: he becomes Jean Genet the thief. The Other binds him to the
concepts of good and evil and wills that shame be his eternal essence. The traduced child undergoes the alienation of conventional
morality. *Saint Genet* is the history of a man's fall into this alienation and his self-generated cure. This was made possible by a salvic
split in the subject's early history.

The argument of *Saint Genet* is difficult to follow for two reasons.
Unlike *Baudelaire*, the book does not flow freely and automatically
from the implied ethical postulates of *Being and Nothingness* but
introduces many ideas not previously found. In this sense *Saint
Genet*, published in 1952, was a new book, whereas *Baudelaire*,
derived to a considerable extent from his earlier thought, was already an old book when it appeared in 1946. The other reason that

Saint Genet is hard to read is its loose organization. Appearing irregularly throughout it is an informal treatise on ethics. During the late 1940s Sartre filled many notebooks for a work on ethics that he had promised at the end of *Being and Nothingness,* but then he abandoned the project because he felt that it made little sense to speak of such matters while vast numbers of people were oppressed in one form or another. The perturbed spirit of this postponed work has found its way into the pages of *Saint Genet.* Sartre's hostility to absolute ethical ideals, which had been evident at least since *The Flies* (1943), in *Saint Genet* receives its first extended justification, providing the thread of Ariadne that alone permits comprehending passage through the book's verbal labyrinth.

Sartre's ethical conception in *Saint Genet* is founded on a refinement of his early idea of freedom. Freedom is said to be a synthesis of two component features: a positive and a negative moment. The positive moment is identified with the Good and Being, with permanence, and with the willing of what is. The negative moment incorporates the potential to negate or disobey, and it demonstrates the idea that history is process. These two components may appear distinct and separate, but their independent existence cannot in fact be hypostatized, for they exist only in the context of the synthesis of freedom, within which they are unified while remaining distinct.

This division is a cause for anxiety. The dichotomy is particularly disturbing to the man whom Sartre sneeringly refers to throughout the biography as *"l'homme de bien"* or *"l'honnête homme,"* who is well pleased with his lot, with the powers that be, with his possessions, and with the passive condition of those who are oppressed. He does not wish to see the world as other than it is, for his vested interests require stability and obedience. Material wealth, power, and influence have been distributed in an agreeable pattern that need not be altered. The right-thinking man wants history to come quietly to an end so that he can dwell peaceably in his Eleatic utopia. But this changeless state is impossible, for he cannot confirm without simultaneously being possessed of the potential to deny; he cannot confirm without being capable of doing the opposite: "If he pretends to respect a social constraint, at the same time his freedom suggests to him that he violate it, for it is the same to give oneself laws and to create the possibility of disobeying them" (p. 30). In the negative moment the just man encounters within himself the possibility of a world disconcertingly dissimilar to his own ideal. Hegel remarks that man is good only inasmuch as he has the possibility of being evil. *L'homme de bien* will do what he can to mask this possibility and, in the process, will be the negation of negation.

The just man's solution to this internal menace is to transform it into an external one so that it can be safely fought, to label it with the term *evil*, and to project it upon a metaphysical scapegoat who will be hounded into a frozen, adjectival existence. "Evil is projection," Sartre remarks (p. 34). This evasive strategy is another in the *catalogue raisonné* of temptations that haunt the for-itself. The scapegoat, being the collective projection of the negative moment and the embodiment of evil, allows the Just to sleep peacefully in the knowledge that they alone are the Good. To ease their conscience, to unburden themselves of the complete experience of freedom, the Just band together to create an untouchable caste of alienated object men, more or less permanently dispossessed of their subjectivity. "Many psychologists," observes Morton Schatzman "have dwelled upon the motives of the person who projects; few have pondered the experience of the person *upon whom* someone else projects parts of himself."[2] Sartre's project is to relive the experience of one such man who was the unhappy host of the undesired component of the Just.

The projection upon another of the negative moment of freedom results in the conventional notion of moral evil. In sundering his freedom, *l'homme de bien* gives birth to the abstract dichotomy of good and evil. A valid separation of these concepts is impossible because such a split would involve breaking apart the synthesis of freedom, itself an impossibility. In a crucial footnote, perhaps the most important single passage in the book, Sartre summarizes his view of the good and evil dichotomy and its relation to moralities both true and false:

> Either ethics is nonsense or it is a concrete totality that realizes the synthesis of Good and Evil. Because Good without Evil is Parmenedian Being, which is to say death; and Evil without Good is pure non-being. To this objective synthesis corresponds the subjective synthesis of the recuperation of negative freedom and its integration into absolute freedom, or freedom properly speaking. It . . . is not at all a question of a Nietzschean surpassing of Good and Evil, but rather a Hegelian "Aufhebung." The abstract separation of these two concepts simply expresses the alienation of man. The fact remains that this synthesis is not realizable in the present historical situation. Thus any ethics that does not declare itself today to be impossible contributes to the mystification and the alienation of men. (p. 177)

This abstract separation expresses the alienation of man for two reasons. First, in divorcing the two concepts, *l'homme de bien* separates both himself and the pariah from their human nature, which is freedom understood as a synthesis of a positive and a negative moment. Second, alienation results because the censorious just man must treat the pariah as an object. If instead he understands the pariah as a free man, permitting the pariah to think of himself as a free man, the pariah can simply refuse the label of evil and his disgraced condition. In this case the displacement of a negative moment of freedom is impossible, and the just man is obliged to live with the unsettling experience of the totality of freedom. The proper synthesis will be realized only in a context of economic justice and permanent revolution, when men no longer have cause to fear the negative moment. In these circumstances the ideal of reciprocity may be possible; each man will experience the other, not as an object, but as an object-subject. Sartre defines this reciprocity: "The righteous give names and things bear these names. Genet is among the named objects, not among those who name. The righteous are of course objects for one another . . . But if I am named, I may in turn name. Thus naming and named I live in reciprocity. Words are thrown at me. I catch them and send them back at others" (p. 44).

In *Being and Nothingness* the master-slave alternatives were inescapable. In the world of *Saint Genet* alienation, in the sense of the objectification of the subject, is still inescapable but has lost much of its charge of menace. In most cases it is a matter of a temporary or partial alienation. Sartre's concern is no longer with the easily eliminable though inevitable alienation of *Being and Nothingness* but with a not inevitable and not easily eliminable moral alienation which has an economic foundation unmentioned in the earlier philosophical work. In *Being and Nothingness* permanent alienation occurred only with death, but in *Saint Genet* Sartre shows that something approaching permanent alienation in life is not only possible but prevalent. In short, he distinguishes between two levels of alienation: an ontologically permanent level and an historically intensified one. He is less concerned with men who are able to flit playfully between the conditions of subject and object than with the living dead, who have no such liberty because the Just have reduced them permanently to the status of the thing.

Only when men cease to be definitively designated as objects can they realize Sartre's "ethics of praxis" (p. 177). According to this deeply anarchistic ideal, a man should be nothing other than himself, freely and spontaneously. No Other will be lodged within him to deviate the course of his actions. A man will be a pure, free-flowing transparent movement into the future.

In an ethics of praxis the ego does not distinguish itself from its possibilities and its projects. It thus defines itself by the complex ensemble
of its decisions unified by an original choice and only reveals itself by
and through its acts. It can only become the object of study and ap-
preciation after the fact. As soon as I ask myself *before* a theft, whether
I should steal, I detach myself from my enterprise and am no longer one
with it. I separate the maxim of my act and the intention that I have
from myself, as if it were a matter of a tie and a suit. This abstract
attitude, that is called *nobility,* is ruinous at once for the act and for
man. Because if the *Ego* is no longer the intimate quality that a freedom gives to itself through the alterations that it effects in the world,
it becomes, in one way or another, a reality that is incapable of creating itself, in other words, a substance. (p. 177)

Ideally, questions such as "What shall I do?" or "How shall I live?"
should not even arise. Any polyphony of consciousness is the mark
of alienation. In the *Critique* the fused group formed itself without
prior organization or planning. Lack of spontaneity is an epiphenomenon of alienation. According to Sartre, Baudelaire was totally
devoid of the power of spontaneous behavior. Genet and Flaubert
will be similarly emasculated.

In *Saint Genet* Sartre has drawn not only upon his own theory of
alienation but on other sources as well, principally Hegel, Marx,
Engels, and Hesnard. The most powerful outside influence is Hegel.
The master-slave relationship, which influenced Sartre's definition of
alienation in *Being and Nothingness,* reappears in *Saint Genet* as the
framework for the moral questions. Sartre has also adopted Hegel's
dialectical world, in which every idea communicates with all others
and each phase of development is by a natural transition transformed
into its successor. The dialectic operates in the relations between the
two moments of freedom, and good and evil, each pair of which,
as in the Hegelian system, are antithetical components maintaining
their identity in a synthesized state. In *Saint Genet* all issues are
approached dialectically, be they questions of philosophy or individual psychology. For Hegel the task of philosophy is the recovery
of lost unity, the overcoming of oppositions. For Hegel, as for Sartre
in *Saint Genet,* "Division is the source of *the need of philosophy.*"[3]

The distinction between legality and ethics is emphasized by
Hegel. In the *Spirit of Christianity* he expresses a revulsion against
accepted moral attitudes, which may have influenced Sartre.[4] Hegel
especially condemns the legalistic approach of the Mosaic teaching.
The moral life of the ancient Jews is unattractive because within it
the Jews showed themselves to be passively obedient to abstract
and external concepts of right and wrong. The unwholesome split

between the master and the mastered offended Hegel's ideal of freedom. When the Jew obeyed the Mosaic code, his actions did not spring from his own heart but represented the dictates of a foreign authority which he had internalized. Hegel, like Sartre, thought of true morality as individual and lived rather than external and abstract. True morality Hegel found in the teachings of Jesus. Rather than focusing on a prim consciousness of the distinctions between good and evil, and subjecting men to a series of objective commands, Jesus appealed to the notions of love and open-hearted sympathy. Ethical behavior was no longer understood as something engaged in out of obedience to the abstract and external, against inclination, but as something which accorded with inclination, flowing naturally and spontaneously from the love in one's heart. Like Hegel, Sartre objects to the abstraction, dissociation, and externalization of good and evil, as well as to man's enslavement to these false concepts.

Hegel's influence, however, is most apparent in Sartre's description of freedom's uncomfortable experience of the split between its two component features, a concept modeled on the German philosopher's "unhappy consciousness." The *Phenomenology of Spirit* falls into three parts, each treating one of the three principal phases of consciousness. The first phase, termed simply "consciousness," is described as the simple awareness of the object as distinct from the subject. From this phase the mind progresses to a second stage, called "self-consciousness," where the self experiences a division within itself and a split with other men. The self which experiences internal division is labeled "the unhappy consciousness." Sartre refers to this phenomenon in the comment, "the spirit, as Hegel said, is anxiety" (p. 34). The unhappy consciousness is unhappy because it is divided, uncomfortably aware of a schism between two internal selves: an inconsistent, changing, negative self and a changeless, ideal self. The former appears to be a false self, which should be denied, while the latter appears to be the true self, which has not yet been fully realized because of the irritating presence of the former. The unhappy consciousness tries vainly to identify itself purely with the positive self. It does so through religous experience, self-objectification, and self-denial. In *Saint Genet,* Sartre suggests another possible method—the projection of this self upon another. The third phase of consciousness, called "reason," is a synthesis of the earlier phases. Now consciousness is no longer divided against itself or others. Hegel's individual consciousness, without being annulled, becomes at one with itself and others in living union with God, whereas Sartre's unhappy consciousness must resort to a more earthly cure.

Another feature of Hegel's view of the self-conscious mind that influenced Sartre was the relationship between the master and his slave in the second phase of consciousness. Initially the slave derives his consciousness of himself entirely from the master's consciousness of him. His is an inhabited soul; he has so completely internalized the Other that he has no effective sense of himself as a free and autonomous being. The master is his truth, and vice versa, for the master is nothing without the humiliation of his thrall. Hegel describes the sequence of steps the slave must take to liberate his consciousness from its completely derived condition. The slave first attempts to gain self-possession by asserting himself in the minimal possible way. By turning to stoicism, the servile consciousness attempts to liberate itself from domination by intellectually trying to make of the real world a less hostile place. It does not struggle against its condition but rather wills that it be so. Because the slave's own will coincides with the will of nature, the idea of external determination fades from his consciousness. The master-slave division disappears, and if only in the realm of thought, the slave is free. This strategy must fail, however, because of the illusory quality of the solution. An authentic negation of dependence upon outside determination is not the result.

The servile consciousness next resorts to skepticism, which Hegel calls the infinity of negation. By negating all, the slave rises above the vicissitudes of existence. To be consistently negative, the skeptic must be an essentially self-contradictory consciousness, joyfully embracing contradictions for their own sake. The skeptic is always simultaneously what he is and its opposite. Within this world of universal negation the slave has the illusion of freedom because external determination, as well as everything else, is categorically denied. Again failure is inevitable for he has merely masked his truth.

A real turning point is reached only when the slave realizes that it is by working in the world that he can discover his own individuality. As he produces himself in the world, in an object or an act, the slave achieves self-realization, a true sense of autonomy, and rises from a merely relative to an authentic mode of existence. In this final stage of his development the slave opposes himself to the social reality that had revealed itself to be his enemy. Sartre's Genet treads an identical path from servile consciousness to freedom through work. Both Hegel's slave and Sartre's analogous subject begin as men who have been transformed into objects; they try first to negate determination by willing all, then by denying all, and finally escape their psychological servility by realizing their independence through self-objectification in the world. In each case a man gains his freedom by acting upon himself and not by altering his social context.

Within Marxism, the context within which Sartre claims to have written *Saint Genet,* there is a strong tradition of hostility to conventional morality. The two major documents in this regard are *The Holy Family,* the first book-length collaboration of Marx and Engels, and Engels' *Anti-Dühring.* Sartre refers to both works in an essay composed while writing *Saint Genet.*[5]

Marx and Engels held the institution of private property responsible for the existence of abstract ethical idealism, the belief in a universal good and evil. Marx thought that alienation spread throughout every domain of a man's life. The sphere of morality is no exception; it too is under the sway of an inhuman power. Reward for good and punishment for evil are held by both Marx and Engels to be the consecration of differences in social rank. Bourgeois morality is class morality, designed to reflect and further the interests of the dominant class by exalting respect for property and taking strong measures against offenders.

The Marxist dialectic could not admit, in the present, the possibility of ultimate principles of right and wrong that would be the foundation of a final immutable system of ethics. As Engels remarks: "We therefore reject every attempt to impose on us any moral dogma whatsoever as an external, ultimate, and forever immutable moral law on the pretext that the moral world too has its permanent principles which transcend history and the differences between nations. We maintain on the contrary that all former moral theories are the product, in the last analysis, of the economic stage which society has reached at that particular epoch."[6] Ethics cannot be given a sound basis until class antagonisms have been transcended. Until that time a provisional, dynamic ethics will be necessary to guide the actions of men in their struggles. This provisional morality, again necessarily a class morality, a proletarian morality, will hold those acts to be justified which contribute to the destruction of the exploitative society. Ethics are in one sense impossible, but in another necessary.

Sartre agrees: "Thus any ethics that does not explicitly declare itself to be impossible today contributes to the mystification and the alienation of men. The ethical 'problem' arises from the fact that ethics is for us at the same time inevitable and impossible. Action must provide itself norms in a climate of unsurpassable impossibility. It is in this perspective, for example, that we must consider the problem of violence, or that of the relation between means and ends" (p. 177). Against the society that sponsored the sinister fraud of a final impossible ethics, Genet is forced to develop an inevitable provisional ethics. This explains Sartre's complete sympathy for Genet's violations of the conventions of "the righteous," his career as a thief, prostitute, and homosexual. To the extent that these crimes represent a revolt against conventional class morality they cannot be other than ethical acts.

The idea of meting out blame and punishment by external authority was repugnant to Marx and Engels. It contradicted their ideal of free self-realization. With the disappearance of private property the concept of moral judgment passively received from an outside source will fade away. Under truly human conditions, punishment will be nothing other than the sentence freely passed by the culprit upon himself.

In *The Holy Family* Marx and Engels systematically criticize the attitude toward the lawbreaker in a society founded upon economic injustice. The point of departure for their criticism is Eugène Sue's moralistic treatment of the criminal in *The Mysteries of Paris*. Sartre's references to Sue's novel in *Saint Genet* contribute to the suspicion that *The Holy Family* may have played a role in the genesis of his second biography.

The Mysteries of Paris describes the attempts of Rudolph, Prince of Geroldstein, philanthropist and crusader against crime and sin, to rehabilitate criminals. Among those whom he "reforms" are Chourineur, "the son of nature," a butcher become murderer, and Fleur de Marie, a prostitute.[7] The two malefactors are victims of their social context: if their lineage and education had been more privileged, their fate would have been different. Yet according to Marx and Engels, Rudolph's efforts at reform have only a dehumanizing effect. Afterward the criminals are worse off than before. They become guilty and servile, their souls invaded by the image of a demonic economic system. As Chourineur is described after his "reform": "Henceforward all his virtues will be resolved into the virtues of a dog . . . His independence, his individuality will disappear completely . . . Chourineur has accepted a moral identity imposed upon him from outside. He will try to live up to it."[8]

In her unreformed state, Fleur de Marie is characterized by "vitality, energy, cheerfulness, resilience of character . . . She herself is neither good nor bad, but *human*." Absent from the prostitute's experience are the moral abstractions of good and evil: "She is *good* because the sun and the flowers reveal to her her own sunny and blossoming nature." This passage recalls Sartre's association of Genet's initial innocence with his experience of the natural world. Before the arrival of Rudolph, Fleur de Marie was miserable on a material level but nonetheless spiritually free: "In her former most unhappy situation in life she was able to develop a lovable human individuality; in her outward debasement she was conscious that *her human essence* was *her true essence*." But with the intervention of Rudolph she becomes enslaved to the consciousness of sin. With her rehabilitation she is taught shame, discovers the distinction between the sacred and the profane, and learns to judge herself harshly from a Christian point of view. In the guise of good and evil, economics enters her soul: "The filth of modern society . . . becomes her innermost being; and continual hypochondriac self-torture because of that filth becomes her duty, the task of her life appointed by God himself . . . Now self-torment will be her *good* and remorse be her *glory*."[9] A hostile, inhuman force has insinuated itself into her innermost being and stolen her freedom of self-realization. Here, as Adorno writes, "Conscience is the mark of shame of an unfree society."[10]

Genet, who like Sue's wrongdoers was formerly free and at one with nature and his human essence, becomes in *Saint Genet* the serf of the consciousness of sin. The curse of the petrifying glance, which in *Being and Nothingness* existed in an ahistorical vacuum, is analyzed from the perspective of Marxist materialism, and Sartre joins his concept of the objectification by the Other with Marx's point that conventional morality is a theft of one's human essence. The ontological alienation of *Being and Nothingness* is in *Saint Genet* provided with an historical dimension.

Even more evident than the Marxist influence on *Saint Genet* is the influence once again of Hesnard. Sartre could not fail to read Hesnard's 1949 *L'Universe morbide de la faute* sympathetically, for it is prefaced by his old friend Daniel Lagache and it comments favorably on his own *Baudelaire*. Not the least of the work's attractions for Sartre would have been Hesnard's resounding dismissal of some of the Freudian positions that Sartre found most offensive; the sexual etiology of neurosis, and the tripartite division of the self. In *L'Univers morbide de la faute* Hesnard outlines the discipline he calls "ethical psychiatry," which considers mental illnesses not as a disturbance of psychic activity in general but as a disturbance in the individual's moral world.

Mental illness occurs after a child has experienced a traumatic ethical conflict which he is incapable of resolving. Before being integrated into the collective morality that dominates his family and social context, the child's actions are guided by what Hesnard calls "premorality." This atavistic ethic judges to be positive that which is self-serving and negative that which is not. The impact of an action on the larger social context plays no part in the evaluation. Conflict occurs when the child is obliged, by a person whom he loves, identifies with, and is dependent upon, to adopt a foreign ethic which he finds incomprehensible and inferior to his own. The child internalizes the external interdiction. The inquisitor installs himself as a parasitic presence within the child's mind. The latter becomes *"l'automatisé,"* the passive victim of demonic possession.[11] The child is subjected to a moral rape and experiences a catastrophic collapse of self-esteem.

The various morbid configurations of the soul are ways of dealing with the experience of traumatic and irrational guilt: "All psychopathic suffering bears the stamp of Blame (accepted or imputed and denied or combatted) that is more or less recognized by the patient; and every psychopathic reaction is a *Punishment* that is imaginarily justified, or a reaction of preventive defense against this *threat of morality*."[12] The individual suffering from melancholic depression, for example, has absorbed the condemnation of the Other into his character and is resigned to live with it. He considers his character to be permanently petrified and lives, as will Genet at one point in his development, within a timeless world. Unlike the melancholic, who makes an accommodation with the internalized and ubiquitous judge, the schizophrenic escapes a world in which everybody and everything is charged with judgmental menace. He does so by de-realizing all of existence. Therapy must therefore involve the location of the original conflict that is the genesis of mental illness. Once it is discovered, therapy becomes an enterprise of total disculpation. Guilt must be exposed as without foundation. The role of the therapist is to be, in the words of Sartre's Oreste, a "thief of remorse."[13]

With few exceptions, according to Hesnard, all people are deformed innocents. All are the victims of inhuman, narrowly utilitariain ethical systems sponsored by families, states, sects, and parties that are aggressions in disguise. To further their economic and political ends, these groups create Manichean world systems. In order to generate the illusion of security and power, they designate an evil Other. He who is found to be evil by these naive and sadistic ethical systems, and hence excluded, becomes an object of hatred for the Just. They invade his mind and there provoke the torments of bad conscience. The accusatory motto of each of these pseudo-moralities is "find the guilty one."[14] The world must be rid of the concepts of good and evil, the basis of these Manichean world views, because they generate hatred and self-hatred, external and internal barbarism. Otherwise humanity will disappear in a collective suicide. These ethical systems can be gotten rid of only after a revolution puts an end to economic conflict. Only then will a universal ethics based on mutual respect of individual liberties be possible. The present culture of guilt and accusation will be replaced by "the culture of Sympathy."[15] This ethics, which Hesnard labels "a morality of the act," appears to be indistinguishable from Sartre's "ethics of *praxis*."

Although only a collective solution will save humanity from a self-generated perdition, solutions are also possible at the individual level. Psychiatric therapy can reveal to the disturbed individual that the morality which binds him is a mystification. Art can be a self-administered psychiatric cure. Rejecting Freud's view that the source of art is sexual expression, Hesnard maintains that all forms of esthetic creation are used in the protest of human values against the ethical menace. Like the psychopath, the artist is constantly preoccupied with the problems of guilt and expiation. In his artistic creations a man can free himself from external moral authority by establishing a world in which he is permitted to be his own moral conscience. Art does not always liquidate the artist's conflicts in everyday life, but creation frees him at the moment that he creates.

Mutatis mutandis, many of these ideas are applied in *Saint Genet.* Sartre imposes conditions on some of Hesnard's ideas, rejecting, for example, his contention that all artistic creation constitutes a protest against an external authority. In general, however, the tailoring of Hesnard's concepts required is minimal.

Genet's alienation necessarily precedes the moment when he was smitten by the Manichean taxonomy of the Just. Before being labeled a thief, he absorbed other values which made him vulnerable to branding. Young Genet learns first from the adults surrounding him that he is innocent. But innocence too is a false state, a state of alienation that follows the pattern of the objectification of the subject: "It consecrates . . . the priority of the object over the subject, of what one is for others over what one is for oneself" (pp. 13–14). The child Genet is uncomfortable with the label, for he recognizes that there is little correspondence between the adjective and his intimate experience of himself. The label is most inappropriate because he is not at all like the other children to whom the label is generally applied. He has no parents and is in the custody of an institution. His birth has been followed immediately by the maternal rejection that all of Sartre's subjects experience in one form or another. For the term *thief* to have any meaning, Genet must first, however uneasily, conceive of himself as its opposite, as an innocent.

Why does the child steal? In the milieu where Genet lives, property defines Being. He is inevitably conditioned by this value. But the pleasures of possession, and hence the feeling of authentic Being, are denied him. He is accorded board and lodging, but unlike normal children, he is not given these necessities as his right. He submits to the suffocating experience of receiving generosity, described in *Being and Nothingness* as a species of alienation. For Genet "everything is a gift, even the air he breathes" (p. 16). All is experienced as a humiliating peculium.

Sartre speculates that if Genet had been placed in a working-class home in a city, perhaps he would have been infected with the idea that ownership must be challenged. He might have learned that one is also what one does. Instead, his values are handed to him by landowners and farmers for whom "one is formed by what one has" (p. 17). Here Sartre gives a Marxist twist to the categories of Being as described in *Being and Nothingness*. Sartre, the quintessential man of the city, is of one mind with Marx, who thought of rural life as a seat of reaction. The future thief begins his career by learning an absolute respect for property which he can acquire only by resorting to a make-believe form of having: theft.

Through theft he can gain being and avoid the alienation of generosity. As Genet steals from his foster parents and his neighbors, he is not at all challenging the notion of private property but is rather demonstrating his profound respect for this institution. In a consumer society he reproduces in a theatrical fashion the central procedure: he consumes. The child is a fake property owner: "he enacts the comedy of possession just as Barrault plays Hamlet" (p. 20). He seeks only to be like the Other. His mimicry is an act of homage to the values he has faithfully absorbed.

Genet is caught by the Just, who have been passionately awaiting this moment to split the atom of their freedom and to colonize the mind of another with its negative particle. The child is the victim of an ontological malediction. He is free only to be guilty and to live out the sentence of the Just. Much of the same vocabulary used in *Being and Nothingness* in association with alienation appears again in this moment of Genet's life: "he is already dead"; "He is crippled with shame." (p. 26); "he has become an absolute object of horror" (p. 28); "He is paralyzed by the glance of men" (p. 49).

The scorn of the Just would be bearable if it could simply be returned. Although *Being and Nothingness* affirmed that overcoming alienation by objectifying the Other in turn was always a possibility, in the case of Genet, Sartre shows that such retaliation is not always possible. The child is incapable of challenging the value system that has condemned him, for he has absorbed it entirely. Recalling his comment on Baudelaire, Sartre notes: "Unto himself he will be at the same time judge and accused, policeman and thief" (p. 27). The child adores his judges. Free men are able to distinguish the subject they are for themselves from the object they are for others, but Genet cannot. The object he is for others is all that he understands himself to be. The verdict is unconditionally accepted because, "When children, from the earliest age, are forced to submit to a powerful social pressure, when their Being-for-Others becomes the object of a collective representation that is accompanied by value judgments and social interdicts, their resulting alienation can be total and definitive" (p. 32). Genet has become a zombi, an ambulatory corpse in the power of another. He will spend his life paralyzed by the moment of his metamorphosis. Because it is his sacred moment, he will spend his days searching for opportunities to re-create it. He will live outside of time, meditating upon the word that has been used to label him—unless he can find a way out.

Genet's first strategy is, according to Hegel's pattern, the only one possible. He chooses the worst. He decides that rather than merely submitting passively to the Other, he will seize the initiative and choose to be that thing which they have chosen him to be: "I decided to be what crime had made of me" (p. 55). Because he cannot escape the fatality imposed by the Just, he will assume and become that fatality himself. The decision of the Just that he will be a thief will henceforth be his own: "because they make his life unlivable, he will live this impossibility of living as though he had created it expressly for himself" (p. 55). Like Baudelaire, Genet creates for himself the illusion of being self-conceived, of being the cause of his own misfortune.

Genet's first strategy not only seems patterned on the first step in the sequence of the slave's progress toward self-emancipation but also resembles, and perhaps was inspired by, the description of "the beautiful soul" in *The Spirit of Christianity*. Having suffered an unjust attack, "the beautiful soul" neither struggles against its fate nor suffers passively. It weds courage to passivity and wills the accomplished injustice, thus avoiding seeing itself in another's power. Because the soul wills this injustice, it becomes self-created. It renounces everything in order to maintain independence, to experience "a living free elevation above the loss of right and above struggle."[16] This description fits Genet's personal plan exactly.

Sartre explains that this synthesis of courage and passivity was generated by a tension in Genet's thinking between two incompatible ethical systems, which developed from the two dissimilar contexts in which he has been reared. In his person he relives the tension between the city and the country. His original strategy is his imagina-

tive synthesis of the two ethics produced in him by these two environ-
ments. The peasant landowners have obliged him to internalize for
all time the sentence of evil. Sartre suggests that if Genet had had no
experience other than in agrarian France—that "blind tribunal,"
as Blanqui called it—he would have been entirely lost.[17] In a society
which did not recognize freedom and the possibility of change he
would have faithfully absorbed the fact that the label he received
was his passively to accept rather than personally to confirm or
deny. But Genet has also had another experience which provided
him with a saving remnant of subjectivity. He has internalized the
essence conferred upon him by the state-sponsored orphanage. For
this institution he is merely a number, which is not an object but
rather a dim and abstract form of subjectivity. This weak seed of
awareness that he is also a subject prevents him from becoming
totally absorbed in the ethos of the people of Morvan. He is simultaneously inoculated with a slave and with a free will. Genet therefore lives in contradiction, suspended between two irreducible systems of value: Being and Doing. His strategy consists in an attempt
to arrive at a synthesis that will keep his soul from bursting into
contrary directions.

Private property has produced an inferno of division which both
causes Genet's damnation and sets him on his self-emancipatory
course. The Just forcibly divides himself from himself, himself from
the guilty. Private property results in the division of labor, which has
as a consequence the split between country and city. This creates
in turn the saving division within Genet's mind. The first component
of the dialectical movement constituting Genet's life is Being. This
component is nothing other than the life of the Just within him. He
desires to be the perfect instrument of their malevolent will, to
make of himself the absolute and despicable object they declare
him to be: "At the beginning there appears a formal intention to
realize as fast as possible and with all possible means the total
alienation of his person. The first moment of the dialectical progres-
sion is thus alienation: Genet is himself *in the Other:* his consciousness poses the being of the Other as essential and takes itself to
be inessential" (pp. 141–142). Like Baudelaire, "he seeks to confer
upon himself an elusive object status. He struggles to see himself
with borrowed eyes, in order to surprise himself as if he were another" (p. 69). As already shown in both *Being and Nothingness*
and *Baudelaire,* the result of this kind of an effort can only be failure.

The contradictory project of Doing is coextensive with the expression of the autonomy of Genet's will. This component permits
him ultimately to rescue himself. It is responsible for "the superb

project of being self-caused" (p. 73), which is Sartre's loftiest ideal. It allows Genet to make the evil will assigned to him the product of his own will and to expropriate from the Just their power over him.

Sartre seeks to isolate those features of Genet's behavior that derive from the first moment of the dialectic. Like Baudelaire, Genet is said to be a narcissist. He attempts to surprise his image outside himself and then to coincide with it. Erik, the German soldier in *Funeral Rights,* is described: "Sometimes he desired to be an executioner so that he might be able to contemplate himself and to enjoy from without this beauty that he emitted: to receive it." Genet's narcissism, however, has a different cause. To be a narcissist, one must first be guilty: "Narcissus is first of all bewitched. His being was stolen" (p. 77).

Genet's passive homosexuality is described as following directly from his narcissism, which in turn is indistinguishable from the project of Being. Through his sexual experiences Genet seeks to relive the original crisis. The look of the Other has feminized him. His objectivity for others is his essential reality, and he desires to be passively manipulated by the Other in order to become an object in his own eyes. Genet has said that he became a homosexual before becoming a thief, but Sartre, with his perennial certainty that sexuality is never primary, rejects this assertion, arguing that Genet became a homosexual because he was first a thief: "Sexually, Genet was first of all a raped child. This first rape was the gaze of the Other, that surprised and penetrated him, and transformed him forever into an object . . . I am not claiming that his original crisis *resembles* a rape, I am saying that it *is* a rape" (p. 81). Here is the shadow of Hesnard, who three years earlier had described the imposition of a foreign morality on a child as a "moral rape in the same sense as a physical rape."[18] Hesnard also rejected the suggestion that homosexuality had its source in an early confusion of sexual identity. Instead, he found its origins, as does Sartre, in an early delirium of persecution. If Genet is a passive invert, it is out of respectful deference to the will of his persecutors. Acts of passive homosexuality are ceremonial acceptances of the decision of the Other.

Lovers must be chosen carefully. The beloved must be a beautiful appearance and nothing more. He cannot give the impression of being a consciousness. The lover is ideally a mirror of Genet's object state. It is himself that he loves in the form of the beloved, who is reduced to nothing more than the obverse of Genet's freedom. His preference for companions who are criminals is of a piece with this interest. Genet explains that "the criminal is already dead" (p. 99). He is a man-object who, like Genet, has had a destiny imposed upon him. Only such a lover can therefore properly play the role of being the inessential mediation between Genet and himself.

Between the ages of eighteen and twenty Genet roamed about Europe, prostituting himself and begging. During this period he conceived of another ruse to gain access to Being: he would set against his judges another, higher judge. Genet would save himself by calling down the glance of God to rescue him. This God is none other than Genet himself: "For the solipsist and for Genet *I is another* and this Other is God" (p. 141). Genet splits himself in two in order to become both subject and object. Instead of being an object for the Just, he becomes the object of the gaze of an absolute and benevolent witness. His wretchedness is endowed with a privileged, sacred meaning: he has been elected to suffer. Again he makes a choice that had been made by Baudelaire, but Baudelaire could never gain Sartre's sympathy because his narcissistic projects were never, as were Genet's, forms of counterviolence, legitimate reactions to oppression.

Although Genet seems to have escaped only in a lateral direction, from one alienation to another, real progress continues to be made. He has moved from simply being passively alienated by the Other to creating a form of auto-alienation which simultaneously contains, willingly confirms, contests, and masks the original theft of freedom. Within the context of alienation, within the context of his attempts to become an absolute object, he continues on his path to self-liberation.

Yet the project of Being must fail. The primary intention cannot remain uncontradicted, and Genet discovers to his horror that despite all his extraordinary efforts, he remains a subject. He therefore decides to use his subjectivity against itself, to employ this glimmer of freedom in a new kind of attempt to make contact with himself. This he will achieve through what he does rather than through what is done to him. Rather than simply being the evil object, he will do evil. He does evil to be in full possession of himself, to derive his nature from his own decision to do evil, rather than to accept the label passively. A contradiction, however, lies at the heart of this project. Absolute evil can only be an object. One cannot do evil, because by exercising freedom, one cannot be the opposite of a free subject. A subject, as subject, cannot be pure evil. This project is also impossible because of the relationship that exists between good and evil. Evil derives from the love of the good, on which it is dependent for its existence. As in the case of Baudelaire, one can will evil only through a fundamental will to do good. Evil for evil's sake is always impossible because it is always transformed into something else. The idea that evil has only a relative existence is an old one in moral philosophy. Sartre's explanation of the just man's Manicheanism and Genet's failed approach to absolute evil are in part a repetition of Augustine's counter to the Manicheans. Evil, Augustine taught, had no independent existence but was rather parasitic upon the good which alone has real being. For Sartre, however, neither good nor evil has independent being. The efforts of Genet and the Just to arrive at Being must all fail, resulting in an unavoidable return to the unhappy consciousness. When they realize that the split between good and evil is impossible, their freedom will be reestablished in its original synthetic integrity.

Because doing evil is impossible, Genet decides to become a saint, a martyr to the impossibility of doing pure evil. Genet chooses to become a saint, according to Sartre, because the saint is the ideal of the consumer society. The aristocrat, the thief, the warrior, and the saint have in common the fact that they consume without producing and deny the value of work. A society that is based on ostentatious consumption is thrilled by tales of martyrdom and by the myths of the end of the world and the last judgment; healthy societies do not value these tales but instead stress the myths of creation. The aristocrat has his gold smeared on a church ceiling. The warrior goes gladly off to battle in a pointless war. Genet devotes his life to a project that is foreordained to failure. These three people share a single goal: the gratuitous destruction of the world and themselves.

The interaction between these two contradictory systems is the substance of Sartre's interior portrait of Genet at the age of eighteen. All of the phenomena of a person's everyday physical context—the places where he lives and feels comfortable and the things he uses—are for Genet signs of his exclusion from the human race. As Sartre explains, "the industrial products that form the urban landscape are the social will in packaged form; they speak to us of our integration in society. Through their silence men address themselves to us. They are injunctions, recommendations" (p. 241). Tools are the symbols and vehicles of the just man's proper integration into society. At first these objects provoke in Genet a longing to be like everyone else. Through its utensils the society of the Argus-eyed Just condemns the guilty one. Recovering from his initial reaction, Genet turns against these tools with three simultaneous reactions: he willfully refuses to understand them, he steals them in an effort to appropriate the glance of the Other which they represent, and he turns them against their owners.

In *The German Ideology* Marx and Engels claim that man's experience of nature is conditioned by economic forces.[19] This is the case with Genet. He takes no solace in nature because it is the privileged preserve of the Just, who have exclusive access to its pleasures. Nature is their agent. For Genet, "flowers are the ears of policemen; there is a gaze of trees" (p. 251). All of nature is for him that ideal prison which Jeremy Bentham called the "Panopticon."[20] The words and the things they designated are the property of others. The words within his consciousness belong to the Just. "The word is the other" (p. 266). To destroy the look within him Genet will become a poet and obliterate the prose that is the tool of the enemy. He will turn language against itself and hence against the Other by perverting its normal function. "Slang is born of hatred," Céline remarks, and this is precisely its meaning for Genet's fellow prisoners.[21] But Genet is a double exile, from the world of crime as well as from the world of the Just. The other malefactors have contempt for his passivity. Genet is excluded from their world and their language. Since he is doubly an exile, he operates a double perversion of language. His colleagues' expression for making a bed, *"On fait les pages"* (p. 270), is an act of aggression against straight society. Genet adds another level of aggression. In his fantasy life he perverts the meaning of the sentence to give it an erotically charged sense. *On fait les pages* is interpreted to mean that sexual advances are being made on young aristocrats.

At the age of eighteen Genet is not yet really a poet, but neither does he have a prosaic relationship with the world of things and men. For Genet, the poetic emotion recreates the emotion felt at the moment of his original crisis. The thrill caused by an unexpected juxtaposition of terms recalls the moment of his sudden petrification. For his own amusement Genet creates one-line poems, in one of which, "Harvester of cut breaths," Sartre discovers the amazement of the young Genet at his being the victim of a malevolent look. Sartre compares the line to the poetry of Mallarmé as seen by Blanchot. The verse is a trap. The words swallow and then annihilate the being of the world. As is the case in the poetry of Mallarmé, "the universe goes up in smoke" (p. 288). Since Genet is exiled from the universe, he is attentive only to its verbal shell. The only reality he can possess is a perverted verbal reality, and hence his natural language can be only poetry. In this peculiar use of language Genet both destroys the accusing world of the Other and becomes his own victim. These poems are further efforts in his project to be both Genet and the Just, to be both subject and object, both freedom and the negation of freedom.

Genet's pleasure in the discovery of the poetic emotion results in his making a major new decision: he will become an aesthete and live entirely in the imaginary. Genet still wants, however, to obey the command of the Other, who wishes him to be evil. He has discovered that the best way to succeed at being an evildoer is to be a dreamer, for evil can be more completely imagined than actually realized. Resorting to the imagination, because it provides the best opportunity to reject Being (which is synonymous with good), provides the best chance to cooperate simultaneously with the Other and to destroy his world.

Genet derealizes himself as fully as possible. A beggar, he pretends that he is pretending to be a beggar. He puts himself out of reach and does not feel humiliated because he is only an actor playing at being a beggar. Divine, in Genet's *Our Lady of the Flowers,* speaks of himself as a woman but does not care to be a real woman, only an imaginary one. This aesthetic phase corresponds to the skeptical stage of Hegel's slave who derealizes all in order to escape the misery of his condition. Sartre, who considered the departure from real life for the imaginary to be a form of self-alienation and in *What is Literature?* took the surrealists to task for doing exactly that, now praises Genet for doing the same thing. Sartre cannot condemn Genet for this attempt to derealize his life because, at the moment, it is the only possible choice. Genet is like a man unjustly sentenced to death who, before the moment of execution, derealizes his present condition and imagines that he is victorious over those who are about to slaughter him. The escape into self-alienation is the only possible expression of freedom available. Unable to create himself in the world, he instead produces himself as an appearance, a feat that permits him the illusion that he derives from himself alone. As an agent of derealization, he lures the real into the imaginary and there destroys it. Such is his revenge. "Society maneuvers Genet like a marionnette: *he is acted upon* in spite of himself; if he could invent a gigantic snare, he could get even. Society *would be dreamed* in spite of itself" (p. 344). With beauty as his only weapon Genet murders the world. But in derealizing the world, he also necessarily derealizes himself. His assault on the world of the Just is morally a suicide attack. Although he has almost totally disappeared into the imaginary, Genet is still not an artist. He derealizes the world for himself, but not yet for others.

In 1936, at the age of twenty-six, after years of aimless wandering about Europe, Genet returns to France, where he meets a professional burglar who teaches him the techniques of the trade. Genet sees his life as the result of two epochal events. The first, the original crisis, had turned him into a passive dreamer. The second, discussed in *The Miracle of the Rose,* was his discovery of the profession of burglary, a discovery that woke him up, liberated him from his passivity, and opened him to the world of other men and active work. Genet becomes a specialist, a skilled housebreaker, a member of a technical elite. For the first time in his life he can say and understand the word *we.* Earlier he had stolen for his lovers, in obedience to others, but now he steals only for himself. Crime had formerly been a passive and relative activity; now it is an active and independent one dictated by a spirit of individual enterprise. Genet says that burglary made him virile and allowed him to outgrow his femininity and sexual passivity. This time Sartre can accept his subject's explanation since sexuality is not prior to a decision. Formerly Genet had experienced the lover's pleasure as his own, but now he concentrates on experiencing his own. For the first time Genet engages in a true form of praxis. He exteriorizes himself in the world and, in so doing, acquires the moral strength required to reach the end of his path to freedom. He has entered the final stage in the liberation of Hegel's slave.

Until now Genet had been derealizing the real within the confines of a self-enclosed world. His new activism leads him to entertain the idea of realizing the imaginary in a publicly available object in order to challenge society directly with his fictions rather than simply to use them as a means of private escape. Before, his imaginings had depended purely upon his own subjectivity and remained his private terrain of refuge. If he turned mentally away from his fictions, the derealization of the world came to an end. He now seeks to force society to adopt the images he invents and to give them objective form. His dreams will then carry on a life independent of his consciousness. By making cultural objects of his fantasies, he will act upon others. Genet seizes the initiative. He becomes an artist. The Other who had made Genet a permanent object now becomes his means and is used to objectify his imaginings, to give permanent form to his dreams. The revelation of theft frees Genet from passivity and gives him the active instinct which allows him to move from aestheticism to art.

Hesnard noted that in his works the artist can escape the curse of morality since the pure freedom of the artist knows neither good nor evil. Thus Genet is released from the spell case by the Just. At the age of sixteen he had been encouraged to write songs by a well-known writer of lyrics who had taken him under his wing, but it was not until he reached twenty that he wrote his first poem. His intention was narcissistic: "if he speaks it is in order to hear himself as if he were *Another,* if he writes it is in order to read himself" (p. 396). Ten years later he writes another poem. In a jail cell which he shared with a number of other convicts, one prisoner was much admired for the sentimental poems he wrote to his sister. Genet claimed that he could do better. Challenged by the others to do so, he produced the poem "Condemned to Death." His cell mates greeted the work with cries of derision—precisely the reaction that Genet had gleefully anticipated. He understood that bad, derivative verse gives pleasure, so he decided to write a beautiful and original work in order to provoke the contempt of his listeners. By writing poetry, he discovered that he could achieve two of his hopes; to be scorned by the Other and to be the deliberate cause of his own pariah condition. Sartre likens Genet's methods to those of Saint Teresa, who wished to be slandered in order to rise above the men who judged her falsely. Scorned by all, she remained alone in the presence of God.[22] By writing poetry, Genet sought precisely this kind of martyrdom. As a thief, he hoped to be caught and scorned by the Just; he began to write with the same intention.

Genet's turn to prose has its source in his newly discovered activism, but the prose he adopts is intentionally false. Although Genet's writings may well have a revoluntionary function, they are far removed from every essential feature of engaged literature as described by Sartre in *What Is Literature?*[23] Genet in fact stands the old Sartrean ideal on its head and is praised for so doing. A literature guided by a subversive intention is not ipso facto an engaged literature. Genet's novels are in fact false novels. Sartre once wrote that François Mauriac could not be considered a true novelist because his characters were not free. Genet's characters are puppets to an equal or even greater degree. "My books are not novels," explains Genet, "because none of my characters makes an independent decision" (p. 471). A work such as *Our Lady of the Flowers* is far from being the appeal to the reader's freedom that Sartre requires, for the engaged author treats his reader as an end, while Genet manipulates him as an inessential means to the end of the objectification of his fantasies. A novelist who, like the surrealists, seeks totally to derealize the real cannot be said to have redefined beauty as "a density of being," as the true *engagé* must do. Insofar as such a false novel makes of the slave a master and of the master a slave, it is a revolutionary work, but only in a restricted sense, not yet understood by Sartre in 1947. The fact remains that Genet's literary enterprises have as their goal a personal redemption, whereas a literature that is truly engaged also has as its end the amelioration of the fate of other men, for whom Genet has scant fraternal emotion.

Engaged literature is an appeal of one freedom to another. Genet
is not free. Only by creating a literature that is at the antipodes of
engagement can he become so.

Because Genet wants to force the Just to entertain the unthink-
able, crime is his major theme. The Just do not think about crime
for they expel the negative moment of freedom from their minds.
They only punish crime. In his works Genet displays himself as the
object of universal horror and, in so doing, forces the Just to recognize these unseemly thoughts as their own. In the process he obliges
the Just to reabsorb the exiled negative component of freedom.
Genet can perform this operation only on the condition that his
works be beautiful; otherwise he cannot expect them to be read.
Beauty is the trap he uses to drag the Just back to themselves and
to recognize what they have done to him. Years before they had
projected a monstrous ego upon him, and now he is reinstalling it
in them. Just as they had captured his freedom, now he has captured theirs. Just as they had set up a parasitic life within his mind,
now he installs himself in them. As he reads, the reader has no other
ego than Genet's. The Just have now become his object.

In his literary productions Genet reproduces the original crisis
and becomes an object for the Other. But now he has become a
quite different kind of object. This new objectivity is a trap, for
there is no reciprocity of recognition in his writing. The role of the
reader is, as in poetry, passively to objectify the word. Genet offers
himself in his writings as a hateful object, but transforms himself into
a subject who gazes on ironically as the reader incarnates these dis-
tasteful thoughts: "The readers have been had. They damn themselves as a Demiurge looks on. A cynical and peremptory freedom
imposes itself upon them, consuming and manipulating their liberty"
(p. 507). As he appears in his work, Genet is described as a "look-
object" that appears as a thing which steals the world and the subjectivity of the ready-victim, conferring upon him the status of a
seen thing. Alienated by the righteous, the pariah alienates him in
return. Genet has enforced the *lex talionis* of *Being and Nothingness*.
As presented by Sartre, Genet is a literary equivalent of Zola's
Nana. Rising from an oppressed class, he becomes an instrument of
vengeance targeted against the privileged. With beauty as his weapon,
he leads the Just to cooperate happily in an enterprise that will
conclude with their demise.

Genet's purpose in writing remains narcissistic: "The word expresses Narcissus' relationship with himself; he is at once the subject and the object" (p. 423). He draws the world into himself and
there devours it: "This lurking creature . . . like a starfish, projects

outside of its body a visceral and glandular world which is then reabsorbed and dissolved within itself" (p. 417). This passage bears an instructive resemblance to another in Sartre's 1939 essay on Husserl: "We have all read Brunschvig, Lalande and Meyerson. We believed that the Spider-Spirit lured things into its web, covered them with a white slaver and slowly digested them, reducing them to its own substance."[24] Philosophical idealism is taken to task for ingesting the world and reducing it to itself, but Genet is later praised for performing the same operation. Sartre is not contradicting himself, for Brunschvig and the others are guilty of expropriating the world, but Genet is performing the exemplary act of expropriating the expropriator. The world of the Just has done him violence and he is now simply responding in kind.

As an aesthete, Genet derealized the world and himself in the process, thus negating voluntarily his own freedom. If he is to be truly free, he must escape the trap he has set for the world of the Just. Sartre remarks that in his prose Genet has succeeded in doing so. *Our Lady,*" he says, "is a dream that contains its own awakening" (p. 422). Genet has become a cynically lucid dreamer who uses the devices of romantic irony to demonstrate his independence from his creations. Like Lautréamont and Gide, Genet breaks into the narration to destroy the spell of fiction: "Here is Divine all alone in the world. Whom should I give her as a lover?" (p. 420). Sartre does not understand that Genet's use of this impudent technique might possibly be overdetermined. In *Rousseau and Romanticism* Irving Babbitt indicates that those who employ this device do so in order to convey to the reader the illusion of a personality subject to no center, a multiple, transcendental, totally free, and volatile identity which adheres to no fixed point.[25] Through it Genet tells his reader that any attempt to objectify him will fail. Romantic irony is a literary ring of Gyges that functions as a prophylaxis against the alienation of language.

Although Sartre thinks that his Hegelian picaro has escaped the status of the inert thing powerless to exorcise the glance of the Other, it could be argued that he has merely usurped the role of the master. Through his writings, Genet has freed himself of his obsession with crime and of the need for retribution on a large scale; but he remains scarred, for he has yet to be able in his own life truly to universalize human relations, to experience all men equally and simultaneously as subjects and objects. This is evident in the nature of his generosity, his desire to enslave his friends to their benefactor. Once the victim of generosity, Genet now turns it against others. Instead of spreading gifts as widely as possible, he focuses them on selected individuals in an effort to subordinate them to his will. Thus, at the end of his career of self-emancipation, Genet has succeeded in escaping his alienated condition, but he has not escaped the role of the master and the world of conflict between the gazer and the gazed upon. The victory has been relative rather than unconditional. Merleau-Ponty asks whether, in "bringing down the master," the slaves are indeed "on their way to transcending the alternatives of mastery and serfdom." If not, "the world and our existence are a meaningless tumult."[26] This is the world of Genet, but it is not, for Sartre, the only world possible.

In *Being and Nothingness,* three escapes were offered to the master-slave relationship, all of them unfortunately illusory: the elimination of the subject-object relation; the understanding of another man as an end, an unconditional freedom (later said by Sartre to be possible in ideal prose if not in the real world); and the reciprocal and simultaneous understanding of men as both objects and subjects. The conclusion of *Saint Genet* again offers three solutions, two of which remain the same: "If we could all exist in perfect simultaneity and reciprocity, at once objects and subject for and by one another, or if we could sink together into an objective totality or if we could even be, as in the Kantian city of ends, subjects recognizing one another as subjects, separations would cease to exist" (p. 542). The last two of these solutions are not available. People can be a totality of objects only for a transcendent subject. All can become subjects for a transcendent subject, but only on the condition of the impossible liquidation of their materiality. The other is no longer inconceivable: "As far as absolute reciprocity is concerned, it is masked by historical conditions of class and race, by nationalities and the social hierarchy" (p. 542). The block to reciprocity is now thought to be historical rather than ontological. What was declared in *Being and Nothingness* to be "the impossible ideal" continues to be an ideal, but is no longer seen as impossible.[27]

The concept of reciprocity as expressed in *Saint Genet* is vague and incompletely developed. Although Genet is described as an object for the whole world, a state of reciprocity exists between the members of the class of the Just. Sartre seems to be saying that the reciprocity of the Just among themselves is an appropriate ethical model. In the *Critique* Sartre will explain that there are different levels of reciprocity and that reciprocity does not necessarily protect men against reification and alienation. Reciprocity, in all the definitions that Sartre has proposed, excludes the possibility of the permanent objectification of another. But alienation can exist within reciprocity if two people, while fully recognizing each other as free subjects, perceive one another also as means to their separate and mutually exclusive ends. Definitive dealienation can occur only within a certain type of reciprocity. Only when people recognize that they share the same praxis, when they become in effect the same subject and the same object of a shared transcendent end, does pure reciprocity exist.

The ethical ideal of the reconciliation of the subject and object is by no means original with Sartre. The young Marx maintained: "It is only in a social context that subjectivism and objectivism . . . can cease to be antimonies, and thus cease to exist as such antimonies. The resolution of the THEORETICAL contradictions is possible ONLY through practical means, only through the PRACTICAL energies of man."[28] This theme is often found too in Merleau-Ponty, especially in *Humanism and Terror:* "The problems of politics result from the fact that we are all subjects and that nevertheless we see and treat others as objects . . . Marxism seeks to break through the alternatives of subjective and objective politics."[29] Solitude, defined by Sartre as the negative relationship of each to all, the social relationship lived in despair, is the historical consequence of man's inability to achieve a world of pure reciprocity. Genet is alone because he never achieves this condition. As a child, he is the object, experiencing the Just as the subject he can never be. Later in his novels and in his generosity he becomes the subject who petrifies other men. Free mutuality does not exist in either case. In their limited form of reciprocity, the Just also experience solitude, for they are alternately lonely subjects gazing at an object or the petrified means of the Other. Genet displays the human condition writ large for he has gone to the extremes of solipsistic subjectivity and petrified objectivity, exactly as others do on a more prosaic scale in an unredeemed world. Until pure reciprocity is achieved, until the subject and the object are reconciled, men will continue to lurch desperately and relentlessly between the two poles of existence, vainly seeking a point of repose.

Because men are uncomfortably suspended between objectivity and subjectivity, they are constantly tempted to imagine that they are securely one or the other. This is the temptation of bad faith discussed in *Being and Nothingness.* The Just furnish an example of bad faith because they seek to be a pure inhuman gaze to "the guilty one." Men must live their subject-object dichotomy, for it cannot, today, be escaped. Sartre praises Genet for proudly and publicly living this solitude. He has not sought to make life comfortable for himself by feigning that he is uniquely and exclusively a single one of the components of our condition. His struggle has been to secure a position within which he can live in good faith, understand, and oblige others to understand that he is both subject and object. On the other side of the ledger Sartre finds the case of Nikolay Bukharin. One has a choice, Sartre argues, to be either Genet or Bukharin, to live in good faith or bad, to face and live the solitude imposed upon men, or mendaciously to escape it.

Arthur Koestler's novel *Darkness at Noon*, a fictionalized treatment of the 1938 trial of Bukharin, aroused passionate interest when it appeared in French translation in 1946.[30] Merleau-Ponty, who felt that "the book poses the problem of our time," discusses the case at length in *Humanism and Terror*, and Sartre's treatment of Bukharin in the final pages of *Saint Genet* is heavily influenced by his friend's work.[31] Bukharin went on trial for having, twenty years before, advised against rapid industrialization and immediate forced collectivization of Soviet agriculture. He felt that such action was inappropriate because the revolution was supposed not to precede but to follow economic development. For holding this position, Bukharin, who was never other than a passionately committed Marxist, was accused of betraying the state, attempting to restore capitalism, encouraging the enemies of the Soviet Union, and even planning the assassinations of Stalin and Lenin. History had decided that his economic policies were wrong. Although Bukharin did not intend to betray, subsequent events went against him, and Stalin decided that his ideas constituted a betrayal. At the trial his intentions were considered as lacking in significance. It did not matter that, subjectively, he felt at the time that his solutions were the most salutary for the future of the revolution.

Sartre comments inaccurately that Bukharin confessed to all.[32] In declaring himself guilty, Sartre maintains, Bukharin attacks the subjectivity he shares with no one and which isolates him. He confesses with humility to his betrayal. He admits that he was wrong to have thought as a free subject: "he makes himself a stone among stones" (p. 545). He adopts the false solution of the waiter of *Being and Nothingness*. Genet also confesses, but in an entirely different spirit. As he does so, he defiantly proclaims himself to be a subject as well as the object that the Just will him to be: "Genet refuses to be a stone" (p. 539).

Both Genet and Bukharin are the victims of societies with a terroristic proclivity to exterminate the subject. Although Sartre's sympathies are with Marxism, the Moscow trials appear to him to establish the fact that the same malady exists in both Stalin's Russia and liberal France. A plague on both your houses, Sartre seems to say. In one case the disease is an inherent and chronic feature of capitalist societies, whereas in the other it may be only, to borrow Lenin's expression, a childhood disease of communism. In his 1950 preface to Louis Dalmas' *Communisme yougoslave,* Sartre notes that in the Soviet Union the bourgeoisie seemed to have disappeared, but the radical alienation that characterized bourgeois society was still much in evidence.[33] The case of Bukharin is used with a double purpose, both as a criticism of Stalinism and as an example to explain that those who have been horrified by the Moscow trials ought to realize that their liberal societies are every-day performing the same operation, albeit with less fanfare.

Sartre also maintains that men can live these unhappy circum-stances in either good faith or bad. They have a choice between two scandals, two societies with a pathological desire to reduce all, or at least a good number of people, to an inert status. Sartre's position resembles Merleau-Ponty's view that it was equally impossible to be a communist or an anti-communist.[34] In the world of accusation a person has a choice: to be the proud, defiantly solitary subject or to sink into pure objectivity. The unfortunate alternative between the condition of Genet and that of Bukharin can be avoided only if people, on all levels, reconcile the subject and the object. Since this moment is not now in sight, the reconciliation is possible now only in the imagination (p. 550).

Amplifying on the object state of Koestler's protagonist, Merleau-Ponty remarks in *Humanism and Terror:* "He takes a backward path through the road Hegel had traced in the *Phenomenology* from the death of consciousness to History."[35] Hegel had observed that the consciousness of every individual passes through each of the phases through which the *Weltgeist* evolves. Perhaps in this sentence from *Humanism and Terror,* a book revered by Sartre, is the source of the organizing principles in *Saint Genet.* Bukharin has moved backward through the evolutionary path of the Spirit, backward from subjectivity to objectivity. Sartre subsequently discovers in Genet another man whose life history could be clarified by the Hegelian scaffolding and could be used as an instructive comparison with the regressive movement of the career of Bukharin.

The closeness of the parallel between the Hegelian myth and Sartre's Genet raises a question whether Genet has been wrenched and twisted to fit the pre-established harmony of the Hegelian model, whether this life has been rationalistically derived from prior prem-ises instead of being the result of empirical enquiry, whether the Hegelian dialectic has been used to tyrannize the life of Genet rather than to explain it. Sartre often seems to operate on the basis of a coherence rather than a correspondence theory of truth. Propositions are considered true to the extent that they agree, not with empirically verifiable data, but with other propositions in a series. Sartre's curious refusal to accept the chronology of events that Genet himself offered further fuels the suspicion that an a-priori formalism spoils the biographer's analysis.

Sartre's avowed intention in this work is to integrate the tools of Marxist materialism and psychoanalysis. But *Saint Genet* is not the book it advertises itself to be. Throughout it appear the devices of existential psychoanalysis and the thoughts of Hesnard, but Karl Marx plays scarcely more than a supernumerary role. Although the behavior of the Just is given a vaguely materialist base, social and historical categories are insufficiently weighted. The social environment is too abstract. There is no analysis of Genet's place in the struggles between the classes. Sartre does not see the relationship between the righteous and his victim as fundamentally one of class. The specifically Marxist idea of alienation as the theft of praxis is completely absent.

Instead of Marx, Hegel appears at every turn. In *Saint Genet* there is less an integration of Marxist tools than the further absorption of Hegel's system into Sartre's thought. In the case of Genet, freedom from alienation comes about merely from an act of consciousness, which is a Hegelian and un-Marxist idea. Sartre seems to say that, with skill and effort and given the proper elements in one's past, one can become free and happy within society as it is presently constituted. Dealienation is a question of grit. Many Marxists would not admit this possibility. Herbert Marcuse argues that "in a repressive society, individual happiness and productive development are in contradiction; if they are defined as values to be realized within this society, they become themselves repressive."[36] The autotherapy approach found in *Being and Nothingness* is still apparent in *Saint Genet*. For the Marxist, freedom within a structure of slavery is impossible. The means of production must be changed before a single person becomes free. Although Sartre makes the point that Genet is a freakish case, the convinced Marxist would not find this argument agreeable, for liberal society always flaunts exceptions to establish its freedom and benevolence. Sartre even realized that his use of Marxist materialism was inadequate: "It is clear that the study of Genet's conditioning by the events of his history is insufficient, very, very, insufficient."[37] Without fully understanding the extent to which man is an object, molded by overwhelming and inescapable forces, one cannot hope to grasp fully the exact margin of his freedom.

This does not mean that *Saint Genet* makes no contribution to the Marxist tradition in which it pretends to participate. Marx himself recognized that alienation was ubiquitous, but he over-stressed political and economic forms and underplayed its other possible avatars. Trent Schroycr argues that Marx's limited, largely labor-centered definition of alienation must be supplemented, and in order fully to detail the forms of domination in the world, one must return to Hegel's broader definition of alienation, "which is more sensitive to sociocultural processes."[38] Perhaps when he was writing *Saint Genet* Sartre was not yet familiar enough with the early Marx to understand that his theory needed to be expanded. Whether consciously or not, *Saint Genet* uses Hegel to provide the needed complement to the praxis-centered concept of alienation found in Marx. The problem with *Saint Genet* is rather that the complement it provides exists in isolation from the Marxist theory it complements—a difficulty that will be resolved in *L'Idiot*.

In *Saint Genet* biography becomes social drama. Baudelaire's alienation took place outside of history, but Genet's is, however vaguely, a political event. Sartre has discovered that in the capitalist world or in a revolutionary society grown stagnant, men tend to persecute one another. As a consequence of this discovery, biography is understood as paranoia, the chronicle of an individual's delirium of persecution. The word *paranoia* is used here not in a negative or pathological sense but rather in the sense given by David Cooper: "paranoia in our age . . . is a necessary tentative to freedom and wholeness," and further, "paranoia is the beginning of active existence."[39] In *Baudelaire* the Other had invaded the poet's soul, but the invasion was judged to have been Baudelaire's choice. The invasion of Genet was not invited. The aim of the biographer is to be as attentive and as suspicious as possible of the devices and manifestations of the Other as he seeks to impinge on the autonomy of his victim. Psychoanalysis becomes for Sartre what it was for Hesnard and Lacan: the discovery of the invading Other within an unhappy host. Sartre hopes that his acute if not yet systematic vigilance will prove infectious, heightening the suspicious instincts of his reader. Biography is paranoia and incitement to paranoia.

In *Baudelaire* Sartre criticized the poet from the point of view of a timeless relationship that exists between the for-itself and the in-itself, which he thought characteristic of the human ontological condition. In *Saint Genet* he adopts the future as his perspective. "The future is here," Sartre announces in minatory tones, "more present than the present" (p. 549). Again he echoes Merleau-Ponty: "To be a revolutionary is to judge that which is in the name of that which is not yet, taking it to be more real than the real."[40] All men are like Genet, Sartre asserts, in that they too are objects of a glance, gazed down upon by the masked men who will succeed them: "For these future eyes whose gaze haunts us, our time will be an object, a guilty object" (p. 549). In *L'Idiot,* Sartre will have recourse once again to the past, but here too with the intent of discovering the future.

V

Flaubert and the Subjective Neurosis

The family! What an annoyance! What a slough! What a
trap! How one gets swallowed up in it, rots in it, and
dies there a living death! If I had only been born a bastard.

Flaubert

In the *Origin of the Family* Engels gives a tendentious lesson in
etymology.[1] The Latin *familia*, he remarks, originally had a sense
at odds with the usual understanding of the word. *Famulus* meant
domestic slave, and *familia* was the term for the stable of slaves belonging to one man. To read the title of Sartre's latest epic of
alienation, *L'Idiot de la famille*, with this etymology in mind gives
a fair idea of the book's contents. It is the biography of a slave, a
particularly disadvantaged one, who resided in a houschold of
slaves whose duty it was to subordinate themselves to the will of
one man. The master in question is Achille-Cléophas Flaubert, law-
giving Moses of the Flaubert family religion, prince of science, chief
surgcon and director of the Hôtel-Dieu of Rouen. The slave: Gustave
Flaubert, "the patriarch of modern fiction."[2]

Sartre acknowledges that *L'Idiot* is written not only against the
Flaubert clan but against all families.[3] In his personal life and his
writings Sartre has ever expressed little affection for this stubborn
institution. Sartre's first major hostile statement on the family appears in his preface to *The Traitor* (1958), the autobiography of
André Gorz:

It seems that one can still find on earth savages stupid enough to discover reincarnated ancestors in their newborn children. . . . What barbarism! They take a kid who is very much alive and sew him into the
skin of a dead man. He will suffocate in this senile childhood without
other hope than to poison future childhoods after his death. Can one

be astonished after this that he only speaks of himself with the greatest
caution, in an undertone, and often in the third person. This unhappy
fellow is not unaware of the fact that he is his own great uncle.

These backward aborigines are found in the Fiji Islands, in Tahiti,
in New Guinea, in Vienna, in Paris, in Rome, wherever there are men.
They are called relatives.[4]

Some of the black comedy of *Nausea* is directed against the bourgeois
families encountered in Bouville. *The Words* is replete with references to "the family comedy."[5] In Sartre's autobiography the humor
has lightened, but the family remains a subject for ridicule. *The
Condemned of Altona* is suffused with a destructive atmosphere
exuded by a strict sense of family identity. "I am chosen," Frantz
says, "Nine months before my birth my name, duties, character
and destiny were decided."[6] According to the *Critique,* it is within
the family that a child undergoes his class apprenticeship. The
family is a mediating institution, an ideological conditioning device, the primary brain-washing tool of an oppressive society.

Social historian Philippe Ariès has identified two family types in
the modern period.[7] Before the middle of the eighteenth century
the family entered the life of the individual only at critical moments,
such as birth, marriage, and death. Since the demise of this family
type, another type has come to prominence in the West. In this
new family the daily existence of the individual is almost totally
dominated in one way or another by his family relationships. This
family, which invades a man and isolates him from his fellow men,
is the particular target of Sartre's wrath. In *The Words* Sartre tells
how he has personally experienced the family's destruction of the
solidarity that children spontaneously find in groups formed with
their colleagues:

> Our games . . . sometimes transformed our groups into a small
> unanimous crowd that swallowed me up. But we were never able to
> forget for long our parents whose invisible presence caused us to fall
> quickly into the communal solitude of animal colonies. Without a goal,
> or end, without a hierarchy, our society oscillated between total fusion
> and juxtaposition. Together, we lived in truth, but we couldn't help
> feeling that we had been loaned to one another, and that we each be-
> longed to tightly knit, powerful, and primitive collectivities that forged
> spell-binding myths, were nurtured on error, and forced upon us their
> arbitrary power.[8]

In *L'Idiot* an exact repetition of this pattern occurs, in which a
schoolboy group in fusion evaporates because of the pernicious intervention of the family.

In *On a raison de se révolter* Sartre explains that the task of the revolutionary is to uncover those institutions that oppress the free subject. One such institution is the family. The numerous alienations of Flaubert, which are the theme of *L'Idiot,* all evolve out of the alienations experienced at the hands of father and mother. Sartre's biography describes a man "who seeks to escape his family alienations . . . by alienating himself in art" (III, 459). Flaubert spent his whole life fleeing from one alienation to another because, as a child, he was stolen from the world and himself.

In attacking the family, Sartre affiliates himself with the enduring socialist tradition of hostility to the family. In *The Communist Manifesto* the bourgeois family appears as an agent of dehumanization. In the *Origin of the Family,* Engels explains that the nineteenth century father-centered family is a microcosm of capitalist society. The same atmosphere of servitude, jealousy, hatred, and class antagonism is found in the society as a whole and in its cellular form. With the demise of private property, the domestic family as presently constituted will disappear. There is a sturdy tradition of interest in the family in the writings of those who feel, with Sartre, that the tools of historical materialism and psychoanalysis must coexist if social phenomena are to be understood, since there are both subjective as well as objective preconditions for social change. Sartre is closer to such authors as Paul Federn, Wilhelm Reich, R. D. Laing, and D. G. Cooper, who have found no redeeming features in the bourgeois family, than he is to such writers as Adorno and Christopher Lasch, who have found in the family the basis for authentic subjectivity, as well as an agency for perpetuating an authoritarian, patriarchal society.

"I felt that I had an account to settle with him," Sartre remarks of his feeling after reading Flaubert's letters.[9] In *Being and Nothingness,* after explaining the system of existential psychoanalysis, Sartre stated his intention of demonstrating the method in studies of Flaubert and Dostoevsky. Although the book on the Russian novelist was not to be, Sartre's knowledge of the literature on Dostoevsky was perhaps a key to understanding Flaubert. Although over the years the major currents of Sartre's thinking have shifted several times, he has always found in the life and writings of Flaubert an important resource.

Even as a very young child, Sartre found Flaubert a challenge. In *The Words* the recently literate Sartre is puzzled by the concluding page of *Madame Bovary*.[10] Michel Rybalka noted a "Flaubertian tone" in *Nausea*.[11] Though Flaubert is dismissed in the "Presentation of *Les Temps modernes*" as "a talented man of private means," this contempt contrasts ironically with Sartre's biography, which is one of the longest books ever written by one man about another.[12]

In about 1954 Roger Garaudy suggested to Sartre that together they study a given individual. Sartre was to employ the method of existentialist psychoanalysis, and Garaudy was to use Marxist tools. The division of labor proposed by Garaudy, however, was now uncongenial to Sartre, who already, as shown in *Saint Genet*, felt that the two approaches were inseparable. Within a year Sartre had written a thousand pages. He abandoned the book briefly, but having become disgusted with his habit of aborting his own projects, returned to work.

After three volumes Sartre has again abandoned his Flaubert. The fourth volume, projected as an analysis of *Madame Bovary*, will almost certainly never appear. It will have to be entered in Sartre's phantom bibliography along with *L'Homme*, *La Reine Albemarle et le dernier touriste*, the second volume of the *Critique*, and the books on Mallarmé and Tintoretto. But the fourth volume of *L'Idiot* is not nonexistent in the same sense as are these others, for Sartre claims that within the first three volumes he has already said all he has to say. His conclusions about *Madame Bovary* are implicit in what he has already written about how Flaubert became the idiot of the family, how his inadequacy served as a springboard to a victory that was false, how the mechanisms of the primary series of alienations and the compensations were developed to escape them, which were also alienations. What remains unexplored is the extent to which *Madame Bovary* reveals this tangle of vipers.

L'Idiot has two principal divisions. Sartre's aim throughout the first two volumes is to describe the subjective neurosis of Flaubert. The third volume is devoted largely to the objective neurosis of the writer and the society of Flaubert's day. Sartre tries to explain the providential relationship between these two maladies. This system of organization seems to have been inspired by Hegel and Dilthey. The phrase "objective spirit," which appears as the title for the second division of *The Phenomenology of Mind*, designates all the principles and relationships that constitute the moral and social life of man. Hegel contrasts this spirit with "subjective mind," which includes all processes and activities within the individual consciousness. For Dilthey, the objective spirit designates those enduring expressions of mental life: buildings, roads, systems of ideas, habits, customs, political and cultural institutions, objects of art. These mold the world and essentially determine a person's activities. Through them the past acts upon the present.

Throughout his life Gustave suffered from a deep and hidden

wound inflicted while he was learning to read. Until some time after his seventh birthday he failed to understand the relationship between the written word and the thing it designated. For Sartre, this failure decided the writer's career.

In order to understand Gustave's dyslexia and the immensity of the consequences, according to Sartre, it is necessary to understand the parents and the situation of the family at the time of his birth. Two factors in Caroline Flaubert's attitude toward Gustave were to have a decisive effect on his later development, making inevitable his desperate limitations. The first can be traced to her own unhappy childhood. Caroline's mother died while giving birth to her. As orphaned children often do, she felt rejected by her mother's death and experienced it as a condemnation. Her early years, in which she was passed around to a long series of relatives, were generally unhappy. Sartre speculated that, as an adult, she sought to compensate for these early affectionless years by giving birth to a daughter with whom she would identify and on whom she would shower the love and care that she had been denied by her mother's death. But the expected compensation in the form of a daughter did not appear.

Achille was the first arrival. This was certainly a disappointment to Caroline, but there was still time to neutralize the curse of her childhood. Sartre imagines that she good-naturedly put aside her personal preference for a girl and treated Achille with a satisfactory level of affection. He was, after all, the first-born son, the successor of the feudal father. With Gustave's birth, however, things were quite different. Time having increased Caroline's desire for a daughter, Gustave was taken for a usurper. Disappointment now becomes evident, and the new project of child-rearing is taken on without enthusiasm. While not detesting Gustave, she cares for him dutifully and efficiently, but indifferently: "The newborn is nothing but the *object* of her care" (p. 94). Gustave experiences the first in a long series of alienations. In *Being and Nothingness* Sartre had described the man who experiences indifference as a victim of alienation, for to the indifferent, others are merely forms that pass in the street. To Caroline, the "Stalinist spouse" (p. 135), Gustave is but a neutral object, or at best a means to accomplish her duties as the wife of Achille-Cléophas.

A child who is loved experiences himself as an end: "This monster is an absolute monarch. He is always an end, never a means. If once in his life, whether at three months or at six, a child is able to experience this pride-filled happiness, he is a man. Throughout the entirety of his existence he will neither be able to resurrect this supreme pleasure of reigning, nor forget it. But even in moments of adverse luck he will retain a sort of religious optimism that is founded on the abstract and tranquil certainty of his value" (pp. 136–137). One must first undergo "this happy alienation" and experience "this false happiness" (p. 143) in order to feel free. One must first be fooled in order to discover the truth of freedom. Memory is the source of a sense of freedom that mitigates the most hostile circumstances. An illusion of freedom is maintained despite the betrayal of early expectations. To be a man requires that one have been during the course of one's early childhood this special kind of monster.

Sartre's description of the free man, reminiscent of Freud's characterization of the special destiny of the Jews in *Moses and Monotheism,* suggests that he is once again using the humanistic concept of the subject that made the Marxism of *Saint Genet* suspect. This concept serves to restrict the desire for power, for it indicates that one man, working in isolation on his own soul, can achieve freedom. Marxism, however, discovers freedom at two historical levels. There is the freedom of the postrevolutionary man who is reunited with his species being, and there is the freedom of the prerevolutionary man who is free to the extent that he is aware of necessity. At the time that Sartre was writing the Genet biography his Marxist culture was still deficient, and he did not yet understand this two-tiered definition. Despite the fact that others were slaves, Genet was said to be unconditionally free. No claim is made that the little monster is free in the utopian sense. He is not, for one can be free only on the condition that all are free. But he is free in the sense that his narcissistic integrity can be wounded by forces that threaten his autonomy. He is free to the extent that he is capable of being insulted by unjust power and, however ineffectually, of acting upon his rage.

Because Gustave was never this monster, he will become a monster of a different stripe. He experiences the lack of maternal love as a lack of self-love, as "a nonvalorization" (p. 140). Since the early experience of love results in the confirmation of one's existence and the guarantee of the value of one's mission, Flaubert perceives his whole life as devoid of meaning, as universal monotony. Because he is a nothing and he exists neither as a distinct nor as a valued person, terrible consequences ensue. To provide himself with a sense of identification, he must play a role, for in effect he has no self. Sincerity will be a lifelong impossibility, for a nonself cannot be sincere.

Another crucial factor in Gustave's development was his appearance shortly after and shortly before other children who died in infancy. The result, Sartre speculates, was that as a child, he was overprotected. His slightest needs were attended to immediately, but not lovingly. Sartre draws on the findings of Margaret Mead, who showed that dominant aggressivity or passivity in an individual is immediately related to the manner in which he was cared for. If the child does not have to struggle to get what he needs, a passive constitution results. Such was the case with Gustave. Because aggressivity was never given the chance to develop, Gustave's problem was compounded. He is not merely superfluous but passively superfluous, and constitutionally incapable of saving himself. "For Gustave . . . the ego comes to him through others. He does not dream of ratifying it but only of playing the suggested role as it is offered him in such a manner as to confirm their demands" (p. 176).

Sartre is here distinguishing Flaubert from Genet, who actively confirmed the decision of the Just. Unlike Flaubert, Genet had a favorable wind behind him: he was told that he was an object, but at the same time he suspected that he was a free subject. It would not be possible for Flaubert, however, to feel himself free to alter his circumstances. The illusion of freedom has a source, which is nowhere apparent in his past. Because his will has been completely plasticized, because he is nothing but an object, Flaubert cannot be expected to demonstrate the same moral stamina displayed by Genet.

Within his first two years Gustave is deprived of the cardinal categories of praxis and hence understands himself to be subhuman. Because his praxis has been stolen, his alienation is more real to him than authentic subjectivity. The child therefore lives in a state of radical ennui. Sartre now defines this spiritual malady quite differently than in *Baudelaire,* where it had been understood as the fear of freedom and the pleasure found in self-alienation. Here it is the negative experience of alienation, "life experienced as the impossibility of becoming a man and as the perpetual collapse of the desire to transcend himself toward the human" (p. 145). Gustave understands from his mother's ministrations that his role is to submit. Action is a foreign concept.

Sartre insists that his speculative account is supported by the known facts of Gustave's early years. Caroline Commanville, Gustave's niece, reported her grandmother's recollection that Gustave was an extraordinarily naive and gullible child. Behind this innocence Sartre discovers the parent's cruelty, for gullibility is originally the consequence of defective relations with others and

with the word. It is a stunted kind of knowledge which results from
stunted intersubjective relations. Sartre calls it "a disease of Truth"
(p. 164).

Because of his passivity and lack of a sense of self, Gustave understands the truth as the will of others within him. The assertions of
adults are accepted automatically as truth. This credulity Sartre
describes as hopeless alienation to adults. The child absorbs the
sentence without treating it critically, for the word is experienced
as an imperative. In *Being and Nothingness* the passive experience
of generosity was a form of alienation, where here Gustave experiences the word, received from others, as generosity: it must be believed because it is a gift from his parents. Gustave is incapable of
seizing words as simple signs designating objects. He cannot distinguish between the word's pure signifying values and its magical,
imperative quality: "Meaning becomes matter: it acquires an inert
consistency. Meaning is true, not because of evidence, but because
of density" (p. 21). The word is understood as a pure in-itself, an
incontestable command. Gustave's relations with his parents are
thus to be responsible for his using words as poetry rather than
as prose.

Gustave has difficulty in learning to speak and feels less than
others the need to do so. The word is something that falls from
the sky; it is the property of adults who sometimes deign to bestow
it upon him. To speak is to act, and action is foreign to Gustave.
It is the others who have the power to act and hence to speak, not
he. Commanville reports family members recalling of Gustave that
"he would spend long hours with a finger in his mouth, with a self-
absorbed, almost stupid look" (p. 17). Sartre relates the child's pro-
pensity to lapse into passive stupors to this defective relationship
with the word. Autism and mutism are Gustave's native state. Ad-
ducing his evidence from a reading of the juvenilia, especially
Quidquid volueris, Sartre demonstrates that the young author treats
passive stupors positively. Gustave understands that these states
appear to adults as negative, but to him they are privileged moments. At such times he experiences himself as passively possessed
by the world, as dissolving ecstatically into the in-itself. All his
life he will be more comfortable describing *exis* than praxis, describing ceremonies and objects rather than acts. He compensates for
his verbal malaise by resorting to these ecstasies. The world of language is hostile territory.

"Culture, for him, is theft" (p. 40), states Sartre, playing with
Proudhon's line. Sartre sympathizes with the young Gustave in
this respect, for the pratico-inert of culture inevitably robs a person

of spontaneity. For Gustave, the word is an instrument of the fallen realm of culture, and his stupors are, at this early age, the only escape possible. They are momentary abdications from the world of praxis. Sartre points out that throughout his life Gustave identified with and had great esteem for animals, madmen, and children, creatures who have not yet crossed into the nightmare world of praxis and culture. From early childhood Gustave equates hebetude with poetry. For him poetry is "a silent adventure of the soul, a lived event that is without common measure with language. More precisely, it *takes place* against it" (p. 35). He speaks, but in order not to speak. He speaks not to act but to abandon himself to the comfortably familiar world of the in-itself.

Each of Sartre's subjects has his golden age. Gustave's most unmitigated period of happiness occurred between the ages of three and seven when he escaped from the emotionally frostbitten mother by basking in the affectionate attentions of his father. In his first years his father's warm interest in him almost justifies his existence. The child is taken on the physician's rounds of Rouen and in general finds in his company what he had sought but not found in the presence of his mother. But it is already too late, for Gustave has already been prefabricated, and the love of the father serves only to abet the process of alienation.

The character of Achille-Cléophas was crucial to this new relationship. As the chief physician of Rouen, he was ambitious socially, economically, and intellectually. The son of a village veterinarian, he had advanced the condition of the Flaubert family by becoming the director of the municipal hospital of Rouen. He considered that his family's goal was to arrive at the highest pinnacle of wealth, prestige, and power. Each family member was only a means to this end. For Achille-Cléophas the proper role of each was the rigorous alienation of the individual to the family group. Each is like Marx's worker who finds his essence outside of himself.

The physician was a traitor to two classes. He was in part a royalist, but at the same time he sought to progress through his own class by buying land and socializing with the wealthy bourgeois of Rouen. As Sartre had noted in the *Critique*, a man can rarely be situated in relation to a single class, and the family type created by Achille-Cléophas was indeed tinged by two social strata. His idea of the family was also inherited from a feudal and theocratic society in which the *pater familias* was the absolute monarch by divine right. For the children of Achille-Cléophas "the alienation to the family is lived as a feudal alienation to the father" (p. 78). The goal of the mother and children is to realize the wishes of the father. The family is thoroughly subordinated to his historical enterprise: the economic conquest of Normandy. The poorly equipped Gustave is expected to play his predetermined part. He has interiorized, through association with his father, the Flaubert imperative to glory and the notion that it is his duty to be its vehicle. The child finds himself in what Gregory Bateson calls the schizophrenia-generating "double bind."[13] He has learned that he must be an active tool of the family's grand design, but he has been formed to be passive and to feel worthless.

Gustave's relationship with his father reveals his predisposition to adoration. Because the child is passive, he is conditioned to adore unconditionally. The feudal and theocratic Achille-Cléophas understands this adoration to be his due: "There is a Flaubert humanism that is the human relation of vassalage which he opposed violently to the ideology of his class, at the time when it is organizing itself to overthrow Louis-Phillippe" (p. 335). Conditioned to be a vassal, Gustave realizes himself only by vainly abolishing himself, negating himself to the profit of another. In his later works he consistently holds unreasoning devotion in highest esteem, as witness the examples of Charles Bovary and of Félicité in "A Simple Heart." For Gustave, adoration can only be passive, but for Achille-Cléophas, proper adoration requires that the worshiper reflect the glory of the worshiped. The child's duty is to be an unblemished mirror of the master. But this he cannot be, for perfectly to return his father's image, he must act.

The parents of Gustave have created a monster whom they cannot recognize as a Flaubert, as they discover when they try to teach their second son to read. Commanville recalls that her grandmother, having taught the brilliant Achille to read, undertook the same task with the young Gustave. For a long time he failed to learn, and it was thought that he might be retarded. To read, for Gustave, is to abandon the sweet inertia of the imaginary and become an active agent. In order for him to succeed, it would be necessary to change his being, to detach himself from his native passivity and its epiphenomenal conception of language. After the mother's failure, Sartre conjectures, Achille-Cléophas, unable to believe that a Flaubert might have below-normal intelligence, assumed the task himself. He too failed. The child tried to read, but could not. He knows that it is his duty to succeed, and he is properly imbued with ambition, but the little abecedarian cannot face the oppressive requirements of praxis.

Because the father sees his son as the means of advancing the family enterprise of *semper excelsior,* he greets the inability to read with anger. Thus Sartre imagines that Gustave may have been told, "You will be the idiot of the family" (p. 383). Echoing the fatal voice and look of Genet's story, Sartre imagines that "a surgical gaze descended on the child and a magisterial voice said: 'He is not gifted' " (p. 570). The vocabulary associated with alienation—the fall, the shame, and the look—which had first appeared in *Being and Nothingness* is here repeated. Gustave "knows himself to be *inhabited* by the fixed gaze of a malevolent father who alienates him as he objectifies him, that is to say, infecting with alterity his most intimate subjectivity that becomes *other* to itself" (p. 324). As in *Saint Genet* and Hesnard's *L'Univers morbide de la faute,* the inability to live up to the standards of another plays a crucial role in the genesis of neurosis. The child understands that he cannot be his father's successor or even the equal of his brother, who will inherit the father's metaphysical aura. The sentence imposed by the father can only be definitive, and Gustave's acceptance of it can only be unconditional. At the age of seven he possesses a complete premonition of a life of total and irremediable failure. In consequence, Gustave acquires a fascination with fatality, as becomes apparent in many of his works. *Madame Bovary*, for example, is the tale of a condemnation that is predicted in the first pages, describing Charles Bovary's first day of school.

This new and most significant alienation will have immense consequences. The boy's hebetudes take on the sense of a prideful and resentful return to a paradise from which he had been expelled. He develops a myth to explain his resistance to acculturation: he is a beast, an idiot. He is asked to hate himself, and so he will. Out of obedience to his father's censorious will he will spend his life mimicking self-destruction in a passive rage. He will often entertain the thought of suicide, but his passive constitution forbids it. Instead he will interiorize the sentence of worthlessness in a more polite and docile fashion, opting for a slow, living suicide. He does not hate his father, but as Sartre seeks to show in an analysis of the early story "Un Parfum à sentir," he blames him for his degraded state. The son hopes that his symbolic suicide will shame Achille-Cléophas and bring back the golden age.

Gustave's situation is unlivable without compensatory myths. His primary solace is the thought that he is somehow of greater worth than the others precisely because he is nothing and thus is irremediably miserable. Having interiorized the institutional compulsion to glory, he finds it necessary to feel superior to others. Since he has nothing with which to work to realize this superiority, he makes good account of his nothingness and uses it as a vehicle, the only vehicle available, to set himself above others. He makes of privation a merit, both out of respect for those who condemn him and out of resentment. He affirms the priority of the nothingness that he is over the being that others are and which he can never be. His nothingness is the sign of his election.

His mission, born of a desire for revenge, will be to infect the world with this nonbeing; hence his subsequent option for the imaginary. Sartre's Gustave says to himself, "Because I am roasting in hell, all others should also suffer the same" (p. 442). Because of his passive nature he cannot turn to crime but must instead resort to the imaginary. He will passively condemn his fellow man, and in so doing, he will include himself in the condemnation. His immolation of the world will be a sadomasochistic enterprise. Gustave, however, will escape in the sense that he is superior to the others because of his greater sentience, because he alone is conscious of the nothingness of men and their derisive efforts and desires. He alone understands that all of life is under the sway of an evil destiny, manipulated, as was Gustave by Achille-Cléophas, by the will of an all-powerful and malevolent Other. Flaubert, as author, will turn against other men the condemnation of his father and become "the Lord of Nonbeing." Against the reality that oppresses him, he will become "the Prince of the Imaginary."

A new conflict emerges when Gustave interiorizes the divergent religious attitudes of his parents. Caroline Flaubert, although only moderately devout, teaches him his prayers and has him baptized. This would hardly have been enough to make of him a believer, except that he was already formed to believe uncritically, to have faith. Another reason disposing the child to religious belief was the image projected by Achille-Cléophas and the relationship of adoration that he encouraged. Gustave played the role of the vassal in a feudalized system of interaction: "The inferior is justified by his total alienation to the superior, whoever he might be" (p. 581). A universal hierarchy had been suggested by the father's image. Even if the word God had never been mentioned, Gustave would have invented it.

Gustave also received, however, a contradictory message from his father. Born to believe, Gustave is taught by the doctor that belief is impossible. He finds himself suspended between the cultural postulates of the contradictory ideologies of two classes: feudal hierarchy and bourgeois liberalism. Another double bind disrupts his psyche. The father, after casually permitting his wife to provide Gustave with a minimal religious education, intervenes as the man of science and informs the child that belief is impossible. Gustave learns that life is a complex machine and that analysis will sooner or later reduce all its mysteries to their purely material constituent parts. Man's essence is his medical objectivity. Bourgeois empiricism and analytical atomism enter the child's soul. The spirit of analysis becomes his superego, the truth of his father within him. Gustave, who has already accepted his father's decree that he was worthless, having now absorbed the implied order to believe, accepts as well the skeptic's judgment that belief is an absurdity. Achille-Cléophas throws his son to his knees before God while simultaneously preparing to show him that analytic reason forbids religious emotion. To believe is to obey; to believe is to disobey. Gustave will eventually integrate the harsh analytical glance of his father into his art. Gustave becomes complicit with the look, just as, because of his passivity, he will become complicit with most of the alienations he undergoes.

Although Gustave fully understands that belief is a permanent impossibility, religion will remain a constant temptation. He adopts the idea of God hungrily, for it justifies his passive stupors and his simplicity. His ecstatic hebetudes become elevations and visitations that sanctify his inertia. God could also assist in another sense, functioning as "the Antifather." The child cannot escape the malevolent look of the father by identifying himself with the look because his brother Achille has already done so, having been designated as the only possible choice for the new Achille-Cléophas because Gustave has shown himself unequal to the task. For Achille-Cléophas, Achille is *"the same"* while Gustave is *"the Other"* (p. 499). If the child could only believe, the surgical glance of God would gain ascendancy over the surgical glance of his father and release him from his inessentiality and his destiny. God would be the Antifather who could restore the golden age.

Gustave's attitude toward religion will always be characterized by ambivalence. He will view it positively because belief is his native state, and he will admire those who unreservedly believe. But at the same time he will never forgive religion for not having the power to win the tug of war with analytical atomism in his mind and to win authority away from the glance of his father.

Gustave's experience with religion is crucial to an understanding of his juvenilia. In these works, Sartre explains, the young man often plays the role of an Antichrist, or Satan. He accepts the mechanistic universe of his father but rises above this meaningless aggregate of atoms in his station at the pinnacle of an aristocracy of privation. He has been denied access to the infinite. He is thus Satan, for the fallen angel is damned to have an intense but impossible longing for the infinite. The greatest souls are the most severely punished, for the quality of a man is directly proportionate to the extent of his suffering. "Since the positive infinite is denied me," Sartre's Flaubert reasons, "I will become the negative infinite" (p. 568). By interiorizing his curse, he becomes evil incarnate. This is the origin of the sadistic dream of demoralizing all of humanity that Sartre finds in all of the author's works. Flaubert's feeling that his mission was that of a demoralizer is abundantly clear in his correspondence. In early 1839 he wrote to Ernest Chevalier: "if ever I take an active role in this world it will be as a thinker and a demoralizer. All I'll do will be to tell the truth, but it will be horrible, cruel, and naked."[14] Since he has been deprived of the infinite, out of resentment he will reveal to all the futility of the entire human enterprise. The suicidal pride-filled human cipher who becomes the bearer of ontological bad news to all men is not a new figure in L'Idiot. In "The Childhood of a Leader" Lucien, contemplating suicide, says: "I am killing myself because I don't exist. And you also, my brothers, you are nothingness."[15]

Because of his resentment Flaubert seeks both to humiliate other men and to escape from their midst. Because vertical ascension to God is blocked, he discovers the secret relationship between the high and the low that is one of the major features of his personal philosophy. Since he cannot rise above men, he decides instead to fall into the subhuman. But in sinking below men, he will soar above them. "Baseness pleases me," he wrote to Louise Colet in 1846, "It's the sublime of the lower depths."[16] Throughout Flaubert's life and works Sartre discovers a constant desire to fall, both symbolically and literally. Flaubert symbolically falls when he plays self-degrading pranks as a schoolboy and later as a literary salonard. And he literally falls in January 1844 in the first of his so-called epileptic attacks. Sartre explains the meaning of this fascination with downward movement as a yearning to return to his early childhood, a vain appeal to the mother's hands to take up again the task that should have made of him a man of action and self-esteem.

Gustave's feudal and theocratic background render him a natural royalist. On scant evidence his mother thought herself of noble blood. His father made no such claim, but Sartre insists that Achille-Cléophas was impressed with nobility and was basically a royalist, basing this claim on Gustave's recollection that the happiest moment of his childhood was an occasion when his father took him to see the Duchesse de Berry passing through Rouen. Achille-Cléophas held Gustave above the crowd to afford him a better view of the Duchess. Catching sight of the boy, she had her carriage stop and came over to Gustave and kissed him. He always remembered with intense satisfaction the pleasure this moment provided his father. It gave him what he always sought and what he was soon to lose forever: the joy of being a source of pride to his father. Here Sartre sees the monarchy and the sacred father reflecting in each other's glory. Flaubert will wish for a hierarchically arranged world. He will be a permanent traitor to his class, coming only very late to an unhappy recognition that he has been born a bourgeois.

Up to this point in the first volume Sartre has been examining what was made of Gustave, but a person is more than this. As Sartre noted in the *Critique,* "man is characterized above all by the overcoming of a situation, by what he succeeds in doing with what has been done with him."[17] Through the rest of the first volume and the entirety of the second, Sartre seeks to discover how Gustave acts on the basis of his prefabricated existence and what self-defensive measures he adopts to neutralize the damage he has sustained. For the first time a true praxis will appear and with it the possibility of its alienation. Sartre calls this moment "the *stress.*"

Gustave's childhood ambition was to become a great actor. At the age of seventeen he wrote: "I dreamed of glory when I was a child . . . I would have made, if I had been properly guided, an excellent actor" (p. 660). His interest in acting was no mere velleity, for between 1830 and 1832 he prepared almost thirty plays for family audiences. Yet at the age of ten he suddenly abandoned his theatrical ambitions. The question is why he had wanted to become an actor, and why he abruptly abandoned his hopes.

In the normal child the imaginary is lived as the herald of a real future pleasure. Not so with Gustave. He understands himself to be permanently unreal, to be outside of humanity, and desires to be totally and publicly involved in the imaginary. It does not suffice, Sartre maintains, to choose the imaginary; you must have been chosen by the imaginary. The imaginary must have been at the origin of your misfortune. Gustave was so chosen. He has been told implicitly that he is imaginary, that is, unreal. His being has been stolen. He is a nonperson. The unreal is his malady, but also his means of escaping it.

For himself Gustave has no reality, but he understands that for others he apparently does. At a decisive moment in life he must have understood his identity to lie outside of himself. In the child's mind there is a priority of the "he" that he is said to be by his father over the "me" that he is for himself. Like Marx's alienated worker and the serial man of the *Critique,* Flaubert's identity is located outside of his body, in the mind of the Other. When he appears before an audience, Gustave senses that he has in their eyes a substantial reality which he does not have for himself: "he tries to incarnate *the character he is for the other,* to lend his living and suffering body of this assemblage of abstract determinations" (p. 673). Like the waiter of *Being and Nothingness,* Gustave the actor becomes the "comedian of himself, who grasps himself as a character and not as a person" (p. 673). He seeks to see himself being seen. As did Baudelaire and Genet, Flaubert seeks to direct toward his person the foreign glance. He is alienated to the object that he is for others: "The Other is Me" (p. 771).

Behind Gustave's decision to be a comic actor, to encourage others to laugh at him, lies his sadomasochism. He publicly destroys in his person all human values in order to demonstrate simultaneously that he is unworthy of them and that they are unworthy of his immense and unquenchable desires. Setting himself up as an object of derision, he obediently continues the job of destruction begun by Achille-Cléophas. The choice of the vocation of comic actor reveals Gustave's free assumpton of the refusal that others have imposed on him. He is free only to succeed at a horrified negation of all, himself included. He becomes the public accomplice of those who have declared him worthless. They were right: he is indeed subhuman. This self-abasement, however, has its reward. Having understood from his father that he is "the Other" while Achille is "the same," he can achieve in a comic role the feeling of identification that he has been denied. Self-denunciation is for him a means of identifying with those who condemn him. The subhuman plays a crucial role in Gustave's personal philosophy. Since heaven is empty, the debased is paradoxically the highest thing to which he can attain. As the subhuman object of the world's mirth, the young Gustave becomes sublime.

Flaubert seeks to become not only an actor, but a famous one. He seeks fame for two reasons: in order to demoralize others from whom he derives his renown, and in order to astonish and humiliate his father. It he can manage to become a well-known comic actor, he will have, at least publicly if not internally, neutralized his father's sentence. Fame is revenge. Destined by the surgeon to derealization, he makes it the cause of his celebrity, which in turn will lead to his father's humiliation, both because a glorious Flaubert will appear publicly like a subhuman monster and because the profession of actor is beneath the high social station of the upwardly mobile Rouen family. Obedience and disobedience coincide in the same act.

Sometime between 1832 and 1835 Gustave abandoned his acting ambition. According to Sartre, it is unlikely that Achille-Cléophas or Caroline directly forbade him to consider entering the profession. Instead, they must simply have greeted his plans with indifference. To be a comic actor was not yet a proper middle-class ambition. In an 1846 letter to Louise Colet, Flaubert explained: "During my childhood and youth I had an unbridled passion for the stage. I would perhaps have been a great actor if heaven had caused me to have been born more poor."[18] He was simply not taken seriously as an actor: "Thus even his attempt to make real his derealization becomes derealized" (p. 874). His praxis is stolen.

As a consequence of the frustration of his first vocation, Gustave continues to play a role in order to feel himself real and substantial. He also becomes fixed at an oral level of communication: "he will remain forever alienated to his voice" (p. 877). He writes sounds. The actual meaning of a word is of secondary interest. In this sense he resembles the Giraudoux of *What Is Literature?* He cedes to language the task of meaning.

Forbidden the future of an actor, Gustave becomes an author. He has no choice but to remain a creature of the imagination, for the real belongs to others. He understands that although science is superior to art, he must be an artist because he cannot be a scientist. Gustave falls back on the more accessible career of author because in a sense he is already one. He had begun to write plays when he was eight, although only in order to act them. The passage from actor to author represents an uncomfortable movement away from the social, or identification with others, to secret singularity. The child is thrown back on himself, on his serial individuality. The truth of his terrible solitude reemerges. He becomes a writer in spite of himself; no other choice seems available.

At the beginning literature appears as merely a replacement that is at once urgent and doubtful. The child must flee the derealizing look of others, most especially of his father. In a derealized world Achille-Cléophas is disarmed. The child radically devalues the reality that he is refused and assumes his own lack of reality as a condition of greatness. Gustave makes of the imaginary his supreme value and prides himself on contesting reality and experiencing himself as different, while others remain in the realm of the practical. He comes to realize that literature can meet his needs in a way that acting could not have done. As an author, Gustave continues to derealize himself in a character, as he would have done on the stage, but the character is no longer conceived as a role to interpret and to exteriorize, but rather to interiorize against others. To compensate for his failures and his bored indifference, Gustave invents himself as a sublime superman who laughs in the face of humanity. He also finds that in literature he can obtain the same objectivity he would have sought in the eyes of his audience. At first Gustave tried to surprise himself as the Other that he was for his family and friends through comedy. Now he projects himself into language in order to read himself, to capture himself on the written page. He offers himself as Other to a witness who is really himself.

Sartre supposes that Mallarmé asked himself how one can destroy the world without soiling one's hands.[19] Flaubert was concerned with the same problem and arrived at the same solution as did the poet: one abolishes the world through literary style. The object designated can be made to descend into the word, where it is destroyed. Instead of using words to send the reader to the object designated, Gustave, like the poets described in *What Is Literature?*, focuses on the word itself as object. This subversive use of language is the logical tactic for someone who seeks to disappear entirely into the imaginary: "To choose the sumptuosity of names is already to prefer the universe of the Word to that of things" (p. 934). As he writes and incorporates his fictive superself into his writings, Gustave derealizes himself to an extent that was not possible on the stage.

The decisive conversion to literature occurred between the ages of thirteen and fourteen when Gustave discovered, as he wrote in 1838, that "to write is to take possession of the world" (p. 958). Through literature he learned that he could attempt a counter-creation which would make of him the imaginary equal of God. Literature is an enterprise of both self-possession and self-abolition. Through it one can simultaneously destroy the world and oneself. Gustave understands that his father has in a sense ordered his son's suicide. Out of humility, resentment, and pride Gustave accepts the order, but his very acceptance is used against Achille-Cléophas, forcing the father to recognize that he is a murderer and establishing Gustave as the equal of God: "To disappear is for Gustave to draw the ultimate consequences from the paternal curse in order for it to return against he who pronounced it. It is also *to equate himself with the Creator,* by negating His Work in the person of His witness" (p. 967). The suicidal solution, however, must be found in the imaginary, specifically in literature. There lies the best means to create passively a holocaust of words in which both the author and the world will be destroyed.

Flaubert assumed that the author sacrifices himself in vain so that beauty may exist. For him, literature was an imperative that requires the sacrifice of all. As Flaubert advised Guy de Maupassant in 1878, "For an artist there is but one thing to do: sacrifice all to

Art."[20] Flaubert sees himself as merely the means to the end of beauty. Since under this circumstance Gustave is not his own end but the means to another end, Sartre terms his relationship to literature as one of alienation (p. 975). The artist is conceived as a suicide pilot was destroys himself so that a work of art can come into existence. Gustave did not arrive at this idea on his own but had the help of Alfred Le Poittevin.

Flaubert counted on the friendship of Alfred to compensate for his exile and alienation, but it rather exacerbated them. Alfred was four years Gustave's senior. Between the ages of ten and twenty Flaubert admired Alfred and tried unsuccessfully to imitate him. The friend's most salient trait was his self-destructive mania. He was suicidal and an alcoholic and flirted with a host of other slightly veiled forms of self-destruction. In his youth he seemed to renounce all forms of praxis. The question he asked himself, Sartre reports, was, "How would it be possible to succeed at transcending being without renouncing the immanence of subjectivity?" (p. 1017). This is the familiar ideal of "the for-itself in-itself." Alfred eliminates all action from his life and defines himself against the utilitarian world as "a finality without end" (p. 1018). He is the perfectly useless, superfluous man and thinks of himself as a work of art, a permanent center of derealization. He takes the point of view of death on life which is aestheticism, the conception of art held by the postromantic generation. To become the for-itself/in-itself, one must die to the world of praxis and means and be reborn an inhuman end, an unreal object of beauty.

Gustave sought to imitate Alfred, but the identification could never be complete, because of the relative situations of the Flaubert and Le Poittevin families. Alfred's family has progressed to a more advanced state. For Sartre Alfred is a kind of Hanno Buddenbrook, the decadent, self-destructive aesthete, scion of a bourgeois family that long ago made its money and consolidated its social position. His family has passed the stage of primitive accumulation and gone well beyond the obsessive urge to arrive. The Flaubert family, on the contrary, lives only with the necessary and puts aside the rest of its means with the intention of realizing further social advances which the Le Poittevin family has already achieved. Whereas Alfred learned that he could be an end, Gustave lived in an inferno of means. He was taught to invert the Kantian injunction: "Act in such a way that you treat humanity in your person and in that of the other as a means and never as an end" (p. 1059). He is a means of advancing the family destiny, or he is nothing. Gustave cannot be Alfred because he was not born into the kind of family that was

socially and economically prepared to produce the superfluous man.
A useless work of art, an "in-itself for-itself," he cannot be. Gustave
preserved the ideal, but he cannot be its embodiment, only the
means to its realization. He will be the means to arrive at the
negativity of Alfred. Alfred has taught him to refuse human ends
but not to escape his destiny as a man who can only be a means.

To the intervention of Alfred Sartre attributes Gustave's understanding of himself as an artist rather than a poet. The poet spontaneously exudes superfluous beauty because he is superfluous
beauty. The artist is a far more humble creature. He is not useless
beauty and not a perfect end in himself, but is simply the means to
its realization. As an artist, Gustave will alienate himself totally to
a transcendent end. Since he cannot be beauty, he will make of himself the vehicle of its production.

Richard Ellmann observes aptly that Sartre has created a new
form, "the Gothic biography": "His relentless plumbing of the
mind discovers a chamber of horrors, with distorting mirrors, instruments of self-torture and self-abuse, abasements, refuges, secret
panels, terrible voices that scream to Flaubert, 'You are an idiot,'
as to Genet 'You are a thief'."[21] But it would be even more precise
to term Sartre the father of the "fantastic biography." The bourgeois
imperative absorbed by Flaubert required that he treat himself and
others as means. This idea is a bit of autoplagiarism adapted from
one expressed almost thirty years before. Sartre defined the imperative of the fantastic world of Kafka and Blanchot: "Act in
such a way . . . that you treat the human in yourself and in the
person of others as a means and never as an end."[22] The fantastic
imperative and the bourgeois imperative are one. Sartre has not
created the fantastic biography for the sake of perversity. Rather
the bourgeois, by creating the fantastic world, has forced his hand.
In such a world, as Paul Valéry noted, "The real can only be expressed by the absurd."[23]

At the age of ten the beleaguered Gustave was packed off to the
Collège Royal de Rouen, its halls still haunted by the academic
achievements of his brother Achille who had finished his studies
two years before. Gustave's debilitating family relations follow him
to school, inhibiting his studies and infecting his associations. René
Dumesnil reported that Gustave was a loner at school. For Sartre,
the boy's attitude toward his fellows is more complicated. Although
Gustave does not seem to have had much love for any of his classmates, he heartily appreciated their taste for imitating the extrav-
agances of the romantic protagonists. He also enjoyed a real
popularity and prestige among the other boys. In his correspond-

ence and early writings he sometimes expresses solidarity and sympathy for his mates, whereas on other occasions he says that he was an outsider and was revolted by the stupidity and egotism of the other students. Both hostility and solidarity characterized his relations with his schoolmates. A strange form of gregariousness masked a profound disaffiliation.

The students of the lycée are locked in furious competition for academic prizes. In their school they encounter the world of bourgeois atomism, of the negation of each by all. Every student comes to understand that man is by definition a being who seeks the death of his fellows. At the same time the students, with the exception of Gustave, find a bond in their common hostility to the parents and school authorities who have imposed their hellish circumstances. In terms of the vocabulary of the *Critique,* the boys participate in a group that is simultaneously serial and "a fraternity of terror" (p. 1125). Gustave resembles his fellows in that he understands the group to be a series. He also expresses solidarity with the other boys, but it is a false solidarity, which hides a sadistic trap. The deceit at the heart of this relationship is reflected in the persona Gustave adopted at school, the evil demiurge dressed in motley.

Sometime during the year 1835 Gustave began to play the role of chief organizer of schoolboy pranks at the lycée. This clownish side of his character, which would persist far beyond his school years, Flaubert called "the Garçon." The role is first mentioned in a letter to Ernest Chevalier of March 24, 1837: "When I think of the surprised face of the vice-principal . . . I scream, I laugh. I drink, I sing, ha! ha! ha! ha! ha! ha! and I laugh like the Garçon" (p. 1214). The humor of the Garçon aims at effects that are broad and low. In his pranks the emphasis is heavily on the obscene and the scatological. As he plays the role of the imperfectly housebroken clown, Gustave seeks to personify the lowest depths of vulgarity and to direct the laughter of his school mates, and later the socialites of Paris, at his abased person. For Sartre, this assumed role of self-degradation is indicative, like the early hebetudes, of a primal choice. The new environment and further biographical complications require that the original strategy be implemented in an entirely new form. Again Flaubert tries to sink in order to rise above humanity.

Because his father is a "Prince of Science," his mother of perhaps noble blood, and his brother the most brilliant of students, Gustave is convinced that in the hierarchy of Rouen families represented at the lycée the Flauberts have first place. This institutionalized Flaubert pride must be defended by all family members. In addition, Gustave has a special obligation, for he has been disgraced by his father, and the only way he can neutralize this past humiliation is by achieving success at school. Gustave must win all the prizes. During the hours of recreation the fierce competition ceases for all except the desperate and resentful Gustave: "For the younger Flaubert a student who looks at him is necessarily the aggressor . . . the look is *aggression*" (pp. 1168–1169). In the course of his scholastic wars with his schoolmates, "Gustave suffers a new and incomprehensible alienation, because the competitive serialization forces him into a position of indirect dependance upon others" (p. 1129). In entering the Collège de Rouen, Gustave has entered a world that combines the most nightmarish features of both of Sartre's major philosophical concepts, that of the serialized group in the *Critique* and of the look in *Being and Nothingness*. For the other boys there are moments of respite, but for Gustave no exit is possible.

Although the Flaubert glory and Gustave's early shameful insufficiency require that he excel dramatically, this is going to be difficult. His academic experience can only deepen his sense of inadequacy. Although he is indeed successful at school and wins a fair number of prizes, he does not win all of the prizes, something he would have to do if he were to achieve equality with Achille and meet the requirements imposed by the family honor. His passivity makes academic achievement of the highest level impossible. It facilitates syncretistic thought, Sartre explains, but makes the analytical thought involved in certain disciplines most difficult. Again Gustave finds himself in the same impossible position, stretched incapacitatingly between the two coordinates of his constitution: the despotic patrimony of ambition and passivity. Since he cannot escape either of the two, his only solution is to arrive at a successful synthesis.

Gustave's solution is to become the Garçon, a clown of sadomasochistic temper who will deal both himself and his colleagues a singularly esoteric offense. Since he cannot decisively vanquish his school mates in the classroom, he will have his victory on another terrain. Laughter will be the continuation of the struggle by other means: "He will have the prize for churlishness, the prize for irony, and the prize for blasphemy" (p. 1203). Gustave feels that at school he is mockingly perceived as the odd man out, the other boys somehow understanding his deficiencies and grasping the fact that he is the idiot of the family. He will interiorize their laughter and then reexteriorize it, using it against them as a form of defensive aggression. His strategy will be to exploit his misfortune and to push it to its limits, to display publicly his worthlessness and then turn his unhappiness against his fellow students and the world. As the vulgar class clown, he will simultaneously execute the sentence of Achille-Cléophas and resentfully turn it against all, thus extending universally the personal nullification of which he has been the victim.

Because he cannot succeed academically to the extent that he had hoped, Gustave's solution is to fall beneath comparison. Sartre's Flaubert must be added to the extensive nineteenth-century gallery of underground men, who seek neither to reform nor to cure the world, but to escape by falling beneath its pressures. He admits through his role that he is detestable, but also reveals to his schoolmates that all is ignoble and base. The young comedian sadistically reveals in his person that the individual is comic, not because of his idiosyncracies but rather because of his membership in that irremediably fallen group, the human race. Through his scatological antics Gustave reveals that man is comic, not in his deviation from an accepted social norm, as in the case of Bergson, but in his function as a mirror of humanity in general. The goal of the Garçon is to be a witness to the original and infinite scandal of creation, to personify and convey the transcosmic sneer of the universal nothingness that alone is real. Because his own praxis has been strangled by his upbringing, Gustave will universalize his idiosyncrasy and demonstrate to his friends that all human enterprise is vain and ignoble, that "human praxis vitiated at its foundation by *determination*, is but a consequence of the ontological crime that was Creation" (p. 1191). Self-hatred and misanthropy are synchronized: "man is detestable and the first consequence of this fact is that it is necessary to destroy him everywhere, but first of all in oneself" (p. 1141). He will destroy himself through self-debasing antics, and at the same time he will draw into the general annihilation those with whom he must compete, all of whom represent the unattainable example of Achille. The low pranks of the Garçon are a symbolic holocaust. Suicide, fratricide, and genocide mingle in his laughter.

Sartre's understanding of the humor of the Garçon is borrowed from Georges Bataille's *L'Expérience intérieure*. For Bataille, laughter denounces the human project and is provoked by the consciousness of the radical insufficiency that characterizes the human condition. It is the awareness of "the inanity of the creature that we are."[24] Specific human features and quirks are not comic. Rather the human itself provokes laughter. In a review of Bataille's book, Sartre contrasted Bergson's concept with that of Bataille: "We recognize the laughter of Bataille. It is not the white and inoffensive laughter of Bergson. It is a yellow laughter."[25] That Bataille's concept of the comic is congruent with Flaubert's clear, as shown in an 1854 letter from Flaubert to Louis Colet: "Laughter blends disdain and understanding . . . I love to see humanity and all that it respects debased, mocked, shamed, and hissed."[26]

The relationship of the Garçon to the other boys is described as a system of glances and a system of laughter. Again recalling the vocabulary of *Being and Nothingness,* Sartre writes of the glance of the Garçon as the stare of Medusa (p. 1296). While the boys imagine that they are transforming the Garçon into an object by their derisive looks, it is they who are the victims, they who, with invidious impartiality, are flattened out by the leveling glance. Gustave himself is not the originator of the look. The Garçon is simply the chosen mediator in an infernal continuum of ontological mischief, the transparent lens through which passes the look of the infinite nothingness of the universe, which condemns Gustave, the students of the Collège de Rouen, and all of creation to total absurdity. As the boys laugh, Sartre imagines, the Garçon boasts to himself of his superior sentience. He alone is aware of the humiliating glance of the infinite. This look is modeled on the terrible glance of the chief surgeon, the look that first told Gustave of his personal worthlessness, his personal risibility.

Sartre also sees the relationship of Flaubert and his fellow schoolboys as a system of laughter. In Gustave's philosophy of cosmic *Schadenfreude* there are two laughters: the cosmic and the hypercosmic. In his vulgarity Gustave represents "the enormous uncontrollable laughter of Matter . . . traversed by the infinite, silent, and glacial laughter of Nothingness" (p. 1308). The Garçon gleefully turns the boys' laughter against them and exploits it for his own sadistic ends. Their mirth is the indication that they, no less than he, reflect the nothingness of man and the degraded character of matter and human needs and desires. Gustave has been told that he is an ugly smudge on the Flaubert glory. He compensates by informing the boys of Rouen that they are laughable imperfections before the cruel glance and laughter of the negative infinite. Thus Gustave, if only in his imagination, gains control of his malady and exploits it as a weapon against his oppressors.

The influence of his father has possessed Gustave of a demiurgic temptation to aspire to a sovereign intelligence and efficacity. Through the role of the Garçon and then by imagining a space between himself and the role, he succeeds in imitating his father's position: "At the moment that they devour him and enjoy his atrocious suffering, the martyr, without abandoning his body that is lying in the dust, does not hesitate to slip into the skin of the absent-minded emperor who leans toward the arena and looks without seeing at the last palpitations of this mutilated flesh. Thus the little boy can assure himself that his pain and his death will be disqualified" (p. 1177). The little martyr rises above his tormentors and his martyrdom. Sartre calls this thinking "the Cogito of Nothingness," which holds that "I am nothing, therefore I am" (p. 1177).

After resorting to a perverted version of Descartes, Sartre turns to a blackened Hegelian terminology. Gustave is nothingness, as are his schoolmates, but he is gloriously unique in that he alone is a physically incarnate universal nothingness that is conscious of itself. Since the child cannot imitate in a positive sense the sovereign intelligence of his father, he will do so negatively. As an example of Flaubert's contemptuous perspective, Sartre mentions the description of Emma and Leon traveling through Rouen in a coach. As the two make love in the vehicle, Flaubert the novelist focuses in a wry spirit on the comically erratic external movement of the coach: "The lovers and their embrace have been transformed into a bewitched object: a perfectly inert, hermetically closed black box on four wheels" (p. 1277). Human life is seen as comically senseless, a temporary madness within the world of the inorganic. Flaubert deliberately chooses exterior views of human relations because he has disassociated himself from the human species and allied himself with the negative infinite which glances down scornfully on the comically pathetic actions of the human race. In 1853 he wrote to Louis Colet: "The only way to live in peace is to place oneself with one jump above all of humanity and to have with it nothing in common but eye contact."[27]

Besides the satisfactions of revenge and glory, the persona of the Garçon meets another of Gustave's needs. He must play a role, must grasp himself as objectified by others in order to have a feeling that he exists in a concrete fashion: "Flaubert, dominated by the Other, can only recognize himself in his being for others" (p. 1243). He must make of himself the object of the glance of an impenetrable and sovereign freedom that is not his own. As the Garçon, Flaubert can again capture himself in the eyes of the Other. The glorious days of the child actor are revived.

This role was made possible by the conditions at the school in Rouen, where in the spring of 1831, a year before Gustave was to enter the school, an extraordinary series of events occurred. Although the recent revolution had supposedly separated church and state, the children arrived at school in the fall of 1830 to discover that in their state-supported institution they would still be obliged to go to confession. They sensed that the revolution of their wealthy bourgeois fathers against the rule of Charles X had been betrayed. One student, a political genius named Clouet, per-

suades a few of his fellows to confront the administration with the
disturbing inconsistency by refusing to confess. If students who do
so are expelled, the school officials will be admitting publicly that
freedom of religion does not exist. Eventually the whole student
body expresses solidarity with the refusal of Clouet. The school
authorities are bombarded with insults and eggs. Finally the national
guard is called in to quell the insurrection. Sartre's description of
the schoolboy revolt is the sunniest passage of a grim book. He exults
in the atmosphere of the uprising, his style invigorated by the an-
archic festivities. "What a bash!" he exclaims gleefully, "Power to
the kids!" (p. 1335). For him, it is an ideal insurrection, for it reveals
that power is vulnerable when unjust.

On March 10, 1831, the authorities close the school for the year,
and the children are returned to their families. Expecting to be
welcomed as heroes, the boys are astonished to discover that their
parents have a low opinion of their little revolution. They thought
that they had been fighting for the new rights of their parents, won
in the July Revolution. Instead they learned that their parents were
in fact their enemies. The authorities had returned the students to
their homes for reprogramming, and the parents worked to sunder
the spontaneously achieved revolutionary solidarity. This is the
same experience that Sartre described in *The Words*.

It was in the parents' interest to discredit actions that otherwise
seemed consistent with their own ideology, Sartre explains, because
at the time events such as the insurrection at Lyons and the revolt
at Santo Domingo had thrown a scare into the bourgeoisie. Because they felt their power to be threatened by the dispossessed,
they allied themselves with the interests of the reaction and established a sacred union with the monarchists. The schoolboy
revolution seemed threatening because it communicated the unsettling fact that a revolutionary order, controlled by the oppressed,
was a real possibility. Both parents and children considered each
other to be traitors: "The blackguard Moseses of the bourgeoisie"
(p. 1343) had betrayed their revolution and their children.

The next fall Gustave enters the lycée. Instead of a crowd of
desperate revolutionaries insisting on their rights, he finds the
dispirited victims of a counterrevolution. The former agitators are
in a profoundly ambivalent mood. They perceive the deceit of
their parents but now understand as well that they are themselves
representatives of a specific class and not the fighters for the freedom
of all men that they had taken themselves to be a few months
earlier. They have come to understand and to accept the maxim
of bourgeois alienation: "act in such a manner that you sacrifice

in yourself the man to the owner, that is to say, to the thing possessed" (p. 1350). Each student now grasps that having defines
his being. Each, with the exception of Gustave, understands that
he himself lives in order to inherit and to squash the worker. The
fraternity of man that they sought to implement the year before
now appears as an impossibility, for man is understood to be the
enemy of man. The bourgeois is allied with the aristocrats against
the worker. The schoolboys feel that they have no alternative but
to embrace the world of their fathers.

At the same time they feel shame, for the bourgeois children have
discovered their class affiliation to be a shameful disease. However
much they would like to, they cannot hate their fathers. They no
longer have the concrete and altruistic historical purpose that unified
them the year before, but now must fall into the jungle of bourgeois
atomism. This mentality, according to Sartre, is behind the so-called
second *mal du siècle,* the ennui of the postromantic generation. The
failure of the revolution of 1830 has disillusioned them as to the
efficacy of political action, convincing them that it is inevitably
unsuccessful, for the enemy is within as well as without.

The students continue their disruptive behavior, but it now has
a quite different character and purpose. Their disrespectful antics
take the form of gratuitous violence. Gustave completely misunder-
stands the pranks of his colleagues. Because he is focused on his
own internal difficulties, he does not grasp the specific historical
roots of his schoolmates' low rodomontade. He perceives their unhappiness without reference to the concrete situation, understanding
it as a manifestation of the universal animosity of each against all
which is at the root of human relations. He has no sympathy with
their historical problem because he considers himself an aristocrat,
exempt from the special problems of the bourgeoisie.

The boys first take refuge from their difficulties in romantic literature. Their group in fusion has been shattered, and bourgeois atomism is on the verge of making a final claim on their lives. The young
monads take flight into symbolic satisfactions of the imaginary and
there nurse their anger at being deprived of their praxis. Romantic
literature provides satisfaction on a number of levels. The romantic
author requires the reader to allow himself to be passively absorbed
by his extravagant fantasies. As the boys give in and relinquish their
freedom, they experience the crushing of the dreamer by the dream.
Sartre explains that in this kind of literature, "the novelistic object
is the iron necessity that imposes itself upon their freedom and forces
them to produce the dream of another in a preestablished order" (p.
1378). This reading experience is just what the crushed student

revolutionaries are seeking, in order to find their contradiction justified: "They ask that their fundamental freedom, and the impotence to which the counterrevolution of the fathers reduced them both be valorized" (p. 1379). The romantic work glorifies passivity, as does all poetry and submission to the imaginary. As the ideal romantic reader reads, he collaborates with the author and accepts the inert role that is offered him. The boys see themselves in the romantic protagonists, who themselves are less acting than acted upon. Of Hernani, for example, Sartre explains that he is not the author of his destiny; rather, the will of another—his dead father—prescribed his fate (p. 1382). As the students identify with these glorious figures, they at once contest their mediocre bourgeois destiny and accept it. "Reading is the murder of the father" (p. 1386), but at the same time it is an admission that father is right and that they have been vanquished. In their reading the boys revindicate their right to say no to the bourgeoisie, but as their nay-saying takes place purely in the imaginary, it becomes ineffectual and masks an acquiescence to the will of the genitors.

The young bourgeois eventually discover that they have been the victims of a mystification, since the protagonists with whom they have identified in fact totally condemn the class to which they belong. It dawns on them as they read *Chatterton* for example, that the character with whom they have been empathizing is an aristocrat. They are constitutionally unable to be Chatterton, whom Sartre irreverently tags as "le *desdichado* numéro 1" (p. 1402). The message of *Chatterton,* or *Hernani,* whose bandit protagonist is eventually revealed to be the aristocrat Jean d'Aragon, is that the bourgeois is damned by nature. Instead of aristocratic romantic heroes, the boys of Rouen can only be John Bell, the bourgeois whose role is to persecute the poet and oppress the worker. When they discover that they have been tricked, the students become disgusted with themselves and disillusioned with their hypnotic absorption in romantic literature. Realizing that they cannot escape their class, they reluctantly accept their destiny as bourgeois drones. Their attempt to betray class affiliation through imaginary flight has been thwarted. They hold themselves in horror and, out of spite, say that nothing is beautiful, good, or true. The romantic ideals resist their embrace because they were not born into the class which has a monopoly on them.

At this moment, Sartre claims, postromanticism is born. Revenge will be sought against the fathers who have imposed their bourgeois destiny, against the romantics who made of them silly, passive dupes, and against the nobility, which declares that their birth damns them to social and spiritual nothingness. Where young Clouet believed that a transformation of human relations was a realizable ideal, those who were squashed by the counterrevolution and their younger brothers believe that man is an impostor. Man is not perfectible, as Clouet had thought. Demoralized, they become demoralizers. They seek to "mineralize their lives and push negation to the point of a radical self-destruction" (p. 1428), in short, to adopt the ideal of distinction. Between 1831 and 1835 the students engage in a series of violent pranks, thumbing their noses to authority, to their prefabricated existence, and their class. Their antiauthoritarian antics, however, mask their resignation. As Sartre quotes Camus, "To refuse all and to accept all are one and the same thing" (p. 1432). Because of their fathers' power and their own irreversible programming as bourgeois, an effective revolution is impossible. Yet the fact remains that they hate themselves and must seek an escape. Since the path through identification with the romantic heroes has been barred, they instead create a world of gratuitous scandals devoid of historical purpose. In short, they escape into the imaginary; that is, in a roundabout and noisy manner they shamefully accept the world of the bourgeois as their own.

Gustave reads romantic literature quite differently. Instead of viewing these works as escapes from the world of the middle class, he finds in them a revolt against an offending creation and a scorn for man in general. He is not disturbed to discover that these heroes are aristocrats, for he recognizes the protagonists as his social equals. The romantic hero provides him with a true mirror of himself, while it offers only a fraudulent self-image to the veterans of the school revolt. Whereas Gustave reads romantic works in order to compensate for an individual failure, the other boys read to compensate for a collective and historical failure. Thus Gustave is quite satisfied with what he finds in the works; the other boys are not. The interests of Gustave and of his fellow students come together, however, at a common rallying ground, an acceptance of failure. All find grandeur in their disgust with themselves and with all of existence.

In the Garçon the boys discover a solution to their dilemma. Revolt through laughter replaces revolt via the dream. This is the final depressing phase of the revolt begun by Clouet. The boy's demoralizing failures have made them laughable in their own eyes. Their actions and intentions have been stolen by their bourgeois heritage. Thus they logically gravitate to the comic, which Sartre redefines by drawing upon Marx's idea of stolen praxis: "The human being first affirms himself in his action as sovereign, with the conviction that he is acting upon the world and governing his life.

Chance then intervenes and denounces this illusion. The world is
allergic to man. The comic makes of us witnesses of a procedure of
rejection" (p. 1439). If chance reigns, then man is morally liquidated,
his praxis stolen. Bergson's theory is defective for Sartre because
it does not account for the distinction between the laughable and
the comic. The mirth of Bergson is spontaneous laughter which
denounces the particular individual who takes himself seriously
and has no justification for doing so. Laughter provoked by the
comic, on the contrary, is an epiphany that reveals the ultimate
secret of things: all men are subhuman, since praxis defines humanity, and praxis is precisely what men are without. In the pranks
organized by Gustave the pupils discover the impossibility of being
free men and the necessity to accept the world of stolen praxis that
their bourgeois families impose.

The Garçon is born of a misunderstanding. Unlike his fellows,
Gustave is proud of his birth. He believes himself to be something
of an aristocrat, for he is the son of a noble mother and a Prince of
Science—recalling Rimbaud's line "Science, the new nobility!"[28]
He incarnates the comic in order to gain the position of leadership
he could not achieve in the classroom, to demoralize his comrades,
and to distance himself from his martyred childhood. The boys'
laughter, however, does not demoralize them as the sadistic Gustave
had hoped. Instead it reassures them, because it functions as a
catharsis to purge them of their unease. After their laughter, repre-
senting their imaginary parricide, their ridicule both of romanticism
and of bourgeois vulgarity, they are able to return to the task of
living out their destinies as provincial bourgeois.

Their laughter is the ignominious last gasp of the revolution of
1831. At the time it is a desperate refusal of the bourgeois condition,
but ultimately it is a consent to being assimilated by the hated class.
Laughter becomes an alibi. In 1831 Clouet had been expelled for
fighting for freedom and for the advent of a new kind of human
relations. At the beginning of the academic year 1839 Gustave and
two classmates are tossed out of the school for their gratuitous
persecution of a man named Bezout, a substitute teacher of philosophy. At this moment, Sartre writes, "Postromanticism begins.
These children accept the bourgeois adventure. The socially recuperated Melmouth joins forces with Joseph Prudhomme. He
[postromantic man] will live like everyone else, all the while feeling
that he is worth more than his life, and escaping abjection with the
aid of a constant and imponderable irony, and a sustained self-
disgust" (p. 1463). The destiny of this generation will be to snuff
out the popular revolt of 1848. This section of L'Idiot must be read,

not as an attempt accurately to describe what occurred at the college of Rouen, but as an attempt to create a myth to explain the origins of postromanticism in France.

After passing the *baccalauréat* in August 1840, Gustave found himself in a difficult position. His niece reports that the happy moment of graduation was spoiled by the question of choosing a profession. Realizing that his son could never become a great physician, Achille-Cléophas decides that a career in law would be most suitable. Gustave is terrified, for he had thought somehow that he was above the caste into which his father now tries to insert him. The abyss of the hated bourgeoisie yawns at his feet. His passive constitution makes it impossible for him to contest his father's will. He accepts that his father is right, but only on condition that it can be proved that the son is not a literary genius, a classless superman who sneers down contemptuously upon the entire race. Gustave understands that he has a choice of either proving that he is such a glorious figure or accepting his father's solution as the only valid one.

Between 1838 and 1842 Gustave's life revolves around the problem of creation of the saving masterpiece. He puts off as long as possible an acquiescence to his father's de facto statement that he is no more than a bourgeois, that he is not the equal of Achille, and that he has failed the family glory. In the works that he writes during this period Gustave incarnates himself as an evil artistic genius whose task it is to demoralize man. One of the great questions for him at this time is how, through literature, to flee from the class that is threatening to engulf him. Since he is not born an aristocrat, he cannot escape to the class above and be the "poet," the person who *is* beauty and produces it spontaneously as he lives and breathes. His only alternative is to escape categorically from all social affiliations. He will do so by becoming the "artist," the person who is the means to the production of a transcendent, inhuman end.

In order to escape bourgeois alienation, Flaubert will throw himself into an alienation of a more profound variety which will at the same time valorize and destroy him. By becoming the tool of beauty, he will become the means of a classless, atemporal end. While achieving the beautiful through hard, disciplined work, his subjectivity will be extinguished. The man is subordinated to the product he creates; the artist is a mere living appendage of the work of art. Literature, as conceived by Flaubert, is an alienated product of labor after Marx's model. It is a sacrifice of life, a labor of mortification, a subordination of self to an alien power. Thus is explained Flaubert's ideal of impersonality. To the extent that he absents himself from his creation, he succeeds in becoming a means in the humble service of an inhuman end: Gustave "has escaped from his *finite* alienation by alienating himself to the infinite" (p. 1566). Writing, Foucault has written, "is now linked to sacrifice and to the sacrifice of life itself . . . Where a work had the duty of creating immortality, it now attains the right to kill, to become the murderer of its author."[29] Sartre shows how and why Flaubert is at the origin of this tradition.

During these years Gustave discovers that beauty can be an arm of aggression. In his works he plays the role of a self-hating and misanthropic evil genius who reveals that the world is hell. By demonstrating his scorn for the human race, the imaginary demiurge expresses contempt for himself and resentful hatred for his tormentors and his competitors for social glory. The means he employs is the creation of the beautiful work of art. Through beauty, as Flaubert understands it, one experiences the world in the grip of a cruel necessity. Because of his upbringing Flaubert feels that the world is a perfectly organized system of evil that has irrevocably done him in. By creating beautiful works, he communicates to others that they too are the victims of an incapacitating necessity. As does the comic, beauty shames and dehumanizes, for it declares that praxis is an illusion, that all of existence is in the grip of a terrible necessity: "Beauty demands universal suffering" (p. 1578). The end of literature is to broadcast to the entire species the cosmic bad news that man is an impossibility, and to infect the reader with a stupefying pessimism. By creating a beautiful work, Flaubert, like Genet, will turn the tables on his oppressors. "He will install himself in them *as the other,* by imposing on them the duty of grasping *their* world through the vision of another. In short, he will do to them what they had done to him" (p. 1589).

Here Sartre shows himself to be in disagreement with Marxist writers on aesthetics such as Ernst Bloch, Marcuse, and Adorno who, although they are aware of the ideological content of a work, also find in a work that achieves formal perfection a "cultural surplus" which causes it to rise above its links with a ruling class ethos. Bourgeois art is not always simply reflective of the aspirations of the class, for beauty points to an alternative world that stands opposed to the one in which it takes form. The determinisms of an age are always conserved but can be surpassed at the same moment as well. Where Bloch and Marcuse would find a glimmer of utopia in closed, perfect forms that pretend to abolish the role of chance, Sartre finds only the confirmation of the dominant consciousness. Sartre is by no means simply aligning himself with the predominant orthodoxy of Marxist aesthetics. A literature exists that does not just mirror the prevailing relations of production. But the aesthetic form of Flaubert contains no protest against these relations, no moment of transcendence of the unfreedom that prevails in his milieu and personal life.

The hoped-for masterpiece does not at first materialize. Gustave understands that his father is right, that his destiny is to be a lawyer or a notary. In the fall of 1841 he buys his books and enrolls to study law in Paris, thus officially inscribing himself into the class from which he had long thought to have escaped. Sartre imagines that Gustave found it terribly difficult to concentrate on his studies for in his law books he read of a future that was repellent to his aspirations. On one level he seeks to succeed because of the family pride that haunts him, but this same pride tells him that this future and this discipline are beneath his essentially noble soul and supernatural ambitions.

In August 1842 Gustave fails his first-year law exams. He passes on the second try, but in August 1843 he fails the second year. That fall he returns to Paris, planning to retake the exams in February, but makes virtually no preparations. In January 1844, while visiting his family in Rouen, disaster impends. It is clear to him that he cannot pass the exam, and even if he could, success would lead only to social death. As Sartre explains it, using some of Gustave's own words, "Something quite tragic takes place in the box of his skull" (p. 1766).[30] A powerful and occult countermeasure will be required to save his future.

Gustave now discovers a new and more radical escape through a fall into the subhuman. One evening in January, when he and Achille are returning from Deauville in a cabriolet, with Gustave driving, suddenly he "drops the reins and falls to the feet of his astounded brother" (p. 1767). The diagnosis of epilepsy made by some of Flaubert's contemporaries is acceptable to Sartre only if psychological factors are recognized as the cause. He explains Flaubert's fits on several levels. First the illness is a justification for sequestering himself indefinitely with his family and escaping the career of law and a bourgeois future. The illness is also an act of temporization with a double purpose. A solution to his difficulties can be reached only with the death of the father or of the son. Through his malady, Gustave declares himself provisionally dead. It is a state of hibernation that will end with the death of Achille-Cléophas. "I am awaiting the death of my father" (p. 1674), Gustave seems to say to himself in a tightly censored manner.

The illness in fact receded considerably after the death of

Achille-Cléophas in 1846. To Ernest Chevalier Gustave wrote: "It's been two weeks since it all ended [death of his father]. I am beset, and beseiged on all sides . . . I had to do a lot of haggling over the affairs of Achille. . . . I took charge of the business. In all of this my nerves were so horribly shaken that I no longer am conscious of them. Perhaps I am cured. Perhaps it has had the effect of a cauterization that removes a wart." Also in 1846 he speaks in the past of "the nervous illness that lasted two years" (p. 1797). The death of his father, according to Sartre, thus allows the young man to cure himself. Clearly, at least, the nervous problems lessened after January 1846, and Gustave felt a sense of relief after the death of Achille-Cléophas. In October 1846 he wrote to Louis Colet: "Since the deaths of my father and my sister I no longer have any ambition. They have taken away my vanity in their shrouds . . . Success doesn't tempt me. What does tempt me is the success I give myself, my own approval, and I will perhaps end up dispensing with that, just as I should have dispensed with the approval of the others."[31]

The fall is also a continuation of the strategy of the Garçon and the hebetudes of early childhood. The nervous malady is an attempt to fall below culture, to return to the plentitude of matter, to inhuman nature through the destruction of the trappings of culture. Gustave had wanted to soar above the bourgeoisie, but he felt that he did not have the requisite genius. Through a travesty of innocence he now seeks a dispensation from the pressure that class and culture impose. He discovers that his only alternative is to radicalize his insufficiency and turn it to his advantage. The only solution is to become the idiot of the family. In short, his epilepsy is an act of self-caricature. His father had condemned him to death for disgracing the family glory. Obediently, Gustave dies. By provisionally dehumanizing himself, he realizes his old dream of becoming completely imaginary.

"The super-ego is our god, enemy; and suicide (or any self-defeat) is our obedience and revenge."[32] These words by Norman O. Brown apply to the case of Flaubert. If his "affective" epilepsy is an act of obedience, it is also one of disobedience. Achille-Cléophas is both a demon victorious and a demon overcome. By dropping out of the human race, Gustave throws off the power of his father and superego. The demand to excel cannot be issued to a vegetable. The terrible power of the *pater familias* has been neutralized. Through his fits, Sartre speculates, Gustave was also saying to his father, "Look at what you have made of me." Unloved children are prone to injure themselves in order to evoke the love and pity that has been denied them. Gustave submits to the imposed destiny and pushes it to its limits in order to demonstrate to his father the damage he has done, hoping that he too will die of shame. The malady is thus both an imaginary suicide and an imaginary murder of the father whose demise he awaits. But the victory is false, for in effect he has only radicalized his father's authority by dooming himself to actual ineffectuality in order to gain illusory freedom.

The psychological crisis of January 1844 nevertheless marks, according to Sartre, Flaubert's conversion to optimism. He can indeed become a literary genius, but only after the death of his father, and only on the condition that he fall completely into the subhuman and the imaginary. During the nervous collapse of 1844 Gustave converts to an optimism that feeds on the blackest pessimism.

As a consequence of his conversion, Gustave throws himself into long and taxing literary projects. His labor, like that described by Marx, is neither spontaneous nor free but takes on a frozen, compulsive character. His passivity makes of his work an unbearable *pensum*, but he endures it, for to suffer is to gain. Gustave works expressly in order to suffer. He develops a negative theology consistent wtih the philosophy of "loser wins": "God exists because he does not exist" (p. 2014). Only on the condition of completely despairing of God's existence will the deity appear and justify his life and labors. Literary work can earn him divine grace, but only if he suffers terribly and abandons any hope of reward or recognition.

Although Gustave's thinking is such after the crisis of 1844, the true meaning of the conversion is not directly revealed until the 1875 writing of "The Legend of Saint Julian the Hospitaler." For Sartre this is the moment of Gustave's greatest lucidity. In 1875 the family of Flaubert's niece seemed to be headed for financial catastrophe. The unearned income of the family that permitted Flaubert to live the life of a gentleman at Croisset was threatened. Because Flaubert was a landowner, his essence lay outside of himself, in the hands of others, and this alienation now threatens his career as a writer. In order to work effectively, Flaubert needed his refuge at Croisset, for it was to him the point of view of death on life, the physical "analogon" of the aesthetic distance required by the demiurgic creator to separate him from the world he slanders. Adorno maintained that subjective inwardness arose historically from the mentality of the landowner who maintained an isolated outpost largely unsullied by contact with the productive process.[33] Flaubert's relation with his country home must be seen in this way. Physical detachment was one condition of his genius. Because Croisset seemed lost, Sartre speculates, Flaubert decides to punctuate his career in letters by revealing all in "Saint Julian." He will finally disclose the true character of his relationship with the programmer of his childhood.

The plot of the story is set in motion by Julian's taste for the gratuitous slaughter of wildlife. Sartre finds here Gustave's misanthropic fury, his desire to destroy all men, Achille-Cléophas most especially. A stag wounded by the young hunter predicts to him in a human voice that he will be responsible for the deaths of his parents. After this encounter Julian returns home and is stricken by a strange, immobilizing illness, a malady analogous to the hysterical epilepsy of Flaubert. The illness is a manifestation of the guilt that he feels over the murder in his heart. In order to flee himself and his guilt, Julian takes leave of the family home and resolves to hunt no more, for the fate of his parents seems to hang on his abstention. One night, however, Julian cedes to his passion for carnage, and the lapse results in his inadvertent murder of his parents.

In this tale, as Sartre explains it, Flaubert reveals the origin of his 1844 crisis as the sudden, guilt-filled understanding that he wishes to kill the man who has forced him into an impossible situation. Because of the pure life he leads in penance for his crime, Julian eventually not only gains salvation but becomes a saint. It is precisely because he has killed his father that Julian becomes Saint Julian. The climax of the tale occurs when he kisses the mouth of a leper, at which moment he is transfigured. Like Gustave, Julian degrades himself to the final degree so that he may gain glory. Like Gustave, he plays and wins at the game of "loser wins." Sartre thus enters Flaubert into the history of the concept of decadence. The precondition of fertility is destruction, sickness, impotence, and death.

Gustave can become a genius only after the death of Achille-Cléophas. To become a literary giant, Gustave must die to the world, Sartre asserts, repeating an argument made before him by Jean Bruneau.[34] To enter literature one must have lost all, for to derealize the world one must be totally derealized oneself. Gustave understood that he could not be a literary genius, not because he was mediocre, but because the neutral, impersonal, and totally free creator cannot be suffocated by determinisms. He must be affectless, deracinated. After January 1844 Gustave cuts himself adrift from the aegis of paternal authority. Flaubert at this point is no longer a human being. He has surpassed his confinement to the personal aspects of his particular existence. Thus he is in a position to gain the requisite transcendent perspective, to be nothing but an eye, a speaking gaze. The derealized writer is free to perceive people from the point of view of the inhuman.

Gustave discovers a variety of tactics of derealization, all of which are subsumed under the Russian formalist critic Viktor Shklovsky's term "defamiliarization."[35] Two related means of defamiliarizing the real are to dehumanize the human and to humanize the inhuman. An illustration of the first case is the comically crazed coach in *Madame Bovary*. An instance of the second is the description of the hat of Charles Bovary. In order to derealize the real the human must appear as the inhuman and vice versa. Sartre has always been fascinated with these transformations, as witness his baroque description of the world of the poetry of Francis Ponge: "look at the stone, it is alive. Look at life, it is a stone."[36] Another of Gustave's tactics of derealization is an obsessive attention to detail, which Sartre calls *"l'observation imaginarisante"* (p. 1951). The revelation of more characteristics of the object than ordinary observation would notice results in the detailed derealization of the object. To achieve the total derealization of the world, it is necessary for Flaubert to write works with banal, contemporary settings instead of science fiction, because his black pantheism pushes him to demonstrate that the universal nothingness is present in every detail of the most prosaic of objects.

Gustave also saps the reality from words, another technique of defamiliarization. Sartre, who remarked in *What Is Literature?* that the poet is outside of language, makes the same claim for Flaubert. Flaubert derealizes language by stressing its nonsignifying components, the sound and the plastic beauty of the word, at the expense of what it refers to. He subordinates the informative function of language and dwells on its materiality. For Gustave, literary language is "a language without men" (p. 1978).

Sartre's comments on Flaubert's derealizing literary techniques imply a criticism of subsequent literature, for all of the devices that he finds in Flaubert have been found, by one critic or another, to characterize most of modernist literature. For example, the idea of the inhumanly anafective creator appears in Joyce, who in *The Portrait of the Artist* refers to the author as being "like the God of creation . . . beyond or above his handiwork, invisible, refined out of existence, indifferent, paring his fingernails."[37] Maurice Nadeau describes the aspirations of the narrator in Claude Ollier's *La Mise en scène:* "He wants to be, and is, a pure look."[38] Ortega y Gasset has complained about the "infrarealism," or preternaturally sharp delineation of objects, in twentieth century authors.[39] Peter Löffler defines one of the major themes in the modern drama as "a tendency to transform the human into the inorganic and a tendency to transform the objective into the organic."[40] The "theatricalization of language" is an axiom of twentieth century aesthetics. "I have put the language to sleep," Joyce announced to Beckett, which is explained by Harry Levin as meaning that words are "intended to produce an effect without presenting a picture."[41] In the twentieth century the focus on the sensuous qualities of the word at the expense of its signifying function has gained a political justification. The writers affiliated with the journal *Tel Quel*, for example, include in the defiance of society a defiance of any use of language that smacks of the utilitarian. Sartre would consider this grand refusal to constitute another rat trap. These authors hand over to the opposition one of the few tools a person has to free himself. The superficial illusion of liberty gained through this use of language masks a profound acceptance of domination.

Flaubert, like Genet, began his days as the object of the look of the Other. Flaubert, again like Genet, must recuperate his lost subjectivity by becoming an alienating glance. In the "Legend of St. Julian" he retaliates. Since the title of the story shows that Julian will become a saint, of which the reader is aware in advance, from the point of view of the narrator that celestial destiny has already been realized. Here the point of view of the artist coincides with that of God: both look down on Julian from on high. Whereas earlier the unbelieving Flaubert could not oppose the glance of God to the glance of the oppressing Other, now, because of the philosophy of the "loser wins," things have changed. God appears when all hope of him has been extinguished: "He will live from now on beneath a Gaze. But *only on the condition that he is unaware* of it" (p. 2126). Victimized by the Other, Gustave takes his revenge by opposing to his oppressors the glance of a God whose existence he cannot recognize, in order that he himself may be surreptitiously recognized by God. He performs the tasks that this God requires of him: to be a witness to his own utter abjection and that of all humanity, to communicate the truth that evil reigns on earth, and to relinquish any hope of divine justification.

The philosophy of "loser wins" and its concomitant negative, infralapsarian theology is not appearing for the first time in *L'Idiot.* Flaubert's strategy is identical with that of Goetz: "I will lower myself beneath all, and you, Lord, you will take me in the nets of your night and raise me above them."[42] This idea perhaps owes something to Alfred Adler's concept of the self-punishing hero of suffering, whose humiliation gains him a stature that would not otherwise be available and permits him indirectly to dominate those who may appear to dominate him. The idea also seems to have been touched by Karl Jaspers' concept of "foundering," which maintains that it is in the situation of utter ruin and despair that one perceives not the absence but the existence of transcendence. God appears to man at the moment of the complete collapse of his earthly resources. Foundering is a conversion experience that brings a person at once from the depths of pessimism to the heights of optimism, an optimism that feeds on his very pessimism and total ineffectuality. The recognition of complete failure becomes the source of spiritual strength. Sartre has commented on Jasper's idea in his essay on Bataille in connection with the philosophy of the "loser wins," and again in the *Critique* where he describes the philosophy as a particular temptation of the bourgeois who is uneasily suspended between Christian faith and positivism—which is exactly the case of Flaubert.[43]

Sartre's description of Flaubert's nervous disorder partakes of two traditions of psychoanalysis, Freud's and the antipsychiatrists'. There are a number of striking parallels between his description of the "epilepsy" of Flaubert and the epilepsy of Dostoevsky as analyzed by Freud in "Dostoevsky and Parricide."[44] For Freud, as for Sartre, a neurosis is the consequence of failure to synthesize two conflicting components of one's character. In Flaubert's case the conflict is between his passive constitution and the demands of the family glory. Dostoevsky's conflict was different. Though he called himself simply an epileptic, Freud notes, his disorder was probably an hystereo-epilepsy.

Epilepsy is not a single clinical entity but can be a functional as well as an organic disease. There is an organic and an "affective" epilepsy, which is the externalization of a profound disruption of the psyche. Dostoevsky's neurosis, like Flaubert's, took on the physical symptoms of epileptic seizures. Freud surmises that the initial appearance of the malady might have been due to a sudden scare, as was Gustave's, but that it was subsequently exploited for psychological ends. He sees the Russian novelist's youthful tendencies to lethargy and somnolent states as prophetic of his later epilepsy. Similarly Sartre found in Gustave's passive stupors the same project that was behind the seizures of 1844–1846.

For Freud, attacks of hystereo-epilepsy represent a desire to identify with a dead person, either with someone who is already dead or with someone whose death is desired. Dostoevsky's first seizure occurred in his eighteenth year, after the murder of his father, and his epilepsy is said to be the expression of a deeply ambivalent attitude toward the dead father. It is evidence at once of an admiration for his father, for it signals a desire to identify with him, of a desire to see him dead, and of a hope to die himself. Epilepsy is a sado-masochistic strategy, combining imaginary parricide and guilt-caused suicide. Not until the end of his career, in *The Brothers Karamazov*, did Dostoevsky find the courage to confront publicly and privately the problem of parricide.

On the whole, Sartre's view of epilepsy is so close to Freud's as to suggest an unacknowledged source. In 1959 Sartre prepared an eight-hundred page film script of Freud's life and work for John Houston, and the Dostoevsky essay would have been of special interest to him because of his own announced intention to write a biography of Dostoevsky.

Sartre's thought converges at a number of points with the views of the antipsychiatrists and diverges at others. The major theme of the early work of R. D. Laing is a demonstration of the fact that what is usually termed madness is a strategy adopted by people enclosed in a threateningly social milieu from which there is no apparent escape. Insanity is making the best of a disastrous situation; it is the rationality of those who are forced into impossible conditions. "Everyone," Laing argues, "who has made a close study of the families of schizophrenics appears to agree that much, or even all, the apparent irrationality of the individual finds its rationality in the original family context."[45]

One of Sartre's tasks in *L'Idiot* is to demonstrate that Gustave's malady was of this very sort. In the face of an unlivable situation Gustave found that self-derealization was his only possibility. Sartre takes pains to make clear that Flaubert's behavior was not irrational and inappropriate but on the contrary was a reasonable and appropriate means of coping with his situation. Although Sartre considers that *L'Idiot* is a work of antipsychiatry, he did not need the work of Laing and Cooper to bring him to an understanding of mental illness as caused by the nexus of other persons who constitute one's world, for this concept is already fully operational in *Saint Genet*.

Sartre differs from Laing and Cooper, however, in his view of the family. The antipsychiatrists abstract it from the social context, while Sartre stresses the fact that the family is a mediating institution and can be changed for the better only after the means of production have been altered. Laing glorifies the imagined break with an oppressive reality as the moment of cure. Whereas Sartre sympathetically understands that circumstances are sometimes such that only an imaginary solution is possible, he realizes that such a remedy is a false one and will only ensure that the individual never escapes from the forces that ensnare his mind.

VI

Flaubert and the Objective Neurosis

We are all clowns and charlatans. Bunk and pretension
are everywhere!

Flaubert

I
n the course of her adventures on the other side of the looking
glass, Alice is astounded to make the acquaintance of a unicorn.
No less amazed is the unicorn to encounter Alice, who is for him
the impossible representative of an imaginary race. "Well, now that
we *have* seen each other," offers the unicorn, "if you'll believe in
me, I'll believe in you. Is that a bargain?"[1] The pact that Flaubert
and Second Empire France tacitly strike between them is exactly
parallel. Two imaginary creatures begin a friendship founded upon
a mutual agreement to affirm the suspect reality of the other. Flaubert discovered in the hallucinating world of Louis Napoleon a
society in which he could feel at home, one that confirmed and
honored his flight into illusion. This empire of dreams reciprocally
recognized in Flaubert its special author, the writer whose works
most perfectly mirrored its "reality," the artist who most skillfully
allowed it to continue undisturbed in its headlong flight from its
spiny truth. The mechanics of this providential encounter are the
subject of the third, and most amazing, volume of *L'Idiot de la
famille.*

"Men make their own history," Marx observed in *The Eighteenth
Brumaire of Louis Bonaparte,* "but not of their own free will; not
under circumstances they themselves have chosen but under the given
and inherited circumstances with which they are directly confronted.
The tradition of the dead generations weighs like a nightmare on the
minds of the living."[2] This, as indicated in the *Critique,* is the ex-

perience of all historical men. But Sartre now adds a new refinement. The past may impose contradictory imperatives that cannot be reconciled, or imperatives that cannot be obeyed because present historical circumstances forbid it. The consequence of such a clash, notes Sartre—furthering his efforts to integrate the categories of Marxism and psychoanalysis—is a collective neurosis or "objective neurosis," to use the term he employs to describe a *Weltanschauung* founded upon an irresolvable conflict.

The Second Empire society created by Badinguet was riddled with just such a disease of the spirit. The ailment appeared in one form in the writers of the period and in another in the mind of the triumphant bourgeois. To understand Flaubert dialectically, he must be examined within this neurotic context. The conflicts and products of those who felt compelled to write must be explored, as well as the general ideology of the middle classes of the time. Only then will the differential emerge, explaining both the uniqueness of Flaubert and the reason he came to be the most officially applauded author of the Second Empire.

From 1850 until the end of the century, Sartre states flatly, one had to be mad in order to write. Throughout that period neurosis was "the royal way to the masterpiece" (III, 41). If one set out to write in 1850, the result could only be neurotic, for the context was one of objective neurosis. Sartre quotes the elder Goncourt in this regard: "Consider the fact that our work—and this is perhaps wherein lies its originality—is founded on mental disorder" (III, 43). The writers of the postromantic generation found themselves in an impossible situation. The literary culture in which they wrote imposed imperatives that were hopelessly contradictory and irreconcilable with the requirements of the time. Each would-be author discovers in the literature of the past a range of demands. On all sides ghosts address him with the words, *"Be the writer that we were"* (III, 68). The writer feels himself charged with reproducing in his own times the ideals implicit in the literary masterpieces of the living past. Each imperative appears to be contradicted by another. If a person reads in order to write, he must totalize and unify in a single work these strident and mutually exclusive demands. To write is to have interiorized the literature of the past. If a synthesis of the conflicting imperatives is discovered to be effectively impossible, neurosis will fuel the creative effort. The writer must derealize himself in order to write, finding in dream the only possible resolution to his problem. Examining the cultural givens that confronted the postromantics, Sartre demonstrates that their neurosis was the result of an irresistible logic within the practico-insert of the time.

For these young authors the masters of the eighteenth century were the starting point of living literature. In Flaubert's case, this point is easily documented. In his correspondence he refers to his cult for Voltaire and frequently mentions the great pleasure he takes in reading the eighteenth century's most conspicuous literary figure. From such authors the postromantics learned that literature must have a critical, negative function, must assure the rule of analytic reason, and above all, must be autonomous. Literature was understood as a tool of criticism and demystification to be directed against those with unwarranted political privileges. In these writings the would-be author encounters for the first time what Sartre terms "the high-flying consciousness (*la conscience de survol*)." To be a witness to this time, the author, like Voltaire's protagonists Micromégas and the Ingénu, separates himself from his natural context. The author is a visitor from another continent or planet, an atemporal man from nowhere. He and his avatars represent an egalitarian, abstract, rational, and ahistorical view of human nature. Literature lifts its practitioners above the strictures of class affiliation, for as the author seeks unselfishly the betterment of the race as a whole, he is a representative of human nature at its rational best. The aspiring author also learns from eighteenth-century literary history that the reward for adhering to this ideology is the favor of the enlightened aristocrat. By feigning obliviousness to narrow class interests, the artist undergoes a de facto *déclassement* that liberates him from his origins.

No less significant than the lesson of social autonomy was the eighteenth century discovery of analytical reason. Man came to be understood as a collection of molecules. The final fruits of this atomistic view were the writings of Choderlos de Laclos and the Marquis de Sade. Baudelaire, for one, was an enthusiastic reader of Laclos and was familiar with Sade. Flaubert's passion for the writings of the Marquis is well displayed in his correspondence and in the journals of the brothers Goncourt. The atomistic view of human nature ultimately has the most negative implications epistemologically, ethically, and politically. From Sade and Laclos, among others, the nineteenth-century author is led to wonder: "Between one atom and another can there be any relation other than one of exteriority?" (III, 82). The tools for authentic empathy are not found within the eighteenth century heritage.

After 1830, however, the bourgeoisie definitively takes power and proceeds to demand a class literature that will serve its ends. The man of letters is required to demonstrate that communication between people is impossible; he must establish the "naturalness" of the prevailing system, generate faith in order, and teach the equation of liberty with economic freedom. The bourgeois asks his literary hired gun to defend him on two counts: against the devolved aristocracy, and against the more genuinely threatening claims of the proletariat. The author who has learned from the eighteenth century the lesson of autonomy finds this kind of class servitude impossible. Thus Sartre explains the postromantic rupture between author and public. The new author refuses to associate with and serve the designs of a specific class, not even the powerful class of his birth. The literature of the past century has taught him that literary genius breaks through class structures to a universality which earns for the writer the favor of the enlightened nobility and permits him a symbolic social ascension out of bourgeois mediocrity into a classless pantheon of clerks. Pridefully faithful to the lesson of the previous century, the artist decides that literature will henceforth obey only its own laws. He thus radicalizes and distorts the imperative of autonomy at the moment that its itegrity is endangered.

Whereas in the eighteenth century literature was communication, the postromantic authors find that they must violate this order to be able to preserve it. If they generated an audience within the reading public, it would be at the expense of the cardinal imperative of universal social disaffiliation. There thus develops a split between the idea of writing and that of communication, a split that becomes apparent in the cultivation of occult meanings and of indifference to fame. Leconte de Lisle, for example, held that the popularity of an author was a sure indication of his intellectual inferiority. The artist must write only for other artists. The literary object must become an incommunicable thing; the public is understood to be inessential. The written word, the fetishized signifier, becomes a thing in itself, the main focus of attention. Without readers, the work becomes an inhuman end in itself. The artist becomes the means to the production of an absolute. An inhuman masterpiece requires the sacrifice of its author, who is merely the disposable, inessential tool of its realization. Literature, the postromantic has been told, is a means of real *déclassement,* but since that device is no longer possible, the author can seek only an imaginary escape from social determinisms.

The other model that looms before the postromantic authors is that suggested by the early romantics. The works of these often aristocratic masters display the ideal of writing as an ostentatiously nonproductive activity. The romantics prepared the way for art for art's sake by declaring either directly or implicitly that their poems served no purpose, as, for instance, in Hugo's preface to *Les Orien-*

tales. Such an ideal was appropriate for a class which attached high value to supreme generosity, self-sacrifice, and the gratuitous. In this literature "all is a *gift*" (III, 126). The work is a gift of suffering to man and God, hence antibourgeois for it is antiutilitarian. The romantics introduce the equation of failure and art, as well as the idea of failure that is rewarded. The failure of the aristocratic man of letters is always rewarded because he has received other gifts— power and rank. His suffering and collapse serve only to set in relief the fact that he succeeds no matter what. As he fails, he flaunts his rank in a manner that is not otherwise possible, except in the self-sacrifice of battle. Affiliation with a lost cause is the essence of the aristocrat, as it is the opposite of the utilitarian view of life. The gratuitous is the surest sign of rank; hence the pointless expenditure of self becomes the highest ideal of art.

The young bourgeois authors inherit the scorn of the aristocrats, but the contempt they feel for the values of their native caste is not without damaging consequences. Self-hatred is the inevitable result of their affiliation with the likes of Chateaubriand and Alfred de Musset. The young authors discover, as did Gustave's Rouen school-mates, that it is only the aristocrat who is permitted literary genius. The masters of the previous century told them, "Leave behind your class attachments if you want to write." The message conveyed by the romantics was that it was forbidden for the bourgeois to write. Like all of Sartre's oppressed, the would-be postromantics have been colonized by a scornful look: "These unfortunates have had in-stalled in them the hundred times contested, but nevertheless present scornful glance of an almost abolished class. They are cut off from themselves by this glance of failure and death" (III, 135).

Self-contempt becomes the only source of grandeur, for it is the only thing that raises them above their humiliated condition. They hate the bourgeois in themselves, and through the detested class they come to hate all of humanity, for the bourgeois, after 1830, is conceived as the universal class; the world is bourgeois. That Flau-bert, for one, felt this is confirmed in a 1852 letter to Louise Colet: "The bourgeoisie (which is to say now the entirety of humanity, including the lower classes)."[3]

From the fact that the bourgeois is grasping, envious, competitive, and murderous, it follows that the entire human species is all of these things as well. Human nature is evil, and men must be disciplined and punished simply because they dare to exist. They are sickened by the traits of the bourgeois world that imprisons them, but they are too indoctrinated with its vices to seek its replacement. Their hate is necessarily impotent for they cannot hope to rise above either their class or human nature. Art that entertains these ambitions, the only art conceivable, must conclude in failure. The only art possible is an art that is absolute negation. The work of literature necessarily turns against itself, because it too is a detestable human product and requests, however surreptitiously, to be read, thus violating the imperatives of total autonomy and the refusal to communicate.

The artist tries his best not to be human. He defines himself as *"other than man"* (III, 145). He is brought by the irresistible logic of his situation to pretend complete impersonality and to seek the perspective of *"le survol"* (overflight). In Voltaire *le survol* represented the point of view of a neutral, abstract rationality. In the works of the romantics it affirmed the superiority of a privileged class. But the postromantics use this perspective to declare the metaphysical rupture of the author from the detested species that dares to claim his participation. These writers scornfully look down upon their race from a nonexistent absolute that cannot be attained, declaring, "The world is Nothingness" (III, 140). Art is destined to fail in its attempts to break with the totality of the real, to derealize the world, to negate man and his physical and social world. Since man is a failure, the artist's attempts to extricate himself from humanity must fail as well. Dehumanization, *le survol,* and symbolic escape from class are ideals that are understood to be unrealizable, although the effort must nonetheless be made, for the effort, if nothing else, establishes the artist's superior lucidity. Like Mallarmé's swan, the grandeur of the artist resides in his failed attempt to escape. In his laughable efforts at metaphysical revolt he establishes that he alone is aware that man and the world are beneath contempt. This imaginary superman enters "the Aristocracy of Nothingness" (III, 157) and becomes "a baron of Nonhumanity" or "a knight of Nonbeing" (III, 147), phrases that are perhaps playing with Kierkegaard's "knight of faith." "One can only negate the real on the condition that the real begins by excluding you" (III, 164), explains Sartre, recalling his observation of Gustave in the first volume. An entire generation of authors turns to the unreal because history has rendered its role impossible.

The beautiful work is a denial of the human. Its task is to harm, disarm, and demoralize. Beauty is understood to be a cruel, destructive, and unattainable mistress. Sartre is here supported by the pronouncements of these authors and their descendants. The classic example is Baudelaire's "Beauty," Flaubert's favorite among *Les Fleurs du mal.* In an essay on Mallarmé, Valéry defined beauty as *"that which causes despair."*[4]

The element of chance, the problem that so haunted Mallarmé

and which Flaubert sought to escape through the use of *"le mot juste,"* must be excluded from the artistic product, for it is an absurd chance that caused these authors to have been born into their particular class. In a work unbesmirched by hazard they could be reborn as inhuman aristocrats. If a single word in a paragraph might have been otherwise, then chance reenters the world and all is lost, the effort mocked. If the world is to be derealized, chance must be excluded, for it is the residue of reality erupting in a systematic effort at derealization. This artist is the opposite of the man of action and certain modern artists who realize that they are creatures of chance, who seek to make particular modifications in a real world where they know chance to be a factor. This "creature of chance" takes chance into account and incorporates it into his product. He does not attempt the vain metaphysical gesture of pretending to eliminate chance but prepares himself for its effects and uses it for his ends in order to eliminate to all possible extent its coefficient of adversity. This is Sartre's new prescription for the avoidance of the equation of alienation with objectification. By artificially denying chance, the author falls into the first type of bad faith, the denial of his anchorage in the materiality of the human species. Chance disappears along with reality. When chance does appear in these works, as in *Madame Bovary*, it appears as its opposite, as another face of an inflexible necessity.

If the artist is to derealize man and his world, a derealization of language must also be accomplished. Language must be stolen from men by rendering it unrecognizable, by eliminating the factor of chance from the use of words. Because language is infected with the contingent, its use reveals and denounces man as "a creature of chance." In his struggles to escape this humiliating status the author will always fail because, argues Sartre with reference to Mallarmé's discovery in *Un Coup de dés,* "The author is contaminated by chance even in his efforts to take leave of a world of chance, and can only objectify himself in a work in which chance necessarily plays a role." A toss of the dice can never abolish chance. The problem of the antinomy of necessity and chance cannot be resolved by suppressing the appearance of the contingent. Artists can resolve the difficulty only by accepting and controlling the advent of the accidental, by allowing it a specified place, within the context of the form they impose upon the world. Under these circumstances the work can have the true look of an authentically human enterprise. But such a solution was not entertained by the practitioners of *L'Art absolu,* for to do so would be "to make of the book a human enterprise that partially escapes its author and thus reflects his

facticity as well as his freedom." In other words the artist would fall
into the uncomfortable condition of good faith. Again the artist
discovers the desperate Beckettian imperative of L'Art absolu: "You
must but you cannot" (III, 191). His attempts to become "the Lord of
the impossibility of man" (III, 192), to seize life as an analogy of
death, to derealize the real in an object of art, to create the only
conditions under which he can come to approve of himself, must all
fail because of his historically conditioned bad faith.

Sartre's remarks on the role of chance in art bear a striking resemblance to those expressed by Pierre Boulez in his 1957 article
"Alea."[5] There Boulez rejects both a form of music based entirely
on the accidental and a form that attempts to eliminate chance
entirely. Both, he says, deny choice and are not human. He criticizes
the angry rejection of the arbitrary as mechanistic, fetishistic, and
ultimately impossible. The more the artist seeks to flee chance, the
more certain is its appearance. Instead Boulez advocates a form of
music that allows for chance, but only within a pre-established net-
work which itself is never left to arbitrary forces. In support of this
aesthetic, Boulez, like Sartre, quotes from Mallarmé. Given the
similarities between the views expressed in this essay and L'Idiot,
and the fact that Sartre has expressed great admiration for Boulez,
it is not impossible that "Alea" may have had a role in the genesis
of Sartre's views on the place of chance in art and life.

Because the unreal is the only value esteemed by "the knight of
nothingness," the artistic project is defined as a superhuman effort
that concludes in failure. The author writes a work in order to fail
and, in so doing, to manifest that the greatness of literature lies in its
unsuccessful pursuit of the unreal. The aristocracy of the author is
demonstrated by his inadequacy to the task. The failure itself becomes a value because it reveals the grandeur of art and of its practitioner, who subordinates his life to the production of an inhuman
object. It is possible to create such vain objects only on the condition
that the dissatisfaction which produces them never ceases to denounce
these products. As the artist's project fails, it reveals the demoralizing
failure of all human praxis and thus of the entire species. L'Art-
névrose is thus spiritually akin to the negation of man that was a
feature of the comic as understood by the Garçon. As the work manifests its impossibility, it reveals the triumph and superiority of the
unreal, a privileged status which men must despair of attaining. At
the same time it reveals the relative superiority of the artist, because
he is the only person lucid enough to seek to coincide with Nothing.

The objectively neurotic artist is a double being. He is a dupe who
thinks that the contingent can be chased from art, but he is also

the sadistic *farceur* who writes only to prove that the evasion is impossible. Grandeur consists, as it did for the aristocratic romantic from whom the artist inherited the idea, in the sacrifice of self for a cause that is lost in advance. The double being that Sartre postulates serves to explain the phenomenon of romantic irony, a major theme of postromantic French letters. In the literature of the period it often happens that expansive, utopian moods are deflated by a sudden return to the oppressively quotidian. In Baudelaire's "The Soup and the Clouds" the poet's exalted meditations on the infinite are interrupted by an impatient and abrasive demand that the dreamer finish his soup. In Mallarmé's "The Windows" an ethereal vision concludes with the despairing realization that the "here below is master."[6] Sartre is the first to offer a satisfactory historical explanation for the occurrence of the dupe-farceur pair.

The misanthropic, antisocial artists expected no public. One of their major themes was in fact the contemptibility of those who would normally be their readers. Flaubert's correspondence is replete with references to a certainty that his works will be read only by a few friends. Yet his first published work gained him a considerable success with the public. The reason, Sartre explains, is that the bourgeois recognized itself in this black novel. A rejected public embraced a work that sought its negation. The reason is found in the fact that when these knights of Nothingness published their first works, the revolution of 1848 and the *coup d'état* that followed transformed the bourgeois's consciousness of themselves and hence all of human relations.

Under the old order, humanity was denied to the third estate on principle; by divine right it belonged to the aristocracy alone. After the revolution, however, man came to be defined as a creature who owned property. Before 1830 the bourgeois ideology was optimistic. All men were potential landowners and hence potentially human. Guizot's dictum *"Enrichissez-vous"* was the optimistic call of the bourgeoisie to itself and to the workers. All were free to attempt an entry into the new privileged class. The bourgeois considered himself to be the agent of progress who, through capital investments, knowledge, and managerial skills, lifts all of humanity out of indigence and despair. As the economy expanded, thanks to their generosity and abilities, the bourgeois would watch on benevolently as the workers filed slowly into the earthly paradise of the middle class. The indigent levels of society were asked to cooperate by displaying a modicum of patience and self-discipline, to await peaceably their turn to pass through the pearly gates of material sufficiency.

Beginning in 1830 and culminating in 1848, the bourgeois discovers his previously repressed secret: his comforts are built upon the despair of the proletariat. His justification as the agent of progress and of the "burgherization" of the world is fraudulent. He finds that the poverty of the worker is the condition of his wealth. An improvement in the material conditions of the bourgeois comes only at the expense of the pauperization of the worker. It means increasing the surplus value with the aid of automation and a reduction of salaries. The bourgeois discovers that he can believe in the general progress of the human race at his own peril. In 1866 Flaubert wrote to George Sand, "The reaction of 48 has hollowed out an abyss between the two Frances." After June 1848, notes Sartre of the bourgeois, "they sense themselves to be *seen*" (III, 243). An entire class, like Genet and the man at the hotel room door, has been caught in a reprehensible act.

The workers' revolt of 1848 is squashed by Cavaignac. The toll: 4,000 dead, 25,000 arrested. The bourgeois are obliged to integrate this butchery into their ideology, which can no longer be founded upon the illusion of progress but must be reestablished upon the frank acknowledgment of class hatred. The worker must be encouraged surreptitiously to hate, not the bourgeois in particular, but all of humanity, and himself most particularly. Only thus can the bourgeois hope to defuse the just ire of the proletariat. Only by convincing himself that the entire species is hateful can the bourgeois justify to himself the overt and covert violence he directs at the workers.

"On earth all is bad" (III, 216) is the message that the bourgeois proclaims at every opportunity. Man is the victim of natural, inflexible economic laws to which he must subordinate and reconcile himself. No equality is possible in this life. Sartre illustrates his point with a quotation from the banker become premier, Casimir Perier. After the Lyons insurrection had been squashed, Perier reported to the parliament, "The workers must realize that there are no remedies for them other than patience and resignation" (III, 215). This statement, according to the historian Gordon Wright, "epitomized the outlook of most political leaders and most industrialists of the time" —although there were exceptions, such as the Vicomte de Villeneuve-Bargemont, prefect at Lille, who questioned whether it was "necessary that the worker perish, body and soul, so that the master may climb faster to the summit of opulence"[7] Only by spreading about the idea that "on earth all is bad" could the bourgeois hope to lull the worker into passivity and deaden his sensitivity to his misfortune.

This was a tall order. By 1848 France had been far outdistanced by England in the area of legislative protection for workers. At the time that Perier spoke, out of 21,000 children born in the workers' quarters in Lille, 20,700 died before the age of five. Out of 10,000 men requested to report for military service, 8,980 were found to be physically unfit to serve. Children, Sartre reports, were sent off to work at the age of eight. Even this picture is on the rosy side, however, for a law passed in 1841 outlawing the employment in factories of children below the age of eight was not enforced.

The bourgeois continued to believe in progress, but his new view masked a deep pessimism. Of necessity, he developed a system of knowledge that excluded empathy. Because man is not a for-itself but rather fundamentally an in-itself, he can only be known as an object, and from the outside. Knowledge is a form of suicide, Sartre maintains recalling the similar point made by Foucault. Private property and the accumulation and production of manufactured objects require the increase of knowledge, but its subordination to the end of economic expansion results in a misanthropic epistemology. Man's only grandeur consists in his alienation to an impersonal, disinterested concept of truth. His only value resides in his lucid awareness of his relativity, his utility not to other men but to truth and progress, that is, to the internalized ideal of private property. Man is alienated to science, which in turn is alienated to capital. He is not an end for man but a means of realizing systematic self-immolation and the deification of the inert manufactured object.

This epistemology was a component of the ideology that emerged after 1850, referred to by Sartre as "distinction," the Baudelaire-derived term first appearing in the *Critique*. It is Sartre's label for a style of life that is permeated with hatred. The bourgeois is not simply a *heautontimoroumenos* but "this hateful—hated—self-tor-turing man" (III, 325), who at every moment crushes his organic, human component. "The Creator of antinature must display the fact that he is the master of nature and that it obeys him within as well as outside of his person" (III, 247). Through distinction, the bourgeois demonstrates to all that he hates and crushes the worker. This ideology is the exterior sign of an alienation to the manu-factured object, of the bourgeois destruction of self for the sake of creating an ever-increasing flow of manufactured goods. The bourgeois of constraint is the human symbol of a justified aliena-tion, "the predicted advent of the being—in-itself as a manufactured totality that comes into existence with the consented to abolition of the for-itself" (III, 286).

Such a person demonstrates in himself the duty of the human

species to sacrifice itself for the advent of a nonhuman reality. He is an ambulatory definition of man that excludes the notion of praxis. Man is reduced to his objectivity and becomes a suffering passivity deprived of the potential for self-transcendence. His life style is a sandwich board proclaiming that each person is a means, the servant of the manufactured product, and that exploitation is the norm in this best of all possible worlds. Life is conceived as a permanent sacrifice, "the sacrifice of life to *Nothing*" (III, 185). The essence of man "is to cause himself to be devoured." Man is a vain passion who finds his salvation in the willing loss of self that earns him back no significant reward. "The essence of humanity can only be . . . a very long human suicide, or with a bit of luck, the auto-domestication of men in a barnyard supervised by machines" (III, 195).

Within this "humanism of the inhuman," which exists to further the coming reign of the Thing, the inessentiality of human life reveals itself in the form of a black trinity: profit for profit's sake, science for science's sake, and art for art's sake. The bourgeois reader after 1850 takes pleasure in the *survol* experience for, having internalized the worker's hate, he despises his own class and enjoys an imaginary break with his social affiliation. The reader recognizes himself in the impersonality and impassibility sought by the author. He sees reflected back his own experience of self-destruction for the sake of an unrealizable ideal and the creation of a useless object. Like Capital, Beauty says, "I do not serve men. It is rather they who serve me. I am a demand that no one can fulfill. My servants die with their harnesses on so that a work may be born" (III, 312–313). The genocidal concept of beauty cherished by the art for art's sake movement is the aesthetic avatar of the ideology of distinction. As the bourgeois reads, he recognizes his own reality as the servant of Capital, the manufactured product which is per-petually like the mistress of Baudelaire's poem, *"Sed Non Satiata."* The artist feels that no human enterprise is an end in itself, that all action must serve an inhuman end, and that even this grim task is destined to failure. This reality does not exclude man from the black necessity of having to die senselessly for the sake of a sense-less end.

This occult form of black literature allows the bourgeois to hate in innocence. As he reads, he relives his homicidal desires and finds support for his conviction that evil is the organizing principle of the world, that man is a hateful illusion, and that relations be-tween men are reduced to radical exteriority. His suspicion that contempt is the only possible emotion for his fellow man is justified.

Generosity, love, and goodness are revealed to be an exquisite illusion. In the pages of Flaubert, Gautier, the Goncourts, and Leconte de Lisle, the bourgeois discovers universalized hatred. The only truth is the lie that denounces itself. As he reads, the homicidal bourgeois nods approvingly and says complacently to himself, like Proust's hoped-for reader, *"c'est bien cela."* This art, which pretends to be the simple, innocuous reproduction of the real, has demonstrated man and his world to be without redeeming qualities. Since all men are condemned, the murderers of 1848 are exculpated of their particular historical crimes. Man is guilty, to be sure, but endemically so. The author liberates the bourgeois from his historical guilt and allows him to hate himself, the worker, and the world in good conscience.

To enter this approved order of the knights of Nothingness, Anyone who in 1850, for whatever reason, finds he must write is faced with the necessity of reconciling the conflicting imperatives imposed by the objective spirit. An artist in this context is an objective failure, for to write is objectively impossible. On an objective level the artist has been rejected by reality and hence can become a knight of Nothingness. But not every such knight can become a genius and create a work that his society considers a masterpiece: " 'Genius' will depend . . . upon the coincidence of the subjective and the subjectification proposed by the objective neurosis" (III, 201). In other words, there must have been in the early history of the genius a personal rejection to complement the historical rejection that he experiences as he sets out to escape his class affiliation through the act of literature.

Flaubert was eagerly read, while Leconte de Lisle, whose poetry displayed all of the characteristic themes of "Art-Neurosis," was not. Volumes of poetry at this time, Sartre affirms, had the potential for high sales, so the genre itself does not explain de Lisle's dearth of readers. Rather, it was because his public sensed that his hatred for man was abstract and unauthentic, vitiated by the fact that his pessimism seemed to lack the requisite profundity. This idea was probably suggested to Sartre by Flaubert himself, who in his correspondence makes similar complaints about the work of the poet. Unlike Gustave, de Lisle did not hate himself and had not undergone a rejection in his early life. The reader did not feel that self-hatred was his essence and hence did not recognize himself in what seemed to be insipid, dessicated poems of hate. The bourgeois audience will accept only a hatred that is a true reflecton of its own. De Lisle did not convince, because of his fault of practicing Art-Neurosis without being himself a neurotic. He was, as were

all members of the order, objectively mad, but without being simultaneously subjectively mad. Whereas the bourgeois was truly a
pessimist, de Lisle affected pessimism and was caught in his masquerade.

For "genius" to exist, there must be, as in the case of Flaubert, a
double determination. In the literature produced by Flaubert, the
superstructure corresponds exactly to the needs of the infrastructure,
not as a consequence of an iron rule of congruity, but rather because of a psychological accident. Flaubert was a passive child
from the provinces, who was isolated both from the vanguard of
bourgeois thought and from any experience of the dominant means
of production. He was told that he was an idiot and hence could not
hope to advance the glorious self-image that his family sought to
project. Flaubert's personal experience led him to create a literature
that freakishly met the deepest needs of the class he despised.

The practitioners of Art-Neurosis discovered to their amazement
that in spite of themselves they were providing the despised public
with precisely the pleasures and vindications it sought. In their
work the enemy finds impressive justification of his misanthropic
ethos of distinction. The artist had thought his product to be a protest against the bourgeois, when in fact it functions to validate and
serve the commodity culture. The artist throws away his life on a
useless object to demonstrate his refusal of the world of the manu-
facturer, but instead of reacting with dismay, the bourgeois reader
nods in approval at an occult kinship. He is pleasantly surprised to
discover a justification arriving from a most improbable source.
The artist's alienation thus is doubled. In order to escape the bourgeois variety, he subordinates himself to the production of an in-
solently beautiful, inhuman thing. The intended subversive meaning
of this object is in turn "misread" by the bourgeois, who correctly
assumes it to serve his instrumental rationality. In an alienated society all alienations are symbolic of one another. By exchanging
artistic alienation for the mirroring bourgeois form, the author has
succeeded only in ensuring the imperium of the forces he sought to
escape, for he now lives in the dreamy illusion that he has fled something when in reality he has not: "At this level the alienation to the
Work appears like a peacock who, while scorning a jay, becomes
his supplier of feathers" (III, 312). Accommodation is the final consequence of the artist's systematic scorn.

In the concluding section of *L'Idiot* as it now stands, Sartre shows
how the collective neurosis of the Second Empire and the individual
neurosis of Flaubert mirrored one another. Gustave's 1844 was a
premonition of the bourgeoisie's 1848. Flaubert the artist and Bad-

inguet's empire of dreams were born four years apart and died on the same day. First a man, then an entire class, resigned as agents of history and escaped into illusion. Each flight led to a delusion of triumph that masked an admission of past failure and a prophecy of failure to come. In order to guarantee its economic security against the menace of the newly militant and cohesive workers, the bourgeois handed over its political authority to a military aristocracy, thus compromising with a class that it had already virtually defeated. Similarly in his self-induced attack of 1844 Flaubert had abdicated from the requirements of the world of praxis. Both Flaubert and his world lapsed into the irresponsibility of the minor and fell to a life of dreaming. Both were to awake on September 4, 1870, to the harsh strains of Bismarck's *"Wachet auf!"*

In the period between 1852 and 1870, particularly the years of the so-called liberal phase of the Empire, Gustave felt very much at home. This was the happiest and most productive phase of his life. The imperial government delighted him because it reflected back his misanthropy and pessimism. Flaubert admired and respected Louis Napoleon, for he saw him as a great demoralizer, a vilifier of man. Pécuchet gives his opinion of the emperor: "Because the bourgeois are ferocious, the workers jealous, the priests servile, and the lower classes accept all tyrants, on the condition that they are kept in feed, Napoleon has done well! Let him muzzle, crush, and exterminate them all!"[8] That Flaubert is himself represented in this view is clear from an 1854 letter of his to Louise Colet: "I thank Badinguet. Bless Him! He taught me to scorn the masses and to hate the vulgar herd."[9] The regime of personal power entails the negation of human worthiness and praxis. That no one is worthy of sharing power is the implicit message of the form of government confirmed by the plebiscite of 1852. Badinguet is likened by Sartre to the Caligula of Camus whose self-appointed function was to reveal the absurdity of all, to disclose that human dignity is an ignoble farce: "The Garçon in power: what luck!" (III, 456). Louis Napoleon incarnates the certainty that men are evil. His regime is the political equivalent of the improprieties of Flaubert's schoolboy avatar, and the political equivalent of *"L'Art-Absolu."*

The Empire confirmed and honored the philosophy of "loser wins." In a society that conferred enormous prestige on the false, Gustave could be unembarrassed about his escapism. For once the world seemed to be cooperating. The government seemed to give ontological weight to the imaginary. The imaginary was taken for the real, and vice versa. It seemed finally that the imaginary, man's only grandeur, was not a chimera after all, for the entire society paid homage to the unreal: "the comedy of grandeur and the beautiful, vain homage of man to that which will be refused him to the end" (III, 519). For a moment failure resulted in success.

One of the major themes of Marx's *The Eighteenth Brumaire of Louis Napoleon,* a work that Sartre has valued greatly, is the illusory character of the society formed by Napoleon III. The state is described "as comedy in the most vulgar sense, as a masquerade in which the grand costumes, words and postures merely serve as a cover for the most petty trickery." The government "holds its victims spellbound in an imaginary world and robs them of all sense, all memory, and all understanding of the rough external world."[10] This view of the Empire, since adapted by other historians, is an integral premise of Sartre's third volume. All was blessedly false: "False nephew [an apparent reference to Napoleon's questioned legitimacy], phony emperor, phony war, phony court, phony aristocrats" (III, 532). Paris too was an illusion, which explained its attractiveness to Flaubert. In a 1867 letter to George Sand Flaubert described the city as imaginary, artificial, and dehumanizing: "Paris . . . is becoming colossal. It's becoming mad and excessive. We are perhaps returning to the ancient Orient. It seems to me that idols are going to rise from the earth. We are threatened with a new Babylon. Why not? The *individual* has been negated by democracy to the point of complete abasement, as under the great theocratic dictatorships" (III, 521–522). Flaubert's annual three-month sojourns in Paris were his opportunities not only to rest from his imaginings at Croisset but actually to pass through the looking glass. The Second Empire was a bourgeois society dreaming itself to be legendary, noble, and satanic. Hence Gustave felt it to be his milieu.

Flaubert fully realizes that his society is a mirage, but this understanding is a matter of indifference: "The consistency of the imperial mirage satisfies him to the exact extent that its unreality disappoints. But . . . false and true nobility have in common the fact that they incarnate the discretionary power of man over man, that is to say Evil, and very indirectly, Beauty. Flaubert moves without difficulty from one to the other. Their oppositions do not disturb him at all because, finally, it is a question of two kinds of Nonbeing." (III, 548). On another level the realization that the Empire is false is a crucial component in his pleasure, for it provides another gleefully received proof of the endemic failure of the species. But if only Badinguet's France had at its disposal a serious machine of war instead of imaginary army it deserved, the illusion could have been perpetuated indefinitely.

Besides conferring upon Flaubert the unofficial status of "genius," that false and symbolic nobility to which he had aspired, the Second Empire accorded to him official recognition emanating from the pinnacle of society that Achille-Cléophas had conditioned his son to esteem. Flaubert rubbed elbows with the Emperor and was a great friend of Princess Mathilde. Perhaps because of his own aversion to official awards Sartre is fascinated with Flaubert's relationship with the rosette of the Legion of Honor. Sartre's lengthy treatment of this issue provides indirect justification of his own refusal of the Nobel Prize.

In 1852, when Maxime Du Camp had been named an officer of the Legion of Honor, Flaubert denounced the award given to his friend, although basically he was favorably disposed toward the feudal ideology lurking behind such forms of recognition. Then in 1866 Flaubert accepted the award himself. This made sense, Sartre explains, because in 1852 the award, as far as Gustave was concerned, had a very different meaning. Although Louis Napoleon was then in power, the rosette in Flaubert's mind continued to have the debased meaning it had had under Louis Philippe. Under the citizen king the award had become trivialized by virtue of being disassociated from its original Napoleonic meaning, which was to award soldiers for their devotion to the military causes of the Empire. Because Louis Philippe was the guardian of an abject bourgeois peace, he was without true authority to offer the award. As far as Flaubert was concerned in 1852, the rosette lacked the glorious feudal redolence it had once possessed.

As the Second Empire progressed, however, the original significance of the Legion of Honor was restored. Under Napoleon III's politics of prestige, blood flowed again and the Emperor was once more a god of war. France thus regained its honor, and concomitantly the rosette regained its worth. The award again imparts official recognition on one who throws away his life for his ruler, for an inhuman ideal. It is justly worn only by the person who, for the sake of a bloodthirsty leader and an inhuman prestige, destroys, lives with death, and gladly subordinates himself to a pointless end. Gustave was indeed such a person, for he had subordinated himself to the *pater familias* and the family honor. He had chosen to alienate himself to the Impossible, or Beauty. At least in the imaginary, he had spilt the blood of the enemy: "The artist dies and kills" (III, 564). A proper artist, of the homicidal and suicidal variety, can therefore be a proper recipient of the honor.

It was most fitting, Sartre observes, for Napoleon III, the man who in the social domain tried to create a mirage, the false resurrection of his uncle, to honor Flaubert. From him alone could Gustave accept this phantom, satanic distinction. The writer is rewarded for his fanatical adherence to the ideology of the realm, his fidelity to the maginary, to Nonbeing. By officially recognizing the author of *Madame Bovary,* the government showed it understood that such literature perpetuated the hatred of man for man. The Second Empire does Flaubert the favor of rescuing him symbolically from the class he had always dreamed of escaping. An illusory government has honored and consecrated his anomaly. The strategy of 1844 has been vindicated and rewarded: "Flaubert is named knight of the Legion of Honor inasmuch as he is already a knight of Nothingness" (III, 574).

After Sedan, Flaubert feels that France has lost its honor. In his correspondence he insists that he can no longer wear his cross, which Sartre interprets as an expression of allegiance to the overthrown emperor of dreams, the symbolic sacrifice of the liege man on the tomb of his master. Sartre has Flaubert say:

> When he [Napoleon III] had the aura of the Sacred, he honored me by *consecrating my anomaly,* and as long as the collective dream lasted, that elevated him above men, I had this *other* consciousness of myself: *a saint from day to day, in the throes of mediocrity,* I was able to be a hero in the dreams of others. Now that he has lost everything, even honor, I no longer want to owe to anyone the gift he gave me and that he continued to give me as long as he reigned. To no one, and *especially* not to the wretches who had the audacity to wake from their dream. (III, 574)

The collapse of the Empire in 1870 turns Gustave's world upside down, for it reveals the failure of the strategy of 1844, signaling "the failure of failure" (III, 472). "The soldiers of Being" (III, 543), as Sartre calls the invading army, put to rout "the knight of Nothingness." The triumph of the Prussians is experienced as a condemnation to dream no longer. The escape into the imaginary has turned out to be endemically unsuccessful. Romantic irony enters both Gustave's personal history and that of the Empire. In 1844 he had derealized himself, but he needed a world of illusion to sustain and reinforce his efforts at evasion. The defeat in 1870 reveals that reality and imagination are not the same. With the invasion of the Prussians and the formation of the Republic, Gustave is returned to his intolerable bourgeois reality. The Emperor is evicted from the Elysée Palace, and Flaubert from the imaginary. The true order of reality is reestablished, and the idiot is reduced to his original impotence. He discovers that he had never escaped the patriarchal aegis and that he has been in complicity with his own destruction.

To explain Flaubert's dilemma, Sartre resorts to an extended metaphor that recalls the one organizing *No Exit*. He imagines a drawing room furnished in the ugly Second Empire style. A man in the room is suddenly surrounded with flames and smoke. Realizing that he has only one avenue of escape, he hastily leaves through the door that is the room's single exit. On the other side of the threshold he is terrified to discover that the room he has just entered is an exact copy of the room he sought to evacuate, it too being filled with flames and smoke. For Gustave, the imaginary is this door, this false hope, which only leads him back to the original problem and assures the impossibility of a solution. It confirms that there will be no true solution, only the ineffectual delusion of an escape.

The lesson learned by Flaubert on the fourth of September, when Napoleon III is deposed, is the harsh one implicit in *L'Imaginaire*: the escape into the imaginary is an evasion into bad faith, a self-alienation, a renunciation of power. In 1844 he had fled the superiority of father and brother by leaping through the looking glass. In doing so, he now discovers, he had only confirmed, recognized, and accepted his personal inferiority. By opting for the imaginary in 1844, he had in effect accepted the triumph of the Other. At that time and until the victory of the Prussians he felt that an admission of failure would be only an appearance of failure, upon which he could build a mighty triumph over Achille-Cléophas and the entire race. But as a dreamer, he could be only the object of history, never its subject. He had done nothing but radicalize his father's power over him. His heroic rupture with the human race his transcendental ataraxia, the subordination of his life to the creation of an inhuman beauty, are revealed as a petty game of appearances. Sedan makes him realize that the power of the imaginary is a rat trap. The collective failure of the Second Empire reveals his personal failure. To escape the unpleasant memory of the massacres out of which they were born, both Louis Napoleon and Flaubert had created worlds of false appearance. At Sedan, both relinquish their false authority. In the Third Republic Gustave lives on as a fossil in a new world, a world he suspects will refuse to honor hatred and illusion. After the fourth of September he publishes only a single book.

The French capitulation was an event in family as well as international politics. Before Sedan, the idiot appeared to have come out on top. He was the glory of the family, the most celebrated man of letters of the day. Achille-Cléophas was dead, and Achille had become a mediocre provincial physician, a pathetic shade of his glorious father. Sartre shows convincingly that Flaubert in his correspondence associated the German enemy with utilitarian and scientific values: "Our enemy has science going for him" (III, 595). Because the Germans resembled that other enemy, Achille-Cléophas, they incited the return of the repressed. The defeat resurrects the father and the malediction that the son thought he had escaped with his strategy of failure. The esoteric gambit to outplay the father had failed, and the dead-end logic of Pont-l'Evêque was brutally disproven. Bismarck's ironic glancing down on the dreaming, ineffectual France reactivates the gaze of the exigent ghost of Achille-Cléophas upon his idiot son. The Prussians are the vengeful agents of the father who punishes Gustave for the self-destructive and parricidal temerity of 1844.

On September 4, when Paris received news of the capture of the emperor, a crowd invaded the legislature and at the Hotel de Ville the Third Republic was declared. The American ambassador to France, E. B. Washburne, reported that the announcement of the Republic was "received by every possible demonstration of enthusiasm." Juliette Adam, later to become a friend of Flaubert's, reported that on that day the Place de la Concorde witnessed a marvelous spectacle: "From the chestnut trees of the Tuilleries just as far as the horizon of Mont-Valérien and the hills bathed by the Seine, the scene is on so grand a scale, the crowds feel such a real communion of ideals and desires, that poetry and enthusiasm invade even the coldest and most insensitive hearts."[11] She reported having seen a young worker with a red fez singing the Marseillaise for three hours without a break while supported by a lamp post on a bridge crossing the Seine.

Gustave proved refractory to the contagious republican spirit of the new "riff-raffocracy," as Edmond de Goncourt called it.[12] The death of his friend Gautier in October 1872 seemed the correct occasion for lashing out at the deposition of Napoleon III. To Mathilde he wrote: "He [Gautier] died of disgust with modern life. The fourth of September killed him. That day, the most cursed in the history of France, inaugurated an order of things where the like of Theo have no place . . . I don't pity him; I envy him." On the same day Flaubert wrote to Feydeau: "The fourth of September inaugurated a state of affairs which no longer concerns us. *We do not fit.* They hate and scorn us, it's the truth. And so, good night!" (III, 660). In the guise of Theo, Sartre writes, Gustave is the one who was buried. The fourth of September killed Flaubert. Like the events of 1848, the crisis of Pont-l'Evêque had prophesied the dishonest devices and inevitable fall of the Second Empire. The collapse of Badinguet's France revealed the admission of failure implicit in the daring of 1844. Flaubert's February Revolution was experienced monadically in 1844: a man tried to mask a massacre, a failure, an admission of impotence, with a flight into a self-incurred immaturity and an illusory, hate-filled wonderland. In 1870 the collapse of the mirroring personal and collective strategies of pride and magic are both ingloriously revealed.

Sartre reveals this moment of Flaubert's life in a new way, making the novelist associate the German invaders with the values for which his father stood and feel that the ascendancy of this ethos will put an end to the kind of life he has enjoyed. But Sartre overstates his argument. Flaubert's emotion at this time was certainly not unmodulated by other, more personally significant events. Long before the arrival of the Germans, Flaubert was referring to himself as a fossil surviving in a strange new world. On the basis of the correspondence, Gustave was clearly less disturbed over the arrival of the Prussians than over the deaths of an alarming number of his ideal readers. It seemed to him that no one was left for whom to write. Obsessively he listed to his correspondents the number of friends who had passed: Jules de Goncourt, Sainte-Beuve, Armand Barbès, Gavarni, and most damagingly, Louis Bouilhet. "My intellectual entourage no longer exists," he wrote in July 1870.[13] To say merely that after this moment Flaubert published only a single work is also to distort the picture. Although he did publish less, it is clear from his correspondence that, despite a severe rheumatism that prevented him from holding a pen for very long, he continued to work as hard as ever.

In its baroque extravagance, the imagination of Sartre has soared dangerously beyond the prosaic truth of his subject. Sartre's obsession with ideal types, with a coherence view of truth, with the aesthetically satisfying organizing principle that permits him to find in a life a pat beginning, middle, and end, mars the convincing flow of the argument. Sartre, in all probability, is very much aware of his exaggeration. Like Husserl and Dilthey, he feels that an individual is revealed not by adhering to the "facts" but rather by creating a type. This intentional reduction is for Sartre, as for Dilthey, "a way to overcome experience by means of experience, so that it is felt more intensely than in the truest copy of reality."[14] Sartre would probably feel that only by stripping away the more superficial considerations of Flaubert's physical difficulties and grief over lost friends could be come into contact with the essence of Flaubert's pain.

On one level *L'Idiot* is a very grim book. It is the story of a catastrophe issuing from inescapable contradictions that Flaubert was impotent to resolve, an epic of prefabrication that dramatizes the risk factors which hound even the most sheltered in a world with an instrumental complex, in which the in-itself is the ideal to which people are conditioned to aspire. The cruel economic forces that underlie the prevailing social reality reverberate authoritatively and unopposed through the private and sacrosanct domains of personal life and art. Since Flaubert is inculcated with no countervailing powers, he can escape from one form of bondage only by fleeing to another. Each defensive assertion of the infected will collapses into a new form of alienation. His world appears as a hall of mirrors, each form of alienation reflecting into every other. There is no surface that does not mockingly return the image of a man in fetters.

But within this attempt at a complete catalogue of the snares met with by a single unfortunate are two moments of hopefulness: one sharply localized, the other diffuse and ubiquitous. In *Saint Genet* an illusion of freedom and a concomitant obstinacy of spirit were derived vaguely from the sense of oneself as an anonymous subject free from constricting affiliation. In the *Critique* the subjective preconditions that provide one with the moral stamina to become an agent of history were never adequately explained. Sartre now holds that despite one's total immersion in a world of necessity, one can have a spurring sense of oneself as an insulted freedom as long as the original "valorization" has been experienced. Such a freedom-seeking though ultimately unfree being can be created despite the most malign adversity. He who has experienced this happy moment can never be dissuaded that he has the ability to alter the world for the better. A monster of freedom, like little Clouet, cannot be content until all men are aware of the determinisms that insult their possibilities. This is an important moment in *L'Idiot*, for here Sartre suggests that by itself historical materialism cannot properly interpret revolutionary behavior. There exist psychological factors that are almost entirely unaffected by historical necessity which must be accounted for if men and their actions are to be understood. Also, when Sartre maintains that love and a sense of valorization make critical consciousness possible, he is at the same time saying that there is no universal class which is the carrier of a privileged alternative knowledge.

A heady optimism is also apparent in the critical method that

Sartre employs for the life of Flaubert. Adorno's view that "knowledge is an ethical category" is the case for Sartre as well, as is clear from the *Critique*.[15] To understand the ambitions of his third biography, one must grasp the relation in his thought between epistemology and ethics, between comprehension, the Dilthey-derived means for arriving at a knowledge of other selves, and reciprocity, Sartre's recent ethical ideal. On the first page of *L'Idiot* the author announces that his intention will be to demonstrate a theory of knowledge. In an interview he explained that the *Critique* "is the sequel of *Being and Nothingness,* and the work on ethics can only come afterwards. You can find it for example in the book on Flaubert."[16] The facts of Flaubert's life open out to a large moral conception. *L'Idiot* is ultimately about ethics and the knowledge of other selves. Its hopeful spirit is revealed at the same moment as is the character of the relationship between Sartre's ethical and epistemological ideals.

In *L'Idiot* Sartre restates his belief that positive reciprocity is the most satisfactory relationship: "The fact remains that the fundamental relationship between men, no matter how masked, deviated, alienated and reified, is reciprocity" (p. 816). Reciprocity is the opposite of human relations as they manifest themselves within the series. It occurs at the happy moment when one's relations with others are no longer mediated by the scarcity-contaminated thing. In the series, as in the world of "Art-Neurosis," the Other is perceived as belonging to another, hostile species; he appears as one's demonic double. In reciprocity modified by an atmosphere of lack, "the same appears to us as the antiman inasmuch as this same man appears as radically Other (that is to say, that for us he represents a threat of death)." But within the world of positive reciprocity, "there is no *Other,* there are myselves."[17] The multiplicity of identities is thus disqualified, if not eliminated. Sartre apparently agrees with Hegel, who in *Logic* asserts that "freedom means that the object with which you deal is a second self . . . For freedom it is necessary that we should feel no presence of something which is not ourselves."[18]

James Sheridan strikes to the heart of the meaning of the *Critique* and the work it is intended to preface when he remarks that "comprehension is the noetic correlate of reciprocity."[19] But comprehension is also the intellectual and affective precondition of reciprocity. Sartre's sometime model Dilthey asserts that psychology "is the foundation of all knowledge of historical life, and of all rules for the guidance and progress of society. It is not merely a deeper contemplation of man himself."[20] This is the case as well for Sartre's comprehension, which underlies the possibility of the ethics that overcome reification. For reciprocity and hence freedom to be possible, a certain variety of knowledge founded upon reliving the experience of the Other must also be possible. An understanding of this fact is the key to understanding *L'Idiot*. If one's relations with others cannot be grounded in this empathy-based, tacit knowledge, then human life, as Sartre understands it, is a promise that can never be met. Comprehension is the epistemological basis for the classless society in that it establishes the psychological grounds of solidarity.

The necessary relationship between these ideals is never directly stated by Sartre, but at various moments it is abundantly clear. The reciprocity discovered in the group in fusion is said to involve "the reciprocal translucidity of common individuals." The crucial relation between the ideals is more directly put in the statement that "reciprocity designates the comprehension of the Other as the same."[21] The scandal of otherness can be surpassed only if comprehension is revealed to be a potential of the species. "To understand Adam, is to become Adam," Sartre had noted in his essay on Kierkegaard.[22] The ethical ideal is attained when one becomes another person, without ceasing to be fully oneself, in the group in fusion, or the moment of reciprocity that presupposes the feasibilities of comprehension. If Sartre's epistemological ideal can be realized, then Goetz's separation anxiety can be assuaged, and one is not definitively tied to the serialized world in which Flaubert felt he lived and which he described to Madame Brainne: "We are all in a desert. No one understands anyone."[23]

Sartre wrote the *Search for a Method* to formulate a method of knowledge that would allow for the possibility of an escape from solipsism. In *L'Idiot* he has sought to give concrete proof that this escape can be realized. In *Nausea* the impossibility of biography functioned grimly as a metaphor for the fact that life made little sense. Lukács was right when he commented that "existentialism persists in teaching that it is categorically impossible to know anything at all about man."[24] In *L'Idiot* the practice of valid biography communicates the fact that a positive form of human existence is possible. Sartre once made the peculiar remark that everyone ought to do for their fellows what he has done for Flaubert. At face value this seems to be the statement of a clerkly ideal pushed to an insane extreme, which evokes visions of overtaxed library resources and scribbling billions. But Sartre really means that comprehension must be universalized, because it is the axial component of an ethical world. Just as the experience of the free author of *What Is Literature?* challenged the reader to institute the kingdom of ends, now the biographer enjoins the reader to transform himself in his image. Biography is an insurrection in an armchair, a vicarious experience of a world of freedom and justice, the clerkly equivalent of the task of the revolutionary. Both seek to universalize a condition of comprehension and create a world in which the Other is the same. For Sartre, to play upon the line of Marx, biography must become the world.

The character of ethical relations is determined by the success or failure of an attempt to grasp the reality of the Other. When empathy is not possible, the Other is an object for one, as he inevitably was in the world of *Being and Nothingness*. If selves are finally opaque to one another, as the Bishop of *The Devil and the Good Lord* vainly hoped that he was, then man is finally an object for man, and humanity is definitively divided between the hunters and the hunted. We recognize the world of Flaubert, who wrote: "Hobbes was right: *Homo homini lupus*."[25] Under these circumstances murderous anarchy can be avoided only by recourse to moral laws imposed from without. And this form of alienation, as indicated in *Saint Genet,* is repugnant to Sartre's anarchist bent. If people are mutually transparent, if the Other is the same, then there is no need for laws, or for exterior precepts that arrive from the outside.

The relationship between epistemology and ethics helps to explain certain of *L'Idiot's* problematic features. Biography is quite impossible, Mark Twain reports, because if the task were to be done properly, "Every day would make a whole book of eighty thousand words—three hundred and sixty-five books a year."[26] This discouraging bulk may seem to be approached too closely by *L'Idiot,* and the few who have read the book have often complained about its length. Yet such annoyance derives partially from an ignorance of Sartre's fundamental intention.

Although it is true that the book's length is greater than its insights would seem to warrant, and Sartre is incontinently repetitious, over-killing with examples and laboring his points, the length serves an expressive purpose. The prodigious size of the work is a function of its meaning, a servant of the epistemology that is its pulse, a product of a fusion of form and ethos. Sartre's purpose is to communicate an immediate and oppressive sense of the presence of Flaubert. He wants the reader to be swallowed up by his book, to taste the exact flavor of his subject's grim experience, to live with the text until it disappears and he is confronted with the essence of Flaubert. The singularity of the existence of the Other must be lived as well as thought. The cognitive subject is the human being in its entirety: the rational faculty as well as the hands that hold the three heavy volumes. Man knows not only through rational procedures but also through feeling and imagination, and he eliminates these personal, tacit dimensions at great risk. Knowledge must have affective roots if it is to approach completeness. As Dilthey expressed it, "The cognitive faculty which is at work in the human studies is the whole man."[27] Only when this fact is recognized does life grasp life. Through the exhaustive experience of the months required to read *L'Idiot* and the works they are designed to illustrate and amplify, Sartre hopes that the reader will feel like Hilda, the heroine of empathy of *The Devil and the Good Lord:* "But I suffer in all bodies; they strike me on all cheeks; I die in all deaths."[28] Harry Levin has complained that in this book Sartre seems to be suffering from the delusion that he has become Flaubert.[29] This is quite true, and Sartre hopes that his delusion will prove contagious.

The biographer is entitled to the use of a certain imagination, but when the imagination is used in the life study of an historical individual for the purpose of the unembarrassed invention of fact, the reader becomes anxious. His anxiety with respect to *L'Idiot* is greatest in such moments as the description of the critically deficient maternal offices, of the decisive paternal malediction, and of the birth of the postromantic mentality among the schoolboys of Rouen. Here and elsewhere Sartre has gone off on his own without much in the way of documentation. It is true that these reconstructions are not exactly arbitrary, for they are consistent with what is known of Flaubert. When objectively verifiable material is lacking, Sartre's imagination simply enters the breach to connect two known points. But the fact remains that fiction breaks in upon the realm of fact. Sometimes Sartre lets the reader know that he is speculating, while at other times he does not. The reader might have preferred Sartre to adopt the philosophy of the school of painting restoring which holds that an audience should be clearly apprised of the point at which imaginative reconstruction begins and the known ends. The question is what place this kind of speculation holds in a biography that pretends to total knowledge of a historical man.

Again the answer comes from Sartre's theory of knowledge. As Husserl and Bergson asserted, one knows another self through an imaginative indwelling in his experience. A complete inquiry involves the projection of one's freedom into the domain of the Other. Or as Sartre understands it, empathy, is a mingling of freedoms not a passive mirror experience. Sartre imaginatively reconstructs in order to increase the level of empathy, to heighten the degree of involvement of the inquiring subject and his audience. Knowing rests on something besides the results of empirical demonstration. An "objectivity" that excludes the personal aspects of knowing can never arrive at the sympathetic picture the biographer seeks. The means of knowing must be integrated, all the faculties exercised. By striking together the empirical and the imaginary, distance and empathy, Sartre believes that he can create a living Flaubert. Verifiable facts are essential to the project, for without them there would be no possibility of empathy, but sympathetic identification is the morally prior value, and this is the one that Sartre's boldly speculative reconstructions are designed to serve.

Another notion dramatized by both the length and the unfinished condition of the book is the fact that this form of knowledge is always approximate, always ongoing, never finished. Comprehension, Sartre maintains, "is always in progress because it is nothing other than existence itself."[30] Dilthey expressed the same idea when he chose the verb *nacherleben* as a synonym for understanding in the human sciences. A person can be understood and progressively known, but he is not the object of final knowledge. No finality is possible, even with the dead, for the knowing subject is always evolving, living, and changing. Comprehension is a mode of being rather than an achievement.

"I would like my study to be read as a novel," Sartre has said of *L'Idiot*.[31] The work participates in this genre in the sense that the novel's task has traditionally been to forge an identity that is necessarily a fiction. The biographer, like the novelist, gives shape, a final effect of wholeness, to an individual that he himself never experienced. He causes readers to believe in the existence of a fixed self that is a fiction, at least from the point of view of the living experience of Flaubert. There is always a sense, Sartre would say, from the perspective of the dispossessing glance of the Other, in which I do indeed have an identity. But it is also true, from the perspective of the subject himself, that "all that one can say that I am, I am not."[32] Perhaps Sartre also affiliates Flaubert's biography with the novel because that is the literary form which historically has made the most ambitious attempts to gain the illusion of a perfect knowledge of and identification with another person. What Frederick A. Pottle comments of Boswell in his life of Johnson may also be said of Sartre in *L'Idiot:* "Boswell generally knows his story something as a novelist does . . . It would be naive to suppose that knowledge of subsequent events is not affecting his details meaningfully, to create a significant forward-straining tension."[33] Finally, Sartre may have had in mind the fact that the overriding theme of the European novel, as of *L'Idiot,* has been the conflict between society's constricting requirements and a protagonist's straining for personal freedom.

If this biography is to be labeled a novel, then it is a nonfiction novel, a *Bildungsroman,* a *Kunstlerroman,* and an experimental novel in Zola's sense, for the author tries out hypotheses to test how they mesh with reality and with one another. It is also to no less an extent, though operating under the deepest cover, a utopian novel. The revelation of the negative is only one part of the author's strategy. The biography seeks to be more than narrowly pathographic, more than the means to denounce illusion. Although it is an epic of unfreedom, it also contains a paradigm of unalienated relations. This content will be evident only to readers familiar with the *Critique.*

Comprehension, because of its relation to the ideal of reciprocity, is a method that is no less missionary and prescriptive than diagnostic. A world of freedom and justice is born out of the instrument of knowledge that denounces the world of necessity. An implicit perception of a hoped-for alternative future is concealed within the demystification of the past. As readers relive Flaubert's blighted existence, they glimpse a transfigured reality, for the ever-present method never ceases to whisper in their ear of another kind of world. If, as Sartre insists, the life of someone cannot be accounted for except as the singular universal, then present or past reality cannot be revealed without recourse to a vision of a world in which men are free. Utopia is revealed by the same method that discloses the singular universal, namely the alienated man, because, Sartre insists, today there is no other. A lucid understanding of a negative past or present is not possible without an epiphenomenal revelation of a world which surpasses the one that is directly described. Readers find themselves involved in a hermeneutic circle. Alienation cannot be shown fully without recourse to a vision of salvation, or vice versa. The world of positive reciprocity is disclosed only when readers experience something resembling its opposite.

Sartre's method not only discloses a world that provokes dissatisfaction but simultaneously suggests an alternative to the world which the reader is encouraged to refuse, a microcosmic foretaste of human relations in the ethical world of the future. Utopia is represented without recourse to speculative myth or reified models. The reader, properly prepared by the *Critique,* finds himself on a threshold that opens onto two incompatible realms: one directly seen, the other indirectly sensed. Because of the ubiquitous fusion of the "is," the "was," and the "ought," *L'Idiot* is a work of immanental irony. The two Marxist meanings of freedom appear at the same time: prerevolutionary freedom defined as the awareness of necessity,

and postrevolutionary freedom defined as the unification of man
with his species being. To the extent that he becomes a contemporary
of the alienated world of the Second Empire, the reader becomes a
contemporary of the future. This experience mirrors the Marxist
irony that the matrix of the new man is the most wretched creature
of capitalist society. *L'Idiot* is a lovely dream that is at every moment
blighted, but the blight is simultaneously relieved by the dream that
all might someday be well. The words of Adorno are apposite: "In
the face of despair, philosophy can still be justified if it is the attempt
to consider things as they are seen from the standpoint of salvation.
Knowledge has no light except that which shines from salvation upon
the world."[34] Through his subterfuge Sartre forces the light of salvation to shine on and reflect off Flaubert, whose project it was to
deny the world of any such hope. In a new and far more happy way,
Flaubert's praxis is stolen once again.

A sudden and secret transforming vision of a world into its opposite appears in other Sartre works. In *The Reprieve*, Brunet is intensely aware that war is inevitable while those around him are
seemingly oblivious to its certainty. Gazing at the graceful spectacle
of Paris, Brunet suddenly sees heaps of rubble, the consequence of
the war to come. In *L'Idiot* the reader has an experience that is at once
similar but different. He too sees the opposite of what is immediately
apparent, but the order is reversed. The human rubble of the past
guides the reader to see the graceful world of the future. If Brunet
is a prophet, then Sartre is as Schlegel called Herder, "a retrospective
prophet," the man who finds the future in the past.

Another novel that bears resemblance to *L'Idiot* is *Doctor Faustus*
of Thomas Mann. Each takes the form of an artist's biography.
Mann's protagonist, the demonic composer Adrian Leverkuhn, is
like Flaubert a postromantic artist who seeks to create an empathy-
free, "objective" work of art that expresses hatred and mockery of
the human. Serenus Zeitblom, the narrator-biographer, describes the
mentality of his friend and subject: "It was a state of mind which,
no longer interested in the psychological, pressed for the objective,
for a language that expressed the absolute, the binding and com-
pulsory, and in consequence laid in itself the pious fetters of . . . strict
form."[35] Sartre found all these same impulses in the prose of Flaubert. In the works of both the fictional composer and Flaubert there
is an equation between art, a sadistic, misanthropic laughter, and
death. In the works of both, there is a confusion of the animate and
inanimate. Both seek to attain to an inhuman freedom through
ironic remoteness and the pose of the neutral observer. Both take the
point of view of death on the living, and both find beauty in the

inorganic. In the case of each there is an equating of the detached pursuit of art for art's sake with evil. The terrified Zeitblom says, "Here no one can follow me who has not as I have experienced in his very soul how near aestheticism and barbarism are to each other."[36] This equation is one of the great themes of Sartre's Flaubert. In a letter of 1837 to Ernest Chevalier Flaubert corroborates his biographer: "What is beauty if not the impossible, and poetry if not barbarism."[37]

One of the avowed ends of Leverkuhn is to compose a work that would be the retraction of Beethoven's Ninth Symphony. This new piece would spread hatred and demoralization, thus ironically negating the themes of faith in human nature and universal brotherhood that are affirmed in the finale of Beethoven's work. Conversely L'Idiot represents an attempt to retract, or ironically to undo, the meaning of Madame Bovary as Sartre understands it. The author of the novel ironically becomes the subject of the work that seeks to be its revocation. A work that is a promise of salvation is set against one that is a promise of damnation. A work that tells its readers man has no other future than that of being "the machine of the machine" finds itself opposed by a book that tells its readers man is also a for-itself and may live and be understood as such. In L'Idiot two concepts of the imagination square off: one is based on abstraction and derealization for the sake of derealization; the other is based on empathy, derealization for the sake of realization, that is, deliverance from illusion, or lying for the sake of setting the truth in higher relief. One founds a world of sympathy, the other a world of hatred. Sartre argues that Madame Bovary intends to reveal "the hateful universal" (III, 416). "A work of hatred—that is to say that takes hatred as a point of view—tells the truth of the age" (III, 323). The work of hatred speaks the truth of the middle years of the nineteenth century, whereas the work that reveals the singular universal discloses the falsity of the world of Flaubert and simultaneously the truth of the possible ethical world of the future.

Another theme shared by Doctor Faustus and L'Idiot is the questioning of the validity of fiction. The issue appears explicitly in Mann's novel and implicitly in L'Idiot. In Doctor Faustus Sammael, the angel of death, says to Leverkuhn: "Only the nonfictional is still permissible, the unplayed, the undisguised and untransfigured expression of suffering in its actual moment. Its importance and extremity are so ingrained that no seeming play with them is any longer allowed."[38] Sartre's preference for biography makes the same statement. In Nausea Antoine Roquentin abandons his work on the Marquis de Rollebon and instead entertains the idea of writing a novel. The history of Sartre's own *oeuvre* reveals a clear movement in the opposite direction. Sartre has gradually lost interest in expressing himself through fiction and has devoted most of the postwar years to various autobiographical forms, to biographical theory, and to progressively more ambitious life studies.

Sartre points to the reason for the move when he remarks, "Whatever one does, one refers to an ethics."[39] The shift from fiction to biography can be explained only through an understanding of the development of Sartre's ethical thought. Biography and fiction, as Sartre understands them, depend upon very different ethical systems, one of which has proved to be of greater value than the other.

In *What Is Literature?* Sartre founded the moral dignity of literature on a Kantian ethics. In ideal prose the author is experienced by the reader as a pure and free subject. As he reads, he enters the kingdom of ends. If the work is properly situated in the present and if the characters are properly drawn, the work will encourage the reader to realize this paradigm of unalienated relations in his everyday life. But such a program confronts him with an insuperable difficulty. As shown in *Saint Genet*, a Kantian ethics is an impossibility. When those pages were written in 1951, this conclusion was already far from new with Sartre. In *Being and Nothingness* is the statement: "If I would attempt to act according to the precepts of Kantian ethics, by taking the freedom of the Other as an unconditioned end, this transcendence would become transcended transcendence, simpy by virtue of the fact that I make of it my end."[40] In the *Critique* the description of reciprocity contains the caveat: "Let us not think that . . . we have entered the city of ends and that, in reciprocity, each recognizes and treats the Other as an absolute end. That would only be formally possible if each would treat himself or would treat the human being in himself as an unconditioned end. This hypothesis would send us back to absolute idealism. Only an idea amidst other ideas can pose itself as its own end. But man is a material being in the middle of a material world. He seeks to change the world that crushes him."[41] Since man is embodied existence, Kantian ethics must be rejected as another delusion of idealist thought. The Other can be understood as pure subject only on condition of the impossible liquidation of the reader's materiality. It follows for Sartre that prose fiction rests on an unrealizable ethics. Reality can never be expected to redeem the promise that prose fiction makes.

Biography, however, is affiliated with the ideal of reciprocity, which is founded on a materialist rather than an idealist ground. For reciprocity to be feasible, a certain kind of cognitive and affective event must still be shown to be possible. It thus becomes clear why the vindication of the intrinsic intelligibility of man through comprehension is a life-or-death matter for Sartre. He has written *L'Idiot* in order to demonstrate that this form of knowledge is possible and, by extension, that reciprocity is possible, that the essence of the relation between consciousnesses is not conflict, as he had once thought, but mutuality. With this perception as background it is easier to understand why Sartre has spent seventeen years and almost three thousand pages on his biography of Flaubert. His task has been nothing less than the demonstration of the possibility of a materialist ethics. The reader must understand *L'Idiot* not only as a negative example of how one life can be mangled but also, through attention to the method employed, as an inquiry into how man can be treated in a world in which scarcity and exploitation are things of the past.

Although both can ultimately be only forms of minipraxis, biography is a more important task than the novel. A work of fiction cannot establish the possibility of reciprocity. The understanding of a fictional character is no proof that comprehension is possible in the real world. A work of fiction can provide only the illusion of an idealist ethics. Successful biography, on the contrary, can function as the model, however ineffectual, of an ethical ideal that is attainable. This does not mean that prose fiction is entirely without value. Although for the urgent task of establishing the possibility of ethics, fiction is as useless as biography is crucial, the novel does retain great value when it provides an infectious illusion of an idealist, utopian world of absolute freedom. Both the proof of the possibility of an alienation-free world and the tools for its realization must be found elsewhere. Fiction may contribute, however small its impact, to the freeing of man. But whether freedom is even possible must be established by biography.

Finally, *L'Idiot* is of interest because it functions as a kind of Sartrean *summa*. A disorienting feature of his *oeuvre* has been the dearth of explicit attempts to relate the themes and vocabularies of his various works. His penchant for thinking against himself, his disloyalty to his earlier avatars, his obsession with continually beginning anew, have led him to be reluctant to spend time binding together his concerns of the present with those of the past. But *L'Idiot* is replete with the self-reference, almost the self-parody, that he previously seemed to eschew. The life study of Flaubert functions for Sartre's works as does the coda of *The Past Recaptured:* old friends and themes, disparately encountered, appear together, transformed. Seemingly forgotten issues and terms reemerge and are brought together in an illuminating manner. Sartre explains *L'Idiot* as an attempt to illustrate the ideas found in *Search for a Method*, but it also represents the ingression of many of the features and themes of his earlier work into the world of the *Critique*. In it he feeds on himself in an instructive fashion, restating, extending, historicizing, and amplifying earlier ideas that had languished unmentioned, unintegrated into his late system. The disparate strands of his thought hold reunion; a salmagundi of earlier notions is reconciled and refashioned. The subterfuge of salvic self-perdition is resurrected to help explain Flaubert's conversion. The for-itself/in-itself reappears as the ideal of a world of exploitation. The resort to the imaginary, earlier studied ahistorically, is shown to be the suicidal last resort of a man who has been utterly dispossessed of his being by negative social forces. The comic, treated in the early essay on Bataille, is reconsidered and found to be the refusal of intersubjectivity characteristic of life in the series. Sartre raises again the themes of childhood, found in the stories "L'Enfance d'un chef" and "L'Ange du morbide," and of the family, found in the essay on Gorz and in *The Words*. The doomed schoolboy group in fusion of the autobiography reappears at the Collège de Rouen. Genet, Baudelaire, and Mallarmé return. The events of 1848 and 1871 are once again angrily discussed. Mathieu, like Flaubert, regretted that the formerly gracious Paris was becoming an austere world of instrumental reason. In *Being and Nothingness* man loses himself in vain so that God may be born. In the last biography the bourgeois extinguishes himself in vain in order to generate capital. Just like the paintings of Tintoretto, *Madame Bovary* bears witness to an age that refuses to know itself. *L'Idiot* is a climactic piece and, more than any other work, deserves the title "the essential Sartre."

VII

The Dialectic of Narcissism

The biographer portrays himself in his project.
                                                    Sartre

The philosophical unity of the three biographies resides in their
common concern with the two inextricably related problems of
alienation and the search for a method of knowledge which will
reveal the singular universal and demonstrate that alienation is not
an ontological necessity. But Sartre's enormous biographical enterprise becomes the synthetic totality that he intends only because of
the emotional component of his philosophical concerns. To understand this component, it is necessary to isolate what Sartre's three
biographical subjects have, or do not have, in common with Sartre
himself. Is there a point at which the personal histories of all four
coincide? Sartre has said that he has a habit of writing against himself. Is such the case in these three books, or is Sartre in fact doing
quite the opposite?

Like Baudelaire, Sartre was without a father during his early
years. He had his mother to himself until her remarriage when he
was eleven. Like Baudelaire, he considered the new father to be an
intruder. He explains in *The Words* that he spent his preadolescent
years in the household of his grandparents, where nothing really
belonged to him. Like Genet, Sartre was the victim of generosity. In
the filmed sequel to *The Words* he has mentioned the significance of
his having been caught at pilfering from his mother's purse, which
is another similarity with Genet. In two of the biographies Sartre,
like Saint Jerome battling the ghost of Cicero, may be said to be
struggling against his own early fascination with postromantic
literary myths.

The most striking common feature of the lives of his three subjects is that they all experience the domination of the Other and
internalize that dominion, integrating his will into their character,
where it is simultaneously worshiped and detested. Because all three
have integrated a seemingly hostile and sadistic Other, each subject
is called a *heautontimoroumenos*. Each is, in Hesnard's negative
sense, a narcissist, obsessed with capturing a mirror image of himself. The self with which Baudelaire, Genet, and Flaubert seek to
coincide has been defined not by themselves but by the external
enemy force. As R. D. Laing notes, "The Others have become in-
stalled in our hearts, and we call them ourselves."[1] In this mirror
image they seek to find themselves as a thing rather than a transcendence. As Sartre remarked in *Saint Genet,* one becomes a narcissist when one's being is stolen by the Other. The bereft subsequently seeks to recoup his loss but finds nothing to coincide with
except the self-image imposed by the Other.

Yet Sartre is not writing against his own narcissism, his own lack
of a sense of freedom, and his own worshipful attitude toward a
dominating Other falsely mistaken for himself. He is not the victim
of a remote and vindictive figure of authority. Rather, in these books
Sartre is seeking to eternalize and dramatize that part of himself
which he holds to be most valuable, which sets him diametrically
against his three subjects. The biographies are examples of mirror
writing. Baudelaire, Genet, and Flaubert are primarily inverted self-
images. Through a procedure of symmetrical reversal, Sartre describes himself by describing his opposites. He does not write himself
into his biographies so much as he writes himself out of them.

Sartre considers himself, to the extent that such a thing is possible
in his world, a free man. He once said to Merleau-Ponty, "When
someone speaks to me of freedom, it is as though he spoke to me
of myself."[2] In order to understand how he relates to his biographical
subjects, it is therefore necessary to understand how a secure sense
of freedom is created, which in turn requires an understanding of
Sartre's early years for, as he comments, "everything derives from
childhood."[3]

These psychological considerations do not mean, however, that
Sartre's life has been a suprahistorical drama. The factors that have
created this particular singular universal include, among other circumstances, a family life sheltered from direct contact with the world
of production, lifelong financial security, weakened allegiance to
religion resulting from the influence of positivism on the educated
bourgeois, a Protestant background, the ideal of the clerk, violence
at school, the Parisian café, the revival of interest in Hegel, the influ-

ence of Bergson, Husserl, Marx, Hesnard, and Dilthey, the influence of surrealism and the personalism of Maurice Nédoncelle and Emmanuel Mounier, and the experience of solidarity discovered in the war. None of these character-forming influences can be ignored, and yet the peculiar atmosphere in the house on the rue Le Goff where Sartre spent his first crucial years is of overriding interest and significance.

Merleau-Ponty, in a discussion of the *Introduction à la méthode de Léonard de Vinci*, takes Valéry to task for an inability to explain Leonardo's apparent sense of himself as a totally free person. Merleau-Ponty suggests that such a feeling of freedom must have its source in early childhood. Of the youthful Leonardo he writes: "He had no experience of authority, and . . . trusted only his own judgment, as those who were not brought up in an atmosphere of intimidation and protective power exuded by the father are likely to do." Leonardo's father had abandoned him to the exclusive care of his peasant mother. From his birth to the age of four, Leonardo was without a father: "He learned about the world in the unique company of his mother who appeared to have miraculously created him."[4]

Sartre's experience of his father was similar, as explained in *The Words*:

> The death of Jean-Baptiste was the great event of my life: it returned my mother to her chains and gave me my freedom.
>
> There is no such thing as a good father, it's a rule. It is not men who are to be blamed, rather it is the relation of paternity that is rotten. There is nothing better than to produce children; but to *have* them, what an injustice! Had he lived, my father would have lain on me with all his length and would have crushed me. As luck would have it, he died young. Amidst the Eneases who carry their Anchiseses on their shoulders, I pass from one shore to the next, alone and detesting these invisible sires astride their sons for their whole lives.[5]

Because he had no father, Sartre never learned the concept of obedience, and this explains how he came to experience himself as a free man: "I think . . . that one feels oneself free when one has experienced no family conflict during childhood—I had none myself—, and that one has been loved by one's mother, and, in sum, that one has created for oneself a certain world in which one becomes indispensable; that is to say, that the family treats you in such a way that you believe yourself indispensable to it, so that you sense yourself to be someone who is generous, and who fulfills it."[6]

Because Sartre's subjects did not have a conflict-free early history, because they learned obedience all too well, they are described as narcissistic. Sartre observed of Genet that his being had been stolen. The same occurred to Flaubert. According to the early Sartre, Baudelaire deprived himself of his own freedom. A person whose being is stolen ceases to be autonomous and concomitantly becomes a narcissist in a negative sense, withdrawing from reality and worshiping the Other in the guise of himself. There is, however, another kind of narcissism besides that resulting from alienation, a narcissism which chronologically precedes alienation. In *Civilization and Its Discontents* Freud describes the primary narcissism: "originally the ego includes everything, later it separates off an external world from itself. Our present ego-feeling is, therefore, only a shrunken residue of a much more inclusive—indeed, an all-embracing—feeling which corresponded to a more intimate bond between the ego and the world about it."[7]

Marcuse has commented on this theory of Freud's:

> The concept of primary narcissism implies . . . that narcissism survives not only as a neurotic symptom but also as a constitutive element in the construction of the reality, coexisting with the mature reality ego. Freud describes the "ideational content" of the surviving primary ego-feeling as "limitless extension and oneness with the universe" [oceanic feeling]. And . . . he suggests that the oceanic feeling seeks to reinstate "limitless narcissisms." The striking paradox that narcissism, usually understood as egotistic withdrawal from reality, here is connected with oneness with the universe reveals the new depth of the conception: beyond all immature autoeroticism, narcissism denotes a fundamental relatedness to reality which may generate a comprehensive existential order. In other words, narcissism may contain the germ of a different reality principle.[8]

Sartre too hints at the two forms of narcissism: "There is a profound narcissism in poetry . . . In prose, on the other hand, there is a narcissism, but it is dominated by a need to communicate; this is a more mediated narcissism, that is to say surpassed, in order to communicate with the other."[9] As did Hesnard before them, Marcuse and Sartre recognize both a self-enclosed and an expansive narcissism. Both writers leave this point undeveloped, but it has since been treated systematically.[10] Béla Grunberger, for example, in *Le Narcissisme* recognizes that it is always necessary to speak of two varieties of narcissism: "a centrifugal and a centripetal narcissism, a primary and a secondary narcissism, positive or negative, healthy or pathological narcissisms."[11]

Sartre's description of himself in *The Words* and the ideals he expresses elsewhere accord to a striking degree with the qualities of the centrifugal, positive narcissist. It is in fact impossible to understand Sartre's biographies and their philosophical preoccupations without the dialectic of narcissism. They represent a confrontation between the author and his subjects, between the repressed and the unrepressed narcissist, the centripetal and centrifugal narcissist.

Grunberger remarks that the prime condition for the development of positive narcissism is the absence of an oedipal conflict within the family. Such an absence is possible when the maternal incest of which Hesnard wrote and which Sartre described in *Baudelaire* is not interrupted. Sartre, in stating that the early death of his father was the most significant event of his life, resorts to Freudian terminology: "In truth, the prompt retreat of my father bestowed upon me a very incomplete oedipal experience."[12] In the Freudian system oedipal conflict is crucial to the development of the superego, which is the internalization of external authority. The unrepressed primary narcissist therefore has an underdeveloped superego, whereas the superego of the secondary, repressed narcissist possesses an overdeveloped agency of deferred obedience. Throughout Sartre's dealings with the theme of influence, true consciousness always comes from inside, while false consciousness is imposed from without, as in the case of the synthetic identity imposed by serial structures. All of Sartre's subjects are the unhappy hosts of a hypertrophied internal judge; they are educated into obedience and an easy acceptance of external authority. They are inhabited by the Other. Baudelaire internalized conventional morality, Genet absorbed the morality of the Just, and Flaubert absorbed the oppressive will of his father. Sartre speaks of "the terrible superego" of Flaubert.[13] This superego is none other than the internalization of the ideals of Achille-Cléophas. Of himself, however, Sartre writes, "I readily agree with the verdict of an eminent psychoanalyst: I have no superego."[14] This is an extremely naive remark and points to a damaging blind spot in Sartre's system.

Grunberger notes that the narcissist is hostile to the presence of any foreign force in his psyche. Sartre's three subjects are blemished because they are inhabited souls. "I don't like inhabited souls," Sartre comments in *Saint Genet*.[15] He describes Flaubert as being inhabited by the thoughts of others; "The enemy father was installed in him like an occupying army"; he was "like a Sibyl, inhabited."[16] In opposition to his less fortunate subjects, Sartre considers himself to be uninhabited. In *The Words* he surmises that if he had had a father, "he would have inhabited me." As a child, Sartre confesses, he was "almost nothing, at most an activity without content." The

Hesnard-influenced ethics of praxis in *Saint Genet* requires a self that is "without content." The purely spontaneous behavior that is Sartre's ideal is impossible for an inhabited self. The for-itself always wants to set off anew without any encumbering presence to block its uninhibited rush into the future. It is always, as Sartre says of himself, "the newborn child."[17]

The narcissist understands himself to be self-created. Grunberger observes that he refuses any idea of filiation and establishes himself outside of a hierarchy of cause and effect. In the case of Genet, Sartre admired "the superb project of being one's own cause."[18] In *Being and Nothingness* man is dependent upon himself alone for his freedom; no one can enslave him. The desire to be self-born may be held partially responsible for Sartre's early resistance to psychoanalysis, for as Paul Ricoeur notes, "The understanding that psychoanalysis offers to modern man is difficult and painful because of the narcissistic humiliation it inflicts."[19] *The Words* indicates that Sartre thought of himself as self-conceived: "Son of nobody, I was my own cause." He declares himself to be the "child of my works."[20] If Flaubert had had a constitution that permitted revolt, he could have been, like Sartre himself, "the child of his works."[21] In the fused group, according to Sartre, we are "the children of ourselves."[22] His biographical subjects are, in contrast, the "children of their executioners."[23]

The child described by Grunberger has a sense of the mother's belonging to him alone and hence develops no concept of jealousy or of the necessity for compromise. Sartre writes: "my mother belonged to me alone; no one contested my tranquil possession of her: I knew nothing of violence and hatred. I was spared the hard apprenticeship of jealousy." For the healthy Narcissus there is no sense of rivalry with the mother; the relationship is rather a sibling than an authoritarian one. Sartre's mother was a relatively weak person, not at all regarded by him as an authority figure. In the grandfather's household he and his mother were collectively referred to as "the children." "I had an older sister," Sartre tells in *the Words,* "my mother." Grunberger observes that the narcissistically oriented individual tends to romanticize incest, particularly between brother and sister. In *The Words* Sartre notes briefly the appearance of this theme in his works, mentioning in this connection Boris and Ivich in *The Age of Reason,* Oreste and Electre in *The Flies,* and the blatantly incestuous Leni and Frantz in *The Condemned of Altona.*[24]

Because the child is either ignorant or willfully oblivious of his father's determining role in the fact of his existence, and because he is aware of an exclusive and overpoweringly positive focus on his person, he sees himself as divine and miraculous. Such was the case for Merleau-Ponty's Leonardo, and Grunberger too refers to "the fantasy of the divine child."[25] In *The Words* Sartre also speaks of "my divine childhood." He understood, like Genet, that he was "the child of a miracle."[26] Within the family this self-conception was encouraged by his being referred to as a "marvel," a "treasure," "the gift of Providence." The child described by Grunberger is imbued with an unusually high degree of self-esteem: "He reads his narcissistic confirmation in the eyes of his mother, confirmation because of the fact that he is always unique, that he is esteemed because he is intrinsically valuable." For Sartre, an illusion of being indispensable is crucial to the development of a sense of freedom. The situation described by both him and Grunberger contrasts starkly with the experience of the other sort of narcissist, who undergoes rejection and devaluation at a critical moment in early youth. Grunberger indicates that because of the positive narcissist's high regard for himself, he easily lapses into the role of the hero and has an illusion of being magically all-powerful. In *The Words* Sartre reports that he imagined himself a hero and spent much time in his youth fantasizing about extravagant exploits of generosity. His youth was dominated by the illusion of "my all-powerfulness."[27]

Each bereft child is a solipsistic creature, closed in upon a self defined and dominated by the Other, backed into recoil relationships with others, always moving away. The positive Narcissus, however, does not draw boundaries between himself and others but rather seeks to break through them. He refuses to accept the fact that the distinctions between himself and others are insurmountable. Grunberger refers to the furious quest for fusional relations characteristic of the centrifugal Narcissus. He seeks, without imposing upon the freedom of others or losing his own freedom, to accord his individual will with that of others. Since his conversion to Marxism, Sartre has been interested in balancing solidarity with individual freedom, each of which he feels to be necessary to the realization of the other. In his preface to Gorz's *The Traitor* Sartre remarks: "there are only two possible ways to speak of oneself: in the third person singular, or the first person plural. You have to know how to say 'we' in order to say 'I': this goes without saying. But the opposite is true as well."[28] Goetz wants to accomplish just such a fusion: "*you are not* me, it's unbearable. I do not understand why we are two, and I would like to become you while remaining myself."[29] Sartre's idea of freedom is defined in terms of the narcissistic ideal, as the total refusal of one form of identification and the enthusiastic embracing of another. His epistemological and social ideals incorporate a desire to break through solipsism and establish the relatedness of men, to disprove bourgeois atomism, and to establish the fact that seriality can be overcome. In the fused group the Other is the same. The purpose of comprehension is to realize a victory over the same evils. Comprehension, as Wilfrid Desan puts it, is "the act by which one lives the existence of the other."[30] Solipsism can be avoided if the relation to another is fundamentally a relation of being to being, rather than a relation of knowledge to knowledge.

Grunberger finds that the positive Narcissus seeks to do without the world of the adults and is hostile to adults in general because they represent the threatening experience of heteronomy. In *Saint Genet* and *L'Idiot* Sartre systematically takes the side of his child martyrs against the world of the adult. In *The Words* he reveals that he himself began to write in order to escape the world of adults: "By writing I existed, for I escaped the grownups." Free existence is associated with an escape from their world. In *The Words* Sartre goes so far as to express shame at being an adult.[31]

The positive Narcissus, Grunberger reports, has an ambiguous attitude toward his childhood. He is simultaneously proud and ashamed of his peculiar personal history. He is proud of his past because it is responsible for the fact that he is divine, but he is ashamed because he detests the notion of affiliation and finds it humiliating to be dependent upon others for love and valorization. This divided attitude is evident in *The Words,* where Sartre posits his unusual early history as largely responsible for his sense of freedom, but since he is aware that this admission compromises his wish for pure autonomy, he uses irony to display his distance.

A younger Sartre once insisted that there was no connection between himself and his past. This claim to be an unfathered vapor is consistent with the self-image of the positive narcissist. But Sartre has since come to understand that, in the words of Merleau-Ponty, "There are always links, and most especially when we refuse to admit their existence."[32] *The Words* admits that the child he was is father to the man: "Worn, effaced, humiliated, stashed away, silenced, all my childhood traits remain intact in the quinquagenarian."[33] It is his peculiar upbringing that makes of his biographical enterprise a dialectic of narcissism. It is his unrepressed primary narcissism that elicits his outrage with those men and forces who deprive his subjects of their freedom. And it is his centrifugal narcissism that encourages him to seek a form of knowledge showing that it is not inevitable that men be insuperably isolated or alienated. As Hesnard remarks of positive narcissism, "it permits belief in human liberty."[34] Marcuse explains in *Eros and Civilization:* "The memory of gratification is at the origins of all thinking, and the impulse to recapture past gratification is the hidden driving power behind the process of thought."[35] Sartre's biographies, and his late work in general, attempt to make of "the memory of gratification" and "the different reality principle" a comprehensive theory of man and society.

Sartre's insistence that he is without a superego is naive and points to an insufficient psychoanalytic culture. But the partial truth behind this personal myth helps one to understand possible connections between Sartre's own experience and some of the major features of the biographies. The elimination of parental authority that Sartre says he experienced to a considerable degree does not result in the total absence of a superego but rather fixes the superego at a preoedipal stage. At this point in a child's development, the parents appear as remote, vindictive, and capricious. This impression is allowed to be perpetuated later in life if the child is without exposure to a loving figure of authority which would permit a softening of the demonic vision. The child seeks to extinguish the absent father rather than to identify with him and take his place, for no authority is felt to be legitimate. Such a child divides the world starkly into masters and slaves and refuses to entertain the possibility of a benevolent father figure or institution. The world for this individual, writes Alexander Mitscherlich, "is continually changing in shape and producing sinister surprises."[36] These themes appear in the biographies, and these psychoanalytic insights explain why Sartre was moved to invent what Ellmann called "gothic biography," and why his social thought is marred by a refusal to entertain the possibility that any institution or figure of authority coud have a positive social role.

Against this world of capricious power the narcissistic individual nourishes fantasies of revenge. The most prevalent of these fantasies, Christopher Lasch writes, is that of "a general uprising of the young."[37] The connection is inescapable with young Clouet and the revolt at the Collège de Rouen, the single happy moment in the biography of Flaubert, and the events of May 1968 that seemed to bring to life the myth of the groups of the French Revolution euphorically described in the *Critique*.

Sartre's narcissism is partially responsible not only for his success in illuminating his negative counterpart but also for his vulnerability to the charge of *lèse-dialectique*. Marx stresses that every emerging form of socialization is ambiguous. Each form has not only an oppressive but also a liberating component. But Sartre does not always recognize this complexity. Both *Saint Genet* and *L'Idiot,* in their orgiastic hostility to authority, contain unmitigated hostility to the superego. *L'Idiot,* according to Sartre, is written against all families. Freedom is possible only when a person has experienced no history of family conflict. As the members of the Frankfurt school taught and as Christopher Lasch has repeated, the superego, the interior colony of the father, the intrapsychic extension of social authority, is the seat of negative, oppositional thinking.[38] Born of familial conflict, this faculty is the agency that permits one to challenge authority. It may indeed, as Sartre shows, have an oppressive, debilitating effect on the host, but it also may have a necessary, progressive function to which Sartre seems perilously oblivious. If the superego implants a censor in the mind, it also makes it possible for the censor to be censored.

To liquidate these conflicts and impositions may therefore be counterproductive, for the prototype of the conflict between the individual and society is the conflict within the family that Sartre hopes to extinguish. The man with a weakened superego has no potential for negative thinking, no transgressive sense. Although Sartre believes himself to be unburdened by this agency, his whole career countervails the claim. He advocates a personality type that not only may not be his own but also would lead nowhere. He has eliminated the subjective preconditons for the world in permanent revolution that he would like to achieve.

The roots of radical action can never be an absence of conflict. To jettison the family founded on conflict, the seed bed of negative thought, would be to deprive antitheses of their vital relation and to jettison the idea of revolution. Surversive anger would be replaced by a fatal compliancy that could not resist a prevailing wind. Resistance to assimilation would be extinguished, and people would become helpless before arbitrary power. The world would become ahistorical in a sinister sense, for society would have become a seamless trap. As Arnold A. Rogow remarks, the choice is between the superego and the superstate.[39]

Despite the fanatical opposition to all authority that they seem to contain, the biographies have implications that are perhaps ultimately quietistic. In this perspective, these passionately anarchist works become the negation of negation. Sartre's call for a thoroughgoing transgression issues in a destruction of transgressive potential and hence forecloses the very possibility of an emancipatory subject. There is a question as to whether a society animated by Sartre's ideals would be possible. Even if it were, it is quite certain that it would be founded upon a character ideal that is bankrupt, one that would be incapable of stirring a saving tension between the particular and the universal. Since late capitalism and the superstate seek systematically to weaken the individual, father-centered superego, in order to reduce resistance to its marketing thrusts and to guarantee homogeneous support for policies, it may well be that Sartre's uninflected antiauthoritarianism is in unintentional complicity with their ends. The classical bourgeois family and individual so opposed by Sartre have now all but disappeared. At the end of his strivings, when the Sartrean man of unlimited freedom has the boundary- and conflict-free world he seeks, when he has become a fused member of the hoard of the self-generated and the yearned-for fatherless society, he may well discover that he is without the psychic strength to support a stance against domination, or perhaps even to notice its very existence. The philosophical Caspar Hauser, the man without origins, falls from heaven, but only into the uncontestable grasp of his most implacable enemies.

VIII

The Tribunal of Crabs

[Those who think historically] look backwards only in order to understand the present by considering the previous process and to learn to desire the future more energetically.

Nietzsche

The revolutionary has been defined by Sartre as "the man who has a total awareness of his alienation, and who sees opposing this the possible existence of a society if which men would not be alienated."[1] Through his three lives, Sartre pushes progressively toward the fulfillment of each of the duties he prescribes.

Despite the hyperbolic language and lurid anecdotes that the early Sartre brings to his discussion of the concept, alienation is for him a paper tiger. In *Being and Nothingness* a person was free to return the dispossessing glance and to end his self-deceit. The self-alienation of Baudelaire was condemned because the poet had within his grasp the potential to put an end to his malady. Alienation was without a historical dimension. Dealienation required a revolution from within the self.

In *Saint Genet* Sartre reported that the alienating glance can cause irreparable damage to those who are socially conditioned to conceive of themselves as being without retaliatory powers. In this work Sartre struggled to give his own Hegel-derived view of alienation historical roots. As in his first major philosophical work, the world was divided between those with the dispossessing glances and those dispossessed. But despite the book's claim to rely on Marxist tools of analysis, Marx's basic concept of the theft of praxis was not employed. Nowhere in evidence was the axial idea that the human history of production is the history of estrangement. If certain preconditions were met, inner change could be achieved independently from social revolution. The Just, who had projected outward the negative component of their freedom, could not be fully human, but they could nevertheless rest content, because they were, for themselves and for Sartre, free men. It was up to Genet and his ilk to be miserable for them.

This either-or polarity of the free and the unfree later ceased to be a feature of Sartre's thought. The dispossessor is no less alienated than his victim, for power over another is a form of alienation: "The alienation of the bourgeois is that of a man who attained freedom around 1793, and who transformed his freedom into a power that is an alienation. A bourgeois who commands . . . is not free; he is alienated."[2] In the *Critique* the hatred and fear of the worker invade the life of the bourgeois, constricting his every movement. In *L'Idiot* Sartre carries this idea to its conclusion. By integrating the Hegelian and Marxist models of alienation, he dramatizes the degree to which the oppression of the worker results in the oppression of the master. With the Hegelian model Sartre demonstrates how the for-itself can be strangled in a person's crib long before he collects his first paycheck. With the Marxist model Sartre shows how, in an unsuspected and insidious manner, the most seemingly detached forms of self-objectification can be either stolen or infected by malignant social forces which are beyond the control of the isolated individual.

But as Sartre has progressed through the evolution of this idea, another concept has been ongoing as well. His works have been increasingly invaded by the specter of an unborn alternative to the world of alienation. In *Das Prinzip Hoffnung* Ernst Bloch likens past philosophers to Marcus Terrentius Varro, who neglected to include the future tense in his Latin grammar.[3] The same may be said of Sartre in his *Baudelaire,* which is ironic in that the biography accuses the poet of precisely the same sin. Baudelaire is the one for whom the future was only a word, and who found the meaning of the present in the past at a time when Tristan, Michelet, and Marx found the meaning of the present in the future. The future is present in *Baudelaire,* but only in the ahistorical sense of *Being and Nothingness* as the temporal dimension of freedom into which the for-itself launches itself in good faith. Sartre suggests through the inchoate Marxism of the biography that there is an alternative world to our own, but the reader is confused, for he is still squarely within the world of *Being and Nothingness* where people are involved in an endless round of evading, receiving, and meting out dangerous glances. Human solidarity is ontologically impossible. For Sartre's first *heautontimoroumenos* alienation is self-caused and self-cured. No future world of mutuality will solve his problems.

Since *Baudelaire,* however, Sartre has discovered the future and incorporated it in one way or another in his works. This development is not surprising for a Marxist or fellow traveler, because according to the Marxist view, history since the original division of labor has marched inexorably toward a rendezvous with a predetermined future. Whereas for the bourgeois the future is used as an alibi for the misery of the present and a myth of progress is used to quiet those unhappy about their circumstances, for the Marxist the future is what makes the present unlivable. And it is from the perspective of this future that the present must be judged. As Merleau-Ponty notes, "For bourgeois justice the past is the final instance, but for revolutionary justice it is the future."[4] And as Sartre remarks in *L'Idiot,* man's justification is always retrospective; "it returns to him from the future, and from the horizons moves backward through the course of time, moves from the present to the past, and *never* from the past to the present."[5]

In *The Phenomenology of Perception* Merleau-Ponty observes: "One could not hope to explain the relation of the future to the present except by assimilating it to that of the present to the past . . . Prospection would thus in reality be a retrospection, and the future would be a projection of the past."[6] By dealing with the past, a writer creates in his reader what Husserl terms an "analogizing apprehension" of the future.[7] A work that treats of the past necessarily involves an analogical grasping of the future's perspective on the present. In this sense, then, *Baudelaire* also evokes or alludes to the future. Since that work Sartre has progressively sought to make the reader explicitly aware of this experience of analogy. He has commended Ibsen's achievment in this regard: "In *The Doll's House,* which deals with the emancipation of women at a time when it was not yet a question, Ibsen placed himself in the perspective of the future. It is from the point of view of the future that he described the collapse of this worthless and authoritarian husband, and the liberation of Nora."[8]

In *The Condemned of Altona,* Frantz imagines a formidably alien authority, a tribunal of crabs, which in the thirtieth century sits in judgment on the sins of his own time, frosting the present with the sovereign gaze of the future, causing it to be an object of horror in its own eyes. As Sartre describes the effect of this situation.

Our century will be judged, just as we judge the nineteenth or eighteenth century. It will have its place in history that it will have in a certain way created, and which will incite the judgment of an objective morality on men. Through the ravings of my character I would like the audience to feel itself to be in the presence of this tribunal.

I would like the public to witness our century from the outside, as a foreign object. And at the same time it should realize that it is a participant, because it is making this century. The fact that we know that we will be judged is one of the special features of our time.[9]

In these imaginings there appear again Sartre's hunger for wholeness, for a crowned and coherent world, and his eternal nostalgia for an objective and totalistic knowledge that is ultimately aware of itself as only a retrospective possibility. The device of the meeting with the future also functions as an appeal to freedom, for it suggests the relativity of man's frame of reference, his ultimate responsibility for his own time, and stresses that human consciousness is free precisely because it possesses a future.

The conclusion of *Saint Genet* is redolent with prophetic fervor. The future is more real than the real. Sartre describes the masked men of the future before whom the miserable present appears as a guilty object. Yet the future is still incompletely present. The author has properly terrified the reader with visions of an ultimate judgment, but the picture of the redeemed world that the revolutionary owes the reader is absent. At this point Sartre's ideal of reciprocity was imperfectly formulated, and its relation to the concept of comprehension had not been established. Only after these matters had been settled could he manage a work in which the reader is continuously transcending the immediately apparent historical horizon of the text, a work about an alienated man of the past that also esoterically reveals the possibility of an unalienated world of the future. *L'Idiot* has the face of Janus: to the extent that it is a reproach to the past, it is an approach to the future. As a person vicariously becomes the alienated man of the past, he becomes the unalienated man of the future. In comprehension, the two tasks of the revolutionary collapse into one.

Sartre has been called a figure of the past.[10] In some respects this may be true, but in others it is not. Hegel and Marx provide one index for judgment when they suggest that a system of thought ceases to be relevant at the moment the conditions it describes have been overcome. However hyperbolized, Sartre's world of domination has yet to recede into the mists of history. In *L'Idiot* he proposes a suggestive model for discovering the diffuse movements of power, for relating personality and culture, and base and superstructure without resorting to crude equivalencies, for discovering the relationships between alienations that are primarily social and those that are primarily psychological, and for demonstrating how a system can feed upon internal opposition. Since Paris has been in a resolutely anarchistic mood of late, Sartre has once again been denounced as a dupe of the Stalinists. Some of Sartre's Cold War pronouncements make him vulnerable to this charge. But there is another side to the matter that André Glucksmann alone has noted. He recognizes in Sartre the hostility to all forms of power that is currently in fashion: "After World War II Sartre suspected that there was something in common between the spirit of seriousness and fascism, between the spirit of seriousness and the bourgeois, between the bourgeois and the Marxist."[11]

The utility of a book that pretends to clarify the relays of power is, however, another question. The idea of the old-style clerk, who dares to speak for others, who seeks to illuminate the masses from a hygenic distance, is in disrepute. Such an intellectual, suggests Foucault, is a tool of power. His present duty is to demystify his role and disappear from history. Sartre himself has consigned his biographies to the past. He calls *L'Idiot* the product of the old-style intellectual, the well-meaning library fool, the man of the ineffectual and escapist culture of books. The new intellectual will be preeminently a political activist moving among the dispossessed and expressing their point of view with their own words, for it is they who know best and can best express their difficulties.

By becoming a biografiend, Sartre has sometimes placed himself outside the contemporary movement toward the desubjectification of history, and the Nietzschean critique of knowledge. Foucault has said that one of the reasons for his own attempts to write subjectless history is that this method serves to undermine the humanist myth of the autonomous individual. This myth prohibits the desire for power and excludes the possibility of power being seized because it suggests that the individual, in spite of his place in an unfree world, can be free in his private consciousness, that he can rule even though he possesses no economic or political might. Both *Baudelaire* and *Saint Genet* are tales of the intentional I, but the hold of conventional humanism on *L'Idiot* is more apparent than real. Although Flaubert gives to the forces passing through him a particular color, he is in no sense an originating subject; he is not the source of meaning. The biographee is in the full sense helpless. History is made behind his back. To affirm the irreducibility of what the individual lives and suffers is not to fall necessarily into the trap of humanism. Although the humanly subjectless methods serve to dissolve humanism by largely dispensing with the individual, they come close to mirroring the world of objectifying terrorism which they hope to criticize. In *L'Idiot* Sartre shows that it is possible to write desubjectified history that does not exclude empathy.

Sartre figures in a tradition, involving Hegel, Marx, Husserl, and Bergson, that equates freedom and knowledge. As Sartre explains in *What Is Literature?*: "A liberation that pretends to be *total*, must begin with total knowledge of man by himself."[12] Of late this tradition has been coming in for criticism. The major point of Foucault's studies of the history of madness, medicine, and punishment is that the quest for truth is malicious and serves power. In *Les Maîtres penseurs*, Glucksmann has argued that the totalizing search for truth in the writings of Hegel and Marx necessarily has negative political results, for it is intolerant of difference and insults freedom. The self-intoxicated, Wagnerian discourse that seeks to account for all leads straight to the cruelty of Bolshevism. Injustice is implicit in the will to knowledge, for its goal is always to serve the production goals of the state. Stalinism is not an opportunistic or misguided application of Marx but the inevitable consequence of its reckless, totalizing epistemology. "What does the master know?" asks Glucksmann. "To dominate is to know. To know is to dominate."[13] Power is hostile to that which is hidden and seeks to bring about the dystopia of a night without secrets, in order to open up the minds of its slaves and plasticize their wills to further the ends of the state.

Glucksmann alone is aware that Sartre does not always participate in the tradition he denounces. Apparently referring to the final pages of *Saint Genet*, Glucksmann praises Sartre for recognizing in the Moscow trials the same inhuman, objectifying intellectual passion found on display in *The Phenomenology of Mind*.[14] But this dark tradition is evident in the biographies. In the course of his search for the single, all-encompassing truth, Sartre has galvanized his subjects into conceptual identity, rudely forcing the evidence into his dramatic and speculative structures. His sovereign dissections, especially in *Baudelaire*, admit no remainder, pretend to dissipate all shadows, fix existence spatially, in short see death in life. The vital movement of existence is sacrificed to a knowledge of it, the polemical rhythms drown out the lived experience. Sartre has been insufficiently attentive to Dilthey's advice that comprehension must untendentiously linger over the particular for its own sake. The occasional empirical problems in the biographies are more than surface flaws: they reveal the intolerance of a master thinker who is possessed of an uncontestable truth and animated by the means-oriented rationality he pretends to contest. Sartre's ultimate anarchist message must not be accepted without at the same time being wary of his paranoid, over-anxious use of his method. His search for truth is insufficiently detached from the forms of hegemony.

The three biographies constitute a discourse against power that at the same time bears the marks of power. The power that is denied at one level is reasserted occultly at another. The message of Sartre's method is thus ambivalent. It offers and then withdraws an image of utopia. This may be a fundamental and inescapable contradiction of revolutionary discourse and action: the spontaneity that is meant to be liberated is squashed by the dynamism of the very instrument which seeks to force its release. .

Sartre might defend himself with the words of Adorno: "In psychoanalysis only the exaggerations are true." The caricature is what makes empathy possible. He might also reply, to use Adorno again: "The prudence that prevents us from venturing too far ahead in a sentence is usually only an agent of social control, and so of stupefaction."[15] The prudence that would have caused Sartre to brake for complexity would have had the effect of causing the reader's attention to stray from the essential drama of alienation. But the knowledge that Sartre is seeking, at least in *L'Idiot,* is not always the objectifying, distancing knowledge that Foucault, Glucksmann, and others find repellent. It is a knowledge in which the subject and object are one, in which is heard what Nietzsche called "the sigh of the search of knowledge": "Oh, that I might be reborn in a hundred beings!"[16] It is only a certain kind of unfinished knowledge, uninflected with imaginative projection and the saving nonknowledge of empathy, that constitutes a fascist epistemology. Sartre equates the search for an empathy-based understanding with a quest for pure democracy. This is made clear in a passage from *On a raison de se révolter* where he complains about the defective character of representative government. It is not right for one to represent five thousand others; instead, a way must be found for one person to be five thousand others.[17] Biography is paranoia and unanimist rapture. If Sartre is a master thinker, he is a master thinker who has come in from the cold. If indeed he is the old-style intellectual, the impotent expert, as he shamefully admits, then only rarely has the old so well served the new.

Notes

I. Truth and Alterity

1 *The Rambler*, no. 60, *Samuel Johnson: Selected Poetry and Prose*, ed. Frank Brady and W. K. Wimsatt (Berkeley and Los Angeles: Univ. of California Press, 1977), p. 182.

2 Donald Stauffer, *The Art of Biography in Eighteenth Century England* (Princeton: Princeton Univ. Press, 1941), p. 538.

3 Theodore Zeldin, *France, 1848–1945* (Oxford: Oxford Univ. Press, 1977), II, 767.

4 Zeldin, *France, 1848–1945*, II, 768

5 Samuel Clemens, *Mark Twain's Autobiography* (New York: Collier, 1925), I, 2.

6 E. M. Cioran, *Syllogismes de l'amertume* (1952; rpt. Paris: Gallimard, 1976), p. 23. All translations are my own.

7 Andrew Field, *Nabokov: His Life in Part* (New York: Viking Press, 1977), p. 6; James Joyce, *Finnegan's Wake* (New York: Viking Press, 1959), p. 55.

8 Theodore Ziolkowski, foreword to Herman Hesse, *The Glass Bead Game*, trans. Richard and Clara Winston (New York: Holt, Rinehart and Winston, 1969), p. xix.

9 D. H. Lawrence, *Phoenix: The Posthumous Papers*, ed. E. D. McDonald (New York: Viking Press, 1936), p. 528.

10 Bernard Malamud, *Dubin's Lives* (New York: Farrar, Straus and Giroux, 1979), p. 299.

11 Jean-Paul Sartre, "Qu'est-ce que la littérature?" *Situations II* (Paris: Gallimard, 1948), p. 320n (cited hereafter as "Littérature").

12 Sartre, *L'Idiot de la famille*, vol. I (Paris: Gallimard, 1971), p. 7.

13 Sartre, *Critique de la raison dialectique* (Paris: Gallimard, 1960), p. 9 (cited hereafter as *CRD*).

14 Sartre, *La Nausée* (1938; rpt. Paris: Livre de Poche, 1963), p. 86.

15 Maurice Merleau-Ponty, "Un Auteur scandaleux," *Sens et non-sens*, 6th ed. (1947; rpt. Paris: Nagel, 1966), p. 80.

16 Simone de Beauvoir, *La Force de l'âge* (Paris: Gallimard, 1960), p. 40.
17 Henri Bergson, *Essai sur les données immédiates de la conscience,* 6th ed. (Paris: Alcan, 1908), pp. 141–142.
18 Sartre, "Les Ecrivains en personne," *Situations IX* (Paris: Gallimard, 1972), pp. 11–12.
19 *CRD,* p. 100.
20 Friedrich Nietzsche, *The Gay Science,* trans. Walter Kaufmann (New York: Random House, Vintage Books, 1974), p. 329.
21 *CRD,* p. 10.
22 Sartre, *La Nausée,* p. 25.
23 Sartre, *La Nausée,* pp. 25, 13, 140–141.
24 Sartre, *Saint Genet: comédien et martyr,* in *Oeuvres complètes de Jean Genet,* vol. I (Paris: Gallimard, 1952), p. 118.
25 Sartre, "Sur *L'Idiot de la famille,"* *Situations X* (Paris: Gallimard, 1976), p. 95.
26 Bergson, *Essai sur les données immédiates,* p. 99.
27 Bergson, *Essai sur les données immédiates,* p. 178.
28 Sartre, *L'Idiot de la famille,* I, 154.
29 Sartre, "Une Idée fondamentale de la phénoménologie de Husserl," *Situations I* (Paris: Gallimard, 1947), pp. 34–35.
30 Edmund Husserl, *Cartesian Meditations,* trans. Dorion Cairns (The Hague: Martinus Nijhoff, 1960).
31 Paul Ricoeur, *Husserl: An Analysis of His Phenomenology,* trans. Edward G. Ballard and Lester E. Embree (Evanston, Ill.: Northwestern Univ. Press, 1967), p. 129.
32 *Samuel Johnson,* pp. 181–182.
33 Iris Murdock, *Sartre: Romantic Rationalist* (New Haven: Yale Univ. Press, 1953), pp. ix–x.
34 Sartre, "L'Ecrivain et sa langue," *Situations IX,* pp. 101–102.
35 Angelo Hesnard, *Apport de la phénoménologie à la psychiatrie contemporaine* (Paris: Masson, 1959), pp. 24, 15.
36 Sartre, "Sur *L'Idiot de la famille,"* p. 111.
37 Hesnard, *Apport de la phénoménologie,* p. 59.
38 Sartre, "Les Ecrivains en personne," p. 12.
39 Sartre, "L'Universel singulier," *Situations IX,* pp. 160, 186.
40 Sartre, "Sur *L'Idiot de la famille,"* p. 96.
41 Sartre, *Le Diable et le bon Dieu* (Paris: Gallimard, 1951), p. 182.
42 Sartre, *Le Diable et le bon Dieu,* p. 216.
43 Sartre, "Autoportrait à soixante-dix ans," *Situations X.*
44 De Beauvoir, *La Force de l'âge,* p. 28.
45 Sartre, "Sur *L'Idiot de la famille,"* p. 105.
46 Sartre, "Autoportrait," pp. 141–142.
47 Sarte, *Le Diable et le bon Dieu,* p. 11.
48 Sartre, *Saint Genet,* p. 542.
49 Sartre, *Les Mots* (1964; rpt. Paris: Gallimard, 1975), p. 214.

50   Sartre, "L'Ecrivain et sa langue," p. 65.

51   Sartre, "Sur *L'Idiot de la famille*," p. 112.

42   George Orwell, "Why I Write," *The Collected Essays, Journalism, and Letters of George Orwell,* ed. Sonia Orwell and Ian Angus (New York: Harcourt, Brace and World, 1968), I, 7.

53   Michel Foucault, "L'Oeil du pouvoir," in Jeremy Bentham, *Le Panoptique* (Paris: Belfond, 1977).

54   Domenick LaCapra, *A Preface to Sartre* (Ithaca: Cornell Univ. Press, 1978), p. 141.

55   Sartre, *L'Etre et le néant* (Paris: Gallimard, 1943), p. 644 (cited hereafter as *EN*).

56   *EN,* p. 645.

57   *EN,* p. 648.

58   Stauffer, *The Art of Biography,* p. 324.

59   Michael Ermarth, *Wilhelm Dilthey: The Critique of Historical Reason* (Chicago: Univ. of Chicago Press, 1978), p. 263.

60   Jacques Derrida, *Glas* (Paris: Le Seuil, 1974), p. 36.

61   Roland Barthes, *Sade/Fourier/Loyola,* trans. Richard Miller (New York: Hill and Wang, 1976), pp. 182–184.

62   See e.g. Raymond Aron, *Essai sur la théorie de l'histoire dans l'Allemagne contemporaine* (Paris: Vrin, 1938).

63   Wilhelm Dilthey, "The Understanding of Other Persons and Their Expressions," in H. A. Hodges, *Wilhelm Dilthey: An Introduction* (1944; rpt. London: Fertig, 1969), p. 118.

64   Dilthey, *Wilhelm Dilthey: Selected Writings,* ed. and trans. H. P. Rickman (Cambridge: Cambridge Univ. Press, 1976), p. 181.

65   Hodges, *Wilhelm Dilthey,* p. 28.

66   *CRD,* p. 71.

67   Angelo Hesnard, *L'Univers morbide de la faute* (Paris: Presses Universitaires de France, 1949), p. 271.

68   Perhaps Sartre was here once again influenced by Hesnard, who wrote in *L'Univers morbide:* "But the influence of the period, of the ethnic group or the social class through the intermediary of the child's immediate surroundings, which is identical in today's society with the conjugal, or monagamic type family. A large number of factors outside of the strictly and properly social influences intervene in the life of the child: the place in the family (the psychology of the only child, of the eldest, of the youngest, of the intermediate children, of the small child) . . . and, in a general manner, all the circumstances capable of acting upon the plastic fragility of the young person, his non-maturation, in short, upon his parasitic condition" (p. 301).

69   Paul Valéry, "Introduction à la méthode de Léonard de Vinci," *Oeuvres,* ed. Jean Hytier, vol. I (Paris: Gallimard, 1968), p. 1156.

70   *CRD,* pp. 98, 107, 108.

71   Dilthey, *Wilhelm Dilthey: Selected Writings,* p. 121.

II. Proteus and the Rat Trap

1   Sartre, "Sur *L'Idiot de la famille,*" p. 99.

2   Simone de Beauvoir, *La Force des choses* (Paris: Gallimard, 1963), p. 262.

3   "A Conversation with Jean-Paul Sartre," *Oui,* June 1975, p. 70.

4   Sartre, *L'Idiot de la famille,* I, 351.

5   Sartre, Phillippe Gavi, and Pierre Victor, *On a raison de se révolter* (Paris: Gallimard, 1974), p. 140.

6   Sartre, "Autoportrait," p. 223.

7   Sartre, Gavi, and Victor, *On a raison,* p. 342.

8   See Richard Schacht, *Alienation* (Garden City, N.Y.: Doubleday, 1970); Gajo Petrović, *Marx in the Mid-Twentieth Century* (Garden City, N.Y.: Doubleday, Anchor Books, 1967).

9   Cf. Schacht, *Alienation,* p. 54.

10   Georg Hegel, *Texts and Commentary,* trans. and ed. Walter Kaufmann (New York: Doubleday, Anchor Books, 1966), p. 20.

11   Hegel, *Science of Logic,* trans. W. H. Johnston and L. G. Struthers (London: G. Allen and Irwin, 1951), I, 143.

12   Schacht, *Alienation,* pp. 219–220.

13   See also Erich Fromm, *Marx's Concept of Man* (New York: Ungar, 1969); David McLellan, *The Thought of Karl Marx* (New York: Harper and Row, 1971); Daniel Bell, "In Search of Marxist Humanism: The Debate on Alienation," *Soviet Survey* 32 (April–June 1960): 31.

14   For Husserl, see Schacht, *Alienation,* pp. 219–220.

15   Husserl, *Cartesian Meditations,* p. 78.

16   Roland Barthes, *Roland Barthes par Roland Barthes* (Paris: Seuil, 1975), p. 47.

17   *EN,* p. 349.

18   *EN,* p. 342.

19   *EN,* p. 480.

20   *EN,* pp, 324, 350.

21   *EN,* pp. 97, 81, 334.

22   *EN,* p. 495.

23   Fredric Jameson, *Marxism and Form* (Princeton: Princeton Univ. Press, 1971), p. 207.

24   Sartre, *L'Idiot de la famille,* vol. III (Paris: Gallimard, 1972), p. 515.

25   Sartre, "Sartre par Sartre," *Situations IX,* pp. 133–134.

26   *CRD,* p. 373.

27   Sartre, *L'Imaginaire* (1940; rpt. Paris: Gallimard, 1970), p. 175.

28   Sartre, *L'Imaginaire,* p. 219.

29   Theodore W. Adorno, *Minima Moralia* (Frankfurt: Suhrkamp, 1964), p. 118.

30   Robert C. Tucker, *Philosophy and Myth in Karl Marx* (Cambridge: Cambridge Univ. Press, 1965), p. 101.

31 "Littérature," p. 189.

32 Sartre's use of the word *generosity* in this context is one hint among many that Julien Benda, *La France byzantine* (1945; rpt. Paris: 10/18, 1970), had a role in the genesis of Sartre's essay. Both argue that the author's attitude toward the reader must be one of generosity (Benda, pp. 160–162). Benda makes the same distinction as Sartre between poetry and prose and sharply criticizes authors who focus on the material qualities of the word at the expense of the object signified. Both authors are critical of hermeticism. Both are hostile to most post-romantic authors and schools, especially Flaubert, Baudelaire, the Goncourts, surrealism, Gide, Giraudoux, and Valéry. Both complain about literature being considered "une activité de luxe" (Benda, p. 176) and about "une littérature pour les littérateurs" (Benda, p. 161). The purpose of Benda's book is to ask the question "Qu'est-ce que le littérateur?" (Benda, p. 168).

33 "Littérature," p. 190.

34 "Littérature," p. 296.

35 "Littérature," p. 297.

36 "Littérature," p. 262.

37 "Littérature," pp. 197, 266.

38 Sartre, Gavi, and Victor, *On a raison,* p. 184.

39 Sartre, "Sur *L'Idiot de la famille,*" p. 99.

40 Benjamin Suhl, *Jean-Paul Sartre: The Philosopher as a Literary Critic* (New York: Columbia Univ. Press, 1970).

41 *CRD,* pp. 201, 286.

42 *CRD,* p. 192. Because this noneliminable alienation lies at the heart of Sartre's system, Pietro Chiodi, *Sartre and Marxism,* trans. Kate Soper (Atlantic Highlands, N.J.: Humanities Press, 1976), has accused him of being an inauthentic Marxist. Sartre's riposte would be that without this primitive alienation it would be impossible to explain the possibilty of the Marxist forms.

43 Sartre, *L'Idiot de la famille,* III, 191.

44 *CRD,* pp. 206, 208.

45 *CRD,* pp. 165, 154. Sartre here confuses the reader, for as he himself is careful to note, not all forms of alienation are owing to these two varieties of mediation. By "toute alienation possible" I understand him to mean all historically contingent kinds of alienation.

46 *CRD,* pp. 250, 224.

47 Cf. Schacht, *Alienation,* p. 229.

48 *CRD,* p. 360.

49 *CRD,* p. 309.

50 *CRD,* p. 314.

51 Karl Marx, *Economic and Philosophic Manuscripts of 1844,* trans. T. B. Bottomore, in Fromm, *Marx's Concept of Man,* p. 109.

52 *CRD,* p. 717.

53 Jean Jacques Rousseau, "Lettres écrites de la Montagne," *Oeuvres complètes,* vol. III (Paris: Firmin-Didot, 1883), p. 81.

54 Charles Baudelaire, *Oeuvres complètes,* ed. Y. G. Le Dantec and Claude Pichois (Paris: Gallimard, 1961), p. 1178.

55 Baudelaire, *Oeuvres complètes,* p. 1178.

56 That Dilthey's concept of "the objective spirit" is one source for the idea of the pratico-inert becomes clear in *L'Idiot,* where "l'esprit objectif" and the pratico-inert are used interchangeably. Besides Marx, other possible influences include Hegel, in his idea that the cumulative choices of others becomes an individual's fate, and Bakunin, in his idea of "the authority of society."

57 *CRD,* pp. 369, 359, 200, 358.

58 *CRD,* pp. 362–363.

59 *CRD,* p. 362.

60 *CRD,* pp. 620, 621.

61 *CRD,* p. 303.

62 Sartre, Gavi, and Victor, *On a raison,* p. 170.

63 *CRD,* pp. 421, 529.

64 *EN,* pp. 299, 300.

65 *CRD,* p. 420.

66 Chiodi, *Sartre and Marxism,* p. xi.

67 *CRD,* pp. 442, 456.

68 *CRD,* p. 349.

III. Baudelaire and Bad Faith

1 Sartre, "Sur *L'Idiot de la famille,*" p. 106.

2 *CRD,* p. 10.

3 Sartre, *Les Mots,* p. 60.

4 Sartre, *Les Mots,* p. 152.

5 De Beauvoir, *Le Force de l'âge,* p. 30.

6 Sartre, "Les Communistes et la paix," *Situations VI* (Paris: Gallimard, 1964), p. 274.

7 Sartre, "Présentation aux *Temps modernes,*" *Situations II,* p. 17.

8 George Lukács, "Old Culture and New Culture," *Telos* 5 (Spring 1970): 26.

9 Theophile Gautier, *La Préface de "Mademoiselle de Maupin,"* ed. Georges Matoré (Paris: Droz, 1946), p. 28.

10 *CRD,* p. 49.

11 Sartre, *Baudelaire* (1947; rpt. Paris: Gallimard, 1963), p. 245 (cited hereafter parenthetically in the text).

12 Angelo Hesnard, *L'Individu et le sexe: psychologie du narcissisme* (Paris: Stock, 1927).

13 Sartre, *Saint Genet,* p. 210.

14 Sigmund Freud, *Civilization and Its Discontents* (New York: Norton, 1961), p. 15.

15 Hesnard, *L'Individu et le sexe*, p. 59.
16 Hesnard, *L'Individu et le sexe*, p. 178.
17 Hesnard, *L'Individu et le sexe*, p. 211.
18 Philip Thody, *Jean-Paul Sartre: A Literary and Political Study* (London: H. Hamilton, 1960), p. 148.
19 *EN*, p. 73.
20 Valéry, *Oeuvres*, I, 128.
21 Cf. Maurice Blanchot, *La Part du feu* (Paris: Gallimard, 1949), pp. 137–156.
22 Georges Bataille, *La Littérature et le mal* (Paris: Gallimard, 1957), p. 56.
23 Trent Schroyer, *The Critique of Domination* (Boston: Beacon Press, 1975), p. 56.
24 De Beauvoir, *La Force de l'âge*, p. 57.
25 Sartre, "Sartre par Sartre," p. 113.
26 See also Jules Mouquet and W. T. Bandy, *Baudelaire en 1848* (Paris: Emile-Paul Frères, 1946), pp. 9–11.
27 F. W. J. Hemmings, *Culture and Society in France: 1848–1898* (New York: Scribner's Sons, 1971), pp. 37–38.
28 Baudelaire, *Oeuvres complètes*, pp. 743, 606, 614.
29 Justin Kaplan, "The 'Real Life,' " in *Studies in Biography*, ed. Daniel Aaron, Harvard English Studies 8 (Cambridge, Mass.: Harvard Univ. Press, 1978), p. 2.
30 Sartre's biography of Baudelaire was first published as a preface to an edition of Baudelaire, *Ecrits intimes* (Paris: Editions du Point de Jour, 1946).
31 Cf. Joseph Halpern, *Critical Fictions* (New Haven: Yale Univ. Press, 1976), p. 59; Georges Blin, *Le Sadisme de Baudelaire* (Paris: Corti, 1948), p. 140.
32 Sartre, *L'Idiot de la famille*, III, 13.
33 Sartre, *Le Diable et le bon Dieu*, p. 182.
34 Valéry, "Rhumbs," *Oeuvres*, vol. II (Paris: Gallimard, 1971), p. 622.

IV. Genet and the Just

1 Sartre, *Saint Genet*, I (cited hereafter parenthetically in the text).
2 Morton Schatzman, *Soul Murder* (New York: New American Library, 1974), p. 24.
3 Frederick Copleston, *A History of Philosophy*, vol. V, p. 1, *Fichte to Hegel* (New York: Doubleday, Image Books, 1965), p. 203.
4 Georg Hegel, *Early Theological Writings*, trans. T. M. Knox (Chicago: Univ. of Chicago Press, 1948), pp. 182–301.
5 Sartre, "Faux savants ou faux lièvres," *Situations VI*, pp. 31–32, 45.
6 Friedrich Engels, *Herr Eugen Dühring's Revolution in Science (Anti-Dühring)*, trans. Emile Burns and ed. C. P. Dutt (New York: International Publishers, 1939), p. 109.

7   Karl Marx and Friedrich Engels, *The Holy Family,* trans. Richard Dixon (New York: International Publishers, 1956), p. 193.
8   Marx and Engels, *The Holy Family,* p. 194.
9   Marx and Engels, *The Holy Family,* pp. 198, 200, 205.
10 Theodore W. Adorno, *Negative Dialectics,* trans. E. B. Ashton (New York: Seabury Press, 1973), p. 275.
11 Hesnard, *L'Univers morbide,* p. 176.
12 Hesnard, *L'Univers morbide,* pp. 3–4.
13 Sartre, *Les Mouches,* in *Théâtre,* vol. I (Paris: Gallimard, 1947), p. 72.
14 Hesnard, *L'Univers morbide,* p. 285.
15 Hesnard, *L'Univers morbide,* p. 395.
16 Hegel, *Early Theological Writings,* p. 235.
17 Stewart Edwards, *The Paris Commune, 1871* (1971; rpt. New York: Quadrangle Books, 1977), p. 24.
18 *L'Univers morbide,* p. 180.
19 Karl Marx and Friedrich Engels, *The German Ideology,* ed. S. Ryazanskaya (Moscow: Progress Publishers, 1968), p. 42.
20 Jeremy Bentham, "Panopticon; or the Inspection House," *The Works of Jeremy Bentham,* ed. John Bowring (1838–1843; rpt. New York: Russell and Russell, 1962), IV, 37–172.
21 Patrick McCarthy, *Céline* (New York: Viking Press, 1975), p. 324.
22 Although the title *Saint Genet* was possibly inspired by Jean Rotrou's play *Le Véritable Saint Genest,* an alternative explanation would account for both the book's title and the references to Saint Teresa of Avila. In Rome there are two churches, across the street from one another, with chapels devoted to these two saints. In Santa Susanna is a chapel containing the tomb of Saint Genesius as well as paintings depicting the events of his life. In Santa Maria della Vittoria is the Cornaro Chapel of Bernini, the highlight of which is the dramatic statue *Saint Teresa in Ecstasy.* Perhaps Sartre's many summers in Rome may have had a small role in the genesis of *Saint Genet.* Another possible explanation of the ironic use of the term *saint* in the title may lie in the Marxist tradition of the ironic use of the saintly designation. For example, in *The German Ideology,* Marx and Engels refer to Saint Max and Saint Bruno.
23 Cf. Mark Poster, *Existential Marxism in Postwar France* (Princeton: Princeton Univ. Press, 1975), p. 200.
24 Sartre, "Une idée fondamentale de la phénoménologie de Husserl: l'intentionnalité," *Situations I,* p. 31.
25 Irving Babbitt, *Rousseau and Romanticism* (Boston: Houghton Mifflin, 1919), pp. 240–267.
26 Maurice Merleau-Ponty, *Humanisme et terreur* (Paris: Gallimard, 1947), p. 168.
27 *EN,* p. 479.
28 Karl Marx, *Early Writings,* ed. and trans. T. B. Bottomore (New York: McGraw-Hill, 1963), p. 162.

29 Merleau-Ponty, *Humanisme et terreur*, p. 4.
30 Arthur Koestler, *Darkness at Noon* (London: J. Cape, 1940), translated as *Le Zéro et l'infini* (Paris: Calman-Lévy, 1946).
31 Merleau-Ponty, *Humanisme et terreur*, p. 4.
32 For the trial, see Stephen F. Cohen, *Bukharin and the Bolshevik Revolution* (New York: Knopf, 1973), pp. 372–380.
33 Sartre, "Faux savants ou faux lièvres," p. 39.
34 Merleau-Ponty, *Humanisme et terreur*, p. xvii.
35 Merleau-Ponty, *Humanisme et terreur*, p. 14.
36 Herbert Marcuse, *Eros and Civilization* (1955; rpt. New York: Random House, Vintage Books, 1962), p. 233.
37 Sartre, "Sartre par Sartre," p. 114.
38 Schroyer, *The Critique of Domination*, p. 32.
39 David Cooper, *The Death of the Family* (New York: Pantheon Books, 1970), pp. 9, 11–12.
40 Merleau-Ponty, *Humanisme et terreur*, p. 30.

V. Flaubert and the Subjective Neurosis

1 Engels, *L'Origine de la famille, de la propriété privée*, trans. Henri Ravé (Paris: Carré, 1893), p. 65.
2 Harry Levin, *James Joyce* (1941; rpt. New York: New Directions, 1960), p. 5.
3 Sartre, "Sur *L'Idiot de la famille*," p. 97.
4 Sartre, "Des rats et des hommes," *Situations IV* (Paris: Gallimard, 1964), p. 25.
5 Sartre, *Les Mots*, pp. 61, 74, 81, 96–97, 143, 187.
6 Sartre, *Les Séquestrés d'Altona* (Paris: Gallimard, 1960), p. 107.
7 Philippe Ariès, "Wills, Tombs, and Families," *New Society*, no. 356 (Sept. 25, 1969): pp. 473–475.
8 Sartre, *Les Mots*, pp. 187–188.
9 Sartre, *L'Idiot de la famille*, I, 8 (cited hereafter parenthetically in the text).
10 Sartre, *Les Mots*, pp. 49–50.
11 Michel Contat and Michel Rybalka, *Les Ecrits de Sartre* (Paris: Gallimard, 1970), p. 427.
12 Sartre, "Présentation aux *Temps modernes*," p. 12.
13 Gregory Bateson et al., "Toward a Theory of Schizophrenia," *Behavioral Science* 1 (1956): 258–259.
14 Flaubert to Ernest Chevalier, Feb. 24, 1839, *Correspondance*, ed. Jean Bruneau, vol. I (Paris: Gallimard, 1973), p. 37.
15 Sartre, *Le Mur* (1939; rpt. Paris: Livre de Poche, 1962), p. 179.
16 Flaubert to Louise Colet, Sept. 4–5, 1846, *Correspondance*, ed. Bruneau, p. 328.
17 CRD, p. 63.

18 Flaubert to Louis Colet, Aug. 6 or 7, 1846, *Correspondance,* ed. Bruneau, p. 278.
19 Sartre, "Mallarmé," *Situations IX,* p. 191.
20 Flaubert to Guy de Maupassant, Aug. 15, 1878, *Correspondance,* 8th ser. (Paris: Conard, 1930), p. 136.
21 Richard Ellmann, *Golden Codgers* (New York: Oxford Univ. Press, 1973), p. 7.
22 Sartre, "Aminadab," *Situations I,* p. 132.
23 Valéry, *Oeuvres,* II, 736.
24 Bataille, *L'Expérience intérieure* (Paris: Gallimard, 1954), p. 119.
25 Sartre, "Un Nouveau mystique," *Situations I,* p. 170.
26 Flaubert to Louis Colet, Mar. 2–3, 1854, *Correspondance,* 4th ser. (Paris: Conard, 1929), p. 33.
27 Flaubert to Louis Colet, Apr. 22, 1853, *Correspondance,* 3rd ser. (Paris: Conard, 1927), p. 178.
28 Arthur Rimbaud, *Une Saison en enfer, Oeuvres,* ed. Suzanne Bernard (Paris: Garnier, 1960), p. 214.
29 Foucault, "What Is an Author?" *Language, Counter-Memory Practice,* trans. and ed. Donald F. Bouchard (Ithaca: Cornell Univ. Press, 1977), p. 117.
30 Flaubert to Louise Colet, Aug. 8–9, 1846: "Pour avoir eu ce que j'ai eu il a fallu que quelque chose, antérieurement, se soit passé d'une façon assez tragique dans la boîte de mon cerveau" (*Correspondance,* ed. Bruneau, p. 281).
31 Flaubert to Louis Colet, Oct. 14, 1846, *Correspondance,* ed. Bruneau, p. 389.
32 Norman O. Brown, *Love's Body* (1966; rpt. New York: Random House, Vintage Books, 1968), p. 163.
33 Theodore W. Adorno, *Kierkegaard: Konstruktion des Aesthetischen* (Tubingen: Mohr, 1933), p. 90.
34 Jean Bruneau, *Les Débuts littéraires de Gustave Flaubert* (Paris: A. Colin, 1962).
35 See R. H. Stacey, *Defamiliarization in Language and Literature* (Syracuse: Syracuse Univ. Press, 1977).
36 Sartre, "L'Homme et les choses," *Situations I,* p. 283.
37 Joyce, *A Portrait of the Artist as a Young Man, The Portable James Joyce,* ed. Harry Levin (New York: Viking Press, 1947), pp. 481–482.
38 Maurice Nadeau, *Le Roman Français depuis la guerre* (Paris: Gallimard, 1963), p. 176.
39 José Ortega y Gasset, *The Dehumanization of Art* (1948; rpt. Garden City, N.Y.: Doubleday, Anchor Books, 1956), p. 32.
40 Kurt Lothar Tank, *Gunter Grass,* trans. John Conway (New York: Ungar, 1969), p. 56.
41 Richard Ellmann, *James Joyce* (New York: Oxford Univ. Press, 1959), p. 559; Levin, *James Joyce,* p. 52.
42 Sartre, *Le Diable et le bon Dieu,* pp. 201–202.

43   Sartre, "Un Nouveau mystique," p. 173; *CRD*, p. 21.

44   Freud, *Collected Papers*, ed. Ernest Jones (New York: Basic Books, 1959), V, 222–242.

45   R. D. Laing, "The Study of Family and Social Contexts in Relation to the Origins of Schizophrenia," in *The Origins of Schizophrenia*, ed. J. Romano, International Congress Series 151 (New York and Amsterdam: Excerpta Medica Foundation, 1967), p. 23.

VI. *Flaubert and the Objective Neurosis*

1   Lewis Carroll, *Through the Looking Glass, The Complete Works of Lewis Carroll* (New York: Random House, Modern Library, n.d.), p. 229.

2   Karl Marx, *The Eighteenth Brumaire of Louis Bonaparte, Political Writings*, ed. David Fernbach (New York: Random House, Vintage Books, 1974), II, 146.

3   Flaubert to Louise Colet, Nov. 22, 1852, *Correspondance*, 3rd ser., p. 52.

4   Valéry, "Lettre sur Mallarmé," *Oeuvres*, I, 637.

5   Pierre Boulez, *Notes of an Apprenticeship*, trans. Herbert Weinstock (New York: Knopf, 1968), pp. 35–41.

6   Sartre, Preface to Stéphane Mallarmé, *Poésies* (Paris: Gallimard, 1966), p. 28.

7   Gordon Wright, *France in Modern Times* (Chicago: Rand-McNally, 1960), p. 218.

8   Flaubert, *Bouvard et Pécuchet* (Lausanne: Editions Rencontre, 1965), p. 211.

9   Flaubert to Louise Colet, Mar. 2–3, 1854, *Correspondance*, 4th ser., p. 34.

10   Marx, *The Eighteenth Brumaire*, pp. 197, 211.

11   Edwards, *The Paris Commune, 1871*, p. 54.

12   Edmond de Goncourt, *Journal des Goncourt*, ed. Robert Ricatte, vol. II (Paris: Fasquelle and Flammarion, 1956), p. 904.

13   Flaubert to Mlle. Leroyer de Chantepie, July 8, 1870, *Correspondance*, 6th ser. (Paris: Conard, 1930), p. 132.

14   Ermarth, *Wilhelm Dilthey*, p. 263.

15   Adorno, *Minima Moralia*, p. 376.

16   *Sartre: Un Film* (Gallimard: 1977), p. 98.

17   *CRD*, pp. 208, 420.

18   Tucker, *Philosophy and Myth in Karl Marx*, p. 53.

19   James Sheridan, *Sartre: The Radical Conversion* (Athens: Ohio Univ. Press, 1969), p. 138.

20   Dilthey, "Introduction to the Human Studies," in Hodges, *Wilhelm Dilthey*, p. 129.

21   *CRD*, pp. 456, 526.

22   Sartre, "L'Universel singulier," p. 186.

23 Flaubert to Mme. Brainne, Dec. 30, 1878, *Correspondance*, 8th ser., p. 175.

24 Georg Lukács, *Existentialisme ou marxisme?* (Paris: Nagel, 1948), p. 91.

25 Flaubert to George Sand, July 20, 1870, *Correspondance*, 6th ser., p. 135.

26 Clemens, *Mark Twain's Autobiography*, I, 2.

27 Dilthey, "Introduction to the Human Studies," p. 146.

28 Sartre, *Le Diable et le bon Dieu*, p. 185.

29 Harry Levin, Review of *L'Idiot*, *Journal of the History of Ideas* 32 (1972): 644.

30 *CRD*, p. 106.

31 Sartre, "Sur *L'Idiot de la famille*," p. 94.

32 *EN*, p. 161.

33 Introduction to *Boswell's London Journal, 1762–1763*, ed. F. A. Pottle (New York: McGraw-Hill, 1950), p. 12.

34 Adorno, *Minima Moralia*, p. 333.

35 Thomas Mann, *Doctor Faustus*, trans. H. T. Lowe-Porter (1948; rpt. New York: Random House, Modern Library, n.d.), p. 372.

36 Mann, *Doctor Faustus*, p. 373.

37 Flaubert to Ernest Chevalier, June 24, 1837, *Correspondance*, ed. Bruneau, p. 25.

38 Mann, *Doctor Faustus*, p. 240.

39 *Sartre: Un Film*, p. 99.

40 *EN*, p. 479.

41 *CRD*, p. 191.

VII. The Dialectic of Narcissism

1 Laing, *The Politics of Experience* (New York: Ballantine Books, 1967), p. 74.

2 Merleau-Ponty, "Un Auteur scandaleux," p. 83.

3 Sartre, "Sur *L'Idiot de la famille*," p. 114.

4 Merleau-Ponty, "Le Doute de Cézanne," *Sens et non-sens*, pp. 41, 39.

5 Sartre, *Les Mots*, pp. 18–19.

6 *Sartre: Un Film*, p. 32.

7 Freud, *Civilization and Its Discontents*, p. 15.

8 Marcuse, *Eros and Civilization*, pp. 153–154.

9 Sartre, "L'Ecrivain et sa langue," p. 58.

10 See e.g. Heinz Kohut, *The Analysis of the Self* (New York: International Univ. Press, 1971); Otto Kernberg, *Borderline Conditions and Pathological Narcissism* (New York: J. Aronson, 1975).

11 Béla Grunberger, *Le Narcissisme* (Paris: Payot, 1971).

12 Sartre, *Les Mots*, p. 25.

13 Sartre, *L'Idiot de la famille*, I, 494.

14 Sartre, *Les Mots*, p. 19.

15 Sartre, *Saint Genet*, p. 85.
16 Sartre, *L'Idiot de la famille*, I, 165, 498; vol. II (Paris, Gallimard, 1972), p. 1567.
17 Sartre, *Les Mots*, pp. 76, 130, 201.
18 Sartre, *Saint Genet*, p. 73.
19 Paul Ricoeur, *Le Conflit des interprétations* (Paris: Seuil, 1969), p. 159.
20 Sartre, *Les Mots*, pp. 97, 146.
21 Sartre, *L'Idiot de la famille*, I, 403.
22 *CRD*, p. 453.
23 Sartre, "Des rats et des hommes," p. 26.
24 Sartre, *Les Mots*, pp. 25, 21, 48–49.
25 Grunberger, *Le Narcissisme*, p. 308.
26 Sartre, *Les Mots*, pp. 75, 20.
27 Grunberger, *Le Narcissisme*, pp. 39, 31.
28 Sartre, "Des rats et des hommes," p. 47.
29 Sartre, *Le Diable et le bon Dieu*, p. 182.
30 Wilfrid Desan, *The Marxism of Jean-Paul Sartre* (Garden City, N.Y.: Doubleday, 1966), p. 66.
31 Sartre, *Les Mots*, pp. 130, 185.
32 Merleau-Ponty, "Le Doute de Cézanne," p. 37.
33 Sartre, *Les Mots*, p. 213.
34 Hesnard, *L'Individu et le sexe*, p. 227.
35 Marcuse, *Eros and Civilization*, p. 29.
36 Alexander Mitscherlich, *Society Without the Father* (New York: Schocken Books, 1970), p. 160.
37 Christopher Lasch, *Haven in a Heartless World: The Family Besieged* (New York: Basic Books, 1977), p. 125.
38 See e.g. Adorno, *Minima Moralia*, pp. 21–23; Lasch, *Haven in a Heartless World*.
39 Arnold A. Rogow, *The Dying of the Light* (New York: Putnam's Sons, 1975), p. 79.

VIII. *The Tribunal of Crabs*

1 Sartre, Gavi, and Victor, *On a raison*, p. 341.
2 Sartre, Gavi, and Victor, *On a raison*, p. 343.
3 Ernst Bloch, *Das Prinzip Hoffnung* (Frankfurt: Suhrkamp, 1959), p. 4.
4 Merleau-Ponty, *Humanisme et terreur*, p. 143.
5 Sartre, *L'Idiot de la famille*, I, 143.
6 Maurice Merleau-Ponty, *Phénoménologie de la perception* (Paris: Gallimard, 1945), p. 473
7 Husserl, *Cartesian Meditations*, p. 111.
8 Sartre interview, "L'Auteur, l'oeuvre et le public," in *Un Théâtre de situations*, ed. Michel Contat and Michel Rybalka (Paris: Gallimard, 1973), p. 102.
9 "L'Auteur, l'oeuvre et le public," p. 103.

10 See e.g. Germaine Brée, *Camus and Sartre: Crisis and Commitment* (New York: Dell, 1972), p. 3.

11 André Glucksmann, *Les Maîtres penseurs* (Paris: Grasset, 1977), p. 29.

12 "Littérature," p. 320n.

13 Glucksmann, *Les Maîtres penseurs*, p. 149.

14 Glucksmann, *Les Maîtres penseurs*, p. 199.

15 Adorno, *Minima Moralia*, pp. 56, 107.

16 Nietzsche, *The Gay Science*, p. 215.

17 Sartre, Gavi, and Victor, *On a raison*, pp. 305–306.

Index